Chris Coyle's delightful and detailed account of his family's summer life in a primitive off-the-grid waterfront cabin nestled in a wilderness area of west-central Maine makes me want to visit and explore that natural paradise of ponds, mountains, and wildlife as soon as possible! We Lived in the Woods: *a thoroughly worthwhile and enjoyable read!*

—William Emrich, author
Have Racquet, Will Travel • Wild Maine Adventure • Through One Man's Eyes

With Chris Coyle's We Lived in the Woods, *journey along to a bygone era of a family's summer vacations in the northern woods of Maine. Delight in historical and nostalgic experiences of cabin living on a pond. Relish vignettes centered on Maine moments from loons to geology to recipes to railroads to people and more fully experienced life. You'll want to visit!*

—Clare Green, author
Hearts and Hands on Herbs • The Little Pine Tree • The Legend of the Rainbow

As a person born in Maine, I find We Lived in the Woods *really resonates with my love for Maine and brings back memories that had not entered my thoughts in years!* We Lived in the Woods *makes really enjoyable reading and captures the inherent beauty of Maine during a bygone era!*

—Jeffrey Krasofski, New England outdoor enthusiast

Many people are largely unaware of a unique area of Maine. Residing in the Moosehead area, we traveled through the towns mentioned in We Lived in the Woods—*Mayfield, Kingsbury Plantation, and Wellington, among others. Chris Coyle captures the beauty of living seasonally in the region in a book not to be missed.*

—Everett L. Parker, author and president of Maine Philatelic Society
Railroads of the North Woods • Seboomook—From Native Americans to POWs
The Moosehead Lake Indians—Ethnicity, History, Legends

we lived in the woods

We Lived in the Woods

a memoir from a bygone era

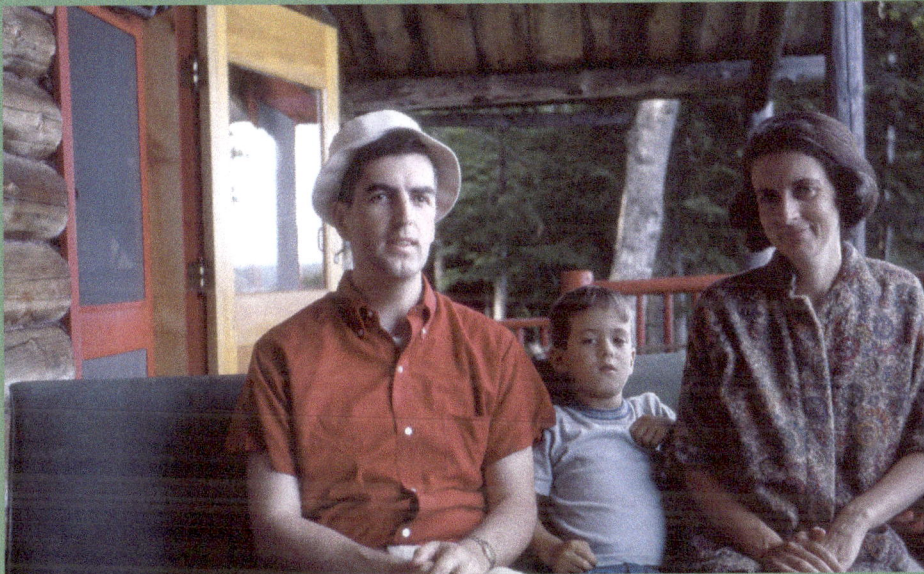

Bob Coyle, Chris Coyle, and Barbara Sherman Coyle

Chris Coyle

with reminiscence by
Bob Coyle

Haley's
Athol, Massachusetts

Haley's
488 South Main Street
Athol, MA 01331
haley.antique@verizon.net • 978.249.9400

Copy edited by Debra Ellis.

Back cover photos by Bob Coyle

International Standard Book Numbers:
978-1-956055-28-3: trade paperback
978-1-956055-29-0: hardback
978-1-956055-30-6: Ebook-Adobe PDF

Library of Congress Number:
2025019555

In memory of my parents

Bob and Barbara Sherman Coyle,

who had quite a hand

in the start of

We Lived in the Woods.

Maine, the way life should be . . .
—sign on Maine Turnpike in Kittery

contents

this is maine

a foreword by Douglas Drown

I am a Bay Stater born and bred. But my paternal family roots extend to Maine. My ninth great-grandfather emigrated from Cornwall, England to Kittery in 1670, so even before I came to know Maine well, felt attracted to the state.

My first visit to Maine occurred in 1959 when I went to Old Orchard Beach for an overnight stay with my parents and other family members. My impression as an eight year old was that with its beach, amusements, and general honky-tonkyness, it resembled Hampton Beach in New Hampshire, with which I was very familiar.

So much for Maine.

Several years later, however, I learned that there is Maine and there is *Maine*!

An inland trip in 1965 took my mother, some friends, and me up through central and MidCoast parts of the state. Holding my ever-present GE transistor radio to my ear and listening to a Red Sox game as we came into the capital city, I heard a station break when the announcer said, "You're listening to Faw-teen hundred, W-Ahh-D-O, Augusta."

I knew I had *arrived*.

In the interesting and delightful book *We Lived in the Woods*, my friend Chris Coyle recounts the many summer days he spent in Upper Kennebec Valley, including the town of Bingham, the former municipality of Mayfield—one of those "don't blink or you'll miss it" locations, and the plantation of Kingsbury, its population so small that town meetings take place around a kitchen table. Readers will come to an awareness of the magnificent beauty of that very rural area, its stalwart and sometimes colorful people, some of its rich history, and the joy of living in a place that had remained largely unchanged for many, many years. I can attest to that, having served as a parish pastor in Bingham for three decades of my life.

Chris has written a wonderfully detailed, very personal testimony as to his experiences and his deep affection for the Pine Tree State where he was born. Such is *Maine*, the place I have come to know and love during my forty-eight years as a resident. As notable Bingham preacher-poet Arthur Macdougall wrote,

. . . the place where the dare began,
Where men and women were face to face
With an ancient silence and wilderness
As black as pines in a nameless place.

Douglas Drown has lived in Maine since 1976 when he became minister of the First Congregational Church of Bingham. Doug is currently minister at North Sedgwick Baptist Church and Saunders Memorial Congregational Church, both on the coast of Maine. A lifelong railfan, he is thoroughly versed in Maine history.

a memoir from a bygone era

an introduction by Chris Coyle

As a child, I had the wonderful experience of growing up part of each year in Maine in a rustic backwoods cabin—a wonderful experience and truly one of the happiest chapters in my life. Although an only child with no other children to play with, I never once felt bored nor could not find anything interesting to do. In the days before cell phones, computers, and even before my folks owned a television set, I found my own amusement and learned from the world around me.

What follows comprises a memoir from a bygone era and time, my boyhood. With reference to my mother's comprehensive journals, I have continued my father's reminiscence of our summers in Maine with additional stories, tales, and yarns as I remember events half a century later. The stories relate how I saw things through my eyes and do not necessarily constitute a historical narrative.

We visited Maine only in summer months. The state experiences long winters and many months of cold weather. I am not able to write about that time of year, as our residency in the Pine Tree State was confined to the warm months.

My mother, Barbara Coyle, kept annual diaries that provide accounts of many of our activities as well as the dates we stayed in Maine each summer. I used it to prepare the Mayfield residency chart included with some entries from her diaries. My mother kept very good records—diaries, bird trip lists, recipes, and such.

Both of my folks proofread sections written during their lives. Although I have written most of the text for *We Lived in the Woods*, the book belongs to them, too, because of their love for the Maine woods and interest in documenting our memories of living there.

the setting

In the wilds of Somerset County, Maine, we called a log cabin home for more than twenty summers. The cabin sits on the north shore of Kingsbury Pond in the unorganized territory of Mayfield Township.

The Coyle family called the cabin on the north shore of Kingsbury Pond, Mayfield Township, Maine, home for many summers, including here in August, 1977.
photo by Bob Coyle

When Omar Sawyer retired as manager of woodlands for the Hollingsworth & Whitney Company, headquartered in Winslow, Maine, he received a 2.5-acre parcel of land on the northwest shore of Kingsbury Pond in Mayfield, where he could build a camp. Since Omar already owned a camp on China Lake, he built the one in Mayfield for his son Donald and his family. Later, the Sawyers purchased additional surrounding land from H&W for a total of ten acres. Except on the pond side, Sawyer land encircled Lea Smith's small camp built much earlier. Don's tract of land then stretched from the shore of Kingsbury Pond to Route 16, including the dirt road into his and the Smith camps and a mountain brook that emptied into the pond at Birch

Point. Red-painted wooden posts marked the original parcel as well as the larger tract later purchased.

In 1951, Omar and Donald Sawyer built the cabin we stayed in. They used logs to build the cabin cut in the spring on the Sawyers' land on Kingsbury Pond. Horses twitched logs out of the woods to the construction site. Charlie Pooler, a Mayfield native who had relocated to Bingham several years previous, was part of the log crew. They used special tools to remove bark while the wood was green. Dan Sawyer, five years old at the time, recalls clouds of ever-present, annoying, gargantuan mosquitoes with appetites to match.

My folks began staying at the cabin in 1958, something that would continue after my birth in 1960 and through 1981. In the early years, the folks sometimes referred to the cabin as Maybury or Mayberry Lodge, from combining the words Mayfield and Kingsbury. In my younger days, I called it our vacation house.

For decades, that part of Maine remained far closer to the spirit of earlier times than to the present and provided one

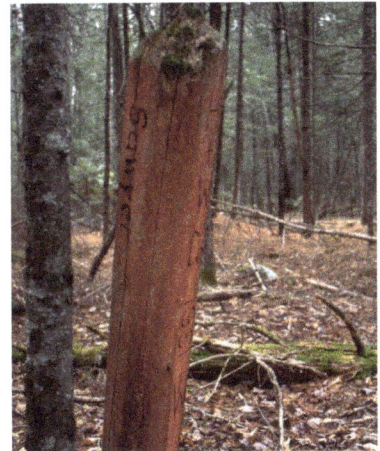

An upright log marked the boundary of Sawyer land and that of Hollingsworth and Whitney Paper Company near Kingsbury Pond.
photo by Chris Coyle

Upper Kennebec Valley with the Ham Farm overlooking Wyman Lake in 1960 shows no evidence of utility poles or wires.
photo by Lowell Flanders, llflanphotography

reason we liked it there so much. We had no electricity, running water, or telephone service. True, the cabin had an ancient crank telephone attached to the wall—an object which provided many hours of amusement for me as a child—but the nearest active wires of the New England Telephone and Telegraph Company were in Brighton. For us, the lack of such modern conveniences provided an easier and more basic lifestyle.

Since the rising sun appeared early across the pond, we tended to retire early in the evening because of our setting in the shadow of the hills in the latter part of the day. Usually, we sat by candlelight for a while after twilight shadows fell. The call of loons on the pond held a captivating if not haunting sound that I shall not soon forget. Once in a very great while, we lit the gaslights. Although they provided considerably more lumens than did candles, their use tended to draw insect no-see-ums or midges through the screens. We had to close all the windows if we lit the lights. Usually, we preferred the ventilation and just curtailed any evening activities that required much light. We also had a kerosene lamp, but since we did not like the smell it produced, we rarely used it.

A 1930 photo from Cook Hill shows farms of Mayfield near Mayfield and Kingsbury ponds.
photo by Milford Baker courtesy of Douglas Drown

Although neither of my parents grew up in the country, they took an immediate liking to living in a log cabin in the Maine woods. My father grew up in the Dorchester section of Boston, while my mother grew up in Weston, a suburb of the same city. While growing up both of my parents spent time at family farms in the country. A landscape architect, my maternal grandfather worked much of his career for Olmsted Brothers based in Brookline, Massachusetts. My mother sometimes accompanied her father to work sites and, in doing so, learned about plants and the natural world.

My folks met at extension classes they took at Harvard University and married in 1953. A graduate of Simmons College in Boston, my mother worked mostly in clerical jobs at universities. While working in an office at Boston University, she became acquainted with the Reverend Martin Luther King Jr. as he earned a PhD in systemic theology.

A skilled typist, Barbara Coyle types a research paper for her husband, Bob.
She also kept a handwritten journal chronicling Maine summers, cabin recipes, and lists of wildlife seen by family members.

photo by Bob Coyle

A skilled typist, my mother frequently typed papers and notes for my father. Their manual Remington typewriter usually made the trip to Maine with us, and as it did not require electricity, it found a lot of use during our stays at the cabin.

In the summer of 1958, my father began his graduate work in geology at Boston University. The summer field program was based at the Mark Emery School in North Anson, Maine. As part of his graduate work, he mapped the bedrock geology of the Kingsbury, Maine US Geological Survey Quadrangle, which necessitated his hiking into many remote areas of this wild part of Maine. After some degree of searching for an appropriate place to stay for the summer near his field work, he found the Sawyer cabin and rented it for the summer.

Mayfield, Bingham, and Skowhegan situated in central Maine.
map by Chris Coyle

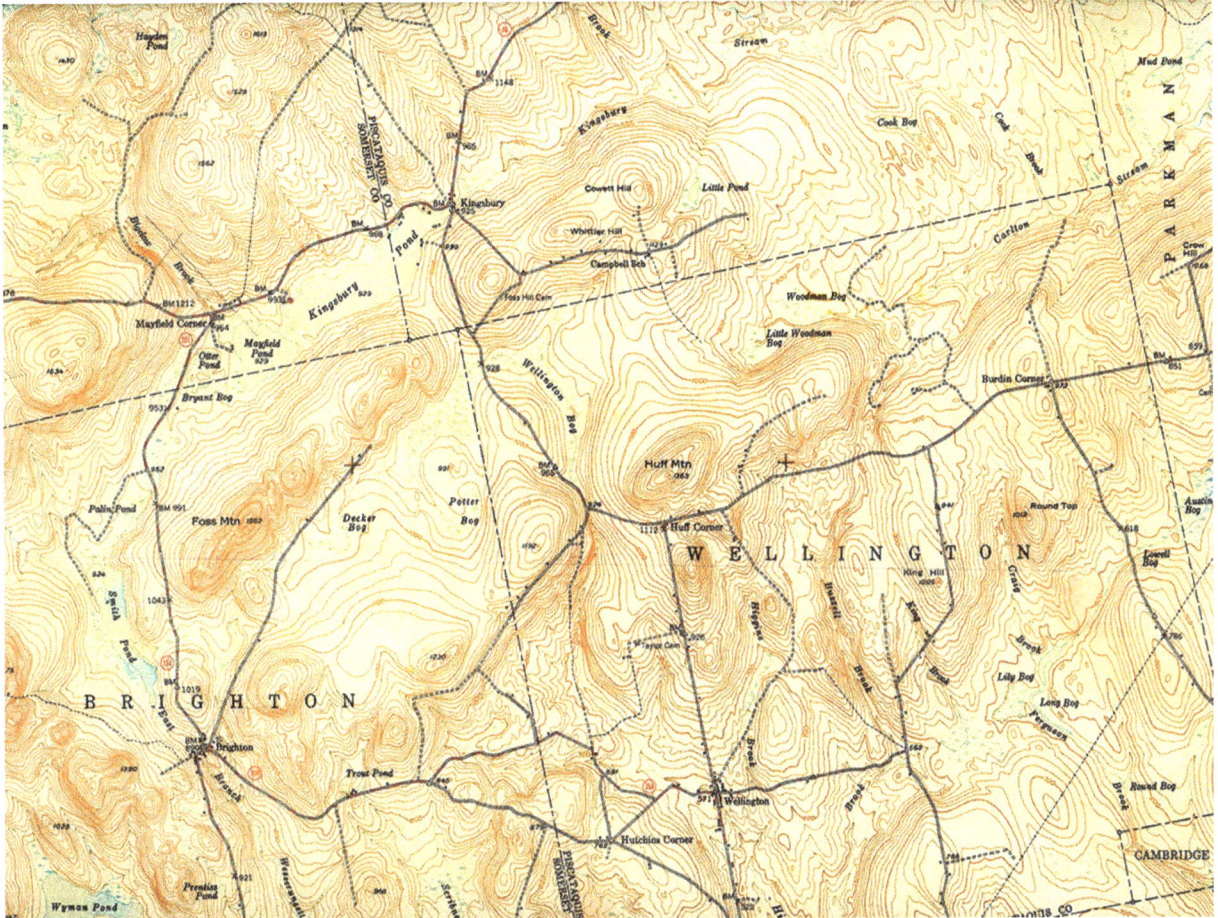

A red dot in the western central section designates the location of the Sawyer-Coyle cabin on the northwest corner of Kingsbury Pond as shown in the 1950 USGS topographic map of the Kingsbury quadrangle.

United States Geological Survey, Kingsbury, Maine, topographic map, 1950

maine's unique municipalities

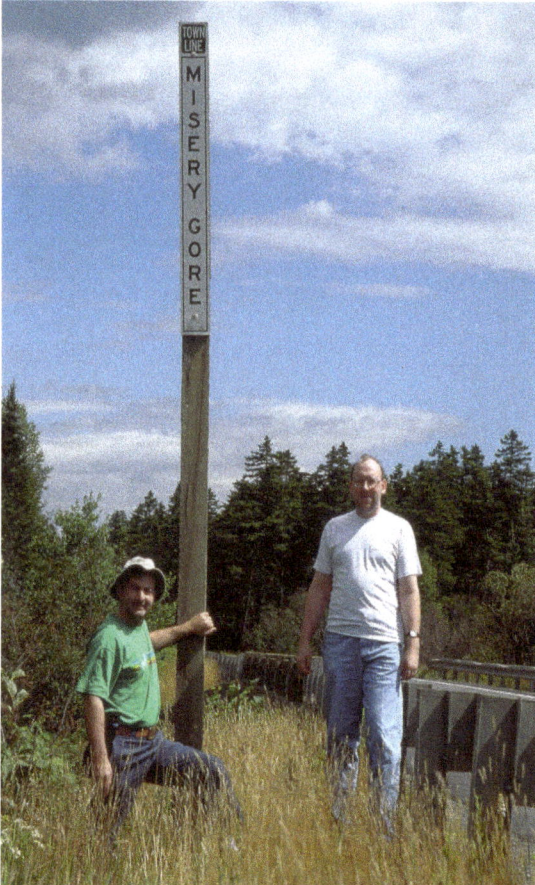

Chris Coyle, left, and Homer Beers stand by the sign at the town line for Misery Gore, an irregularly shaped area in Somerset County.

timed photo by Chris Coyle

The State of Maine has municipalities unique to the state. Like other states, Maine has cities and towns so-called based largely on population. The only state with a plantation land designation, Maine also had thirty-four plantations as of 2023. Plantation designations for Maine plots of land originated in the Massachusetts Bay Colony, which included the area called Maine until 1820, and survive today as a reminder of Maine's past as part of Massachusetts.

Maine's plantations exist as a basic government unit. Most are rural, forested, and lightly populated areas. The vote of the county commissioners organizes Maine plantations, whereas the state legislature votes to incorporate towns. Some Maine plantations have become towns over the years, and some towns have reverted to plantations.

Much of northwestern Maine takes the form of unorganized townships, areas lack local government under direct supervision and taxation by the state. Certain plantations have deorganized to become unorganized townships, often after the population declines to a point that cannot maintain even plantation government. Some such formerly populated settlements are thought of as ghost towns.

Maine also includes municipal boundaries called gores, irregularly shaped lands left over from eighteenth- and nineteenth-century surveying. Some gores have permanent residents, some do not. Somerset County includes Misery Gore and Moxie Gore.

life at the cabin

Our annual trip to Maine from Massachusetts, was usually an all-day affair. We packed the car and then closed the house up. Some years, we stopped to see my grandparents in Weston, Massachusetts, before heading north.

We lived in Boston in the summer of 1961. When it was time to go to Maine, the day arrived during a very hot spell. The folks awoke in the wee hours and decided just to get in the car and head for Maine. They said that, at less than a year old, I slept in the back seat. I woke up about the time we reached Portsmouth, New Hampshire, with a most beautiful sunrise. They said I was in awe of the dawn sky and talked about it for some time afterward.

Another time when I was very young, and I don't remember it, the folks were packing the car to leave for Maine. The very young me wanted to help. I started bringing anything at all that was not nailed down out to the car. Meanwhile, the folks kept bringing that stuff back in. I guess eventually they told me that not everything in the house needed to be taken to Maine for the summer.

The folks generally packed a picnic lunch for the trip. Depending on the time of day, we usually ate either at the Maine Information Center in Kittery or the rest area along the Maine Turnpike near Augusta. After the picnic and what seemed like a very long drive to me, especially when I was young, we left the Maine Turnpike at the Skowhegan-Fairfield exit at Waterville. After we began the drive north on US Route 201, ever-present log drives along the Kennebec River reminded us that we were in the north country.

At Skowhegan, we crossed onto an island by means of an EEE bridge, which takes its name from the sound made by the car going over the open-grate deck. We sometimes stopped for ice cream on the island before crossing a second bridge to reach downtown Skowhegan. Then we drove still farther north to Bingham. When I was young and we still went to Maine for most of July and August, Dad had a roof carrier and gray canvas to cover whatever got placed up there. We really brought a lot up in those days. For many years, it seemed like every time we reached Solon just south of Bingham on Route 201, we got into a rainstorm. The rain might be quite heavy but would be over before we had gone but a couple more miles. Often, the sun had come out by the time we reached the cabin.

Until the passing of Don Sawyer's folks, Omar and Josephine Sawyer, we stopped at their home in Bingham to get the cabin key. Don, his wife, Norma, and children Dan and Pam lived in Pompano Beach, Florida, although they had previously resided in Waterville. Hence, it worked better to pick up the key in Bingham. We might also pick up a few necessary grocery items in Bingham to carry us over to morning when we usually did a full shopping to get set up for our stay. In later years, we sometimes took the route north from Skowhegan through Athens, Harmony, and Brighton along Route 151 to Mayfield Corner, as it shaved a few miles and some very steep hills off the trip.

After driving through Bingham, we reached the north end of town where Route 16 left the main road on its eastward trek out to Kingsbury. Main Street through Bingham was rebuilt around 1970 with a new bridge across Austin Stream. The project widened the first few thousand feet of Route 16 east and bypassed from Main Street east to about where there had at one time been a bridge that connected to Old Canada Road over Austin Stream.

Once a manufacturing office owned by Amon Baker, the Bingham house nicknamed the Cuckoo's Nest reportedly served as a bootlegger stop in the 1930s.
photo by Chris Coyle

I was told that years ago a truck struck and demolished the bridge.

An unusual house stood on the north side of old Route 16 leaving town. The folks nicknamed it the Cuckoo's Nest. In recent years, I learned it had been used as a manufacturing office owned by Amon Baker. Reportedly, it was later a known bootlegger stop. It has stood empty in recent years.

The highway, the largest and steepest length rebuilt in 1961, climbed several miles up out of Kennebec Valley before reaching the summit of what we called Bingham Hill. When we reached the construction area on July 24, 1961, we found a still raging thunderstorm had washed out the until-then-unpaved new highway. We returned to Bingham and stayed overnight at the Yellow Bowl Inn until the next morning when the road had been repaired. Descending the hill going toward Bingham afforded a beautiful view of Wyman Dam.

At the top of Bingham Hill, the road leveled out for a mile or so. Until it was rebuilt, the stretch ran very up and down over low hummocks. Then the road went down a short hill we called Beebe Hill, part of Babbitt Ridge. The name Beebe Hill derived from the highway sign there all shot up, probably with something a little more powerful than a BB gun.

*A washed out construction area on Maine's Route 16 prevented the Coyles
from reaching the cabin on July 24, 1961, according to Barbara Coyle's journals.*
photo by Bob Coyle

Then we climbed a shorter hill up onto a level section for a couple of miles. The town line between Moscow and Mayfield where there was a small bog provided a good place to watch for moose. We sometimes saw Wilder and Lephie Rollins, our good friends from Bingham, parked there hoping to see a moose. The old dirt Lake Road led south to Withee Pond and points beyond left Route 16 to our right. Just west of West Mayfield, the road dropped down and went across a small stream. A long out-of-use concrete bridge stood to the south of the road where years before the highway had been straightened for a couple of hundred feet.

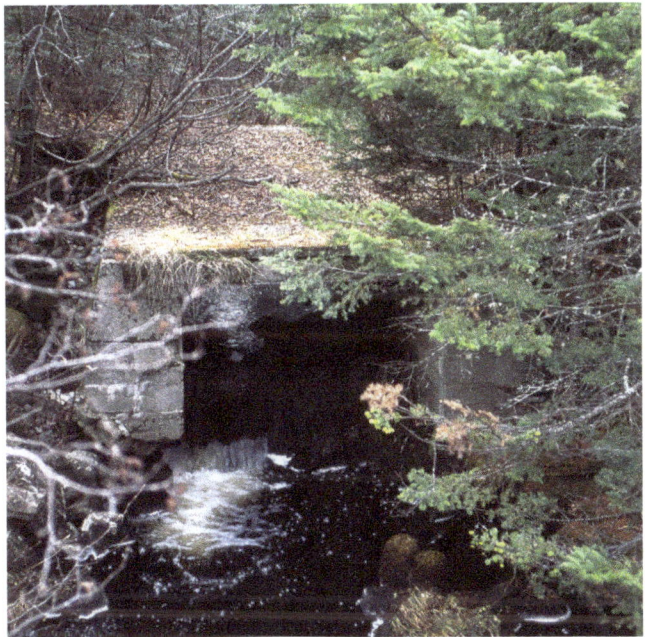

*Abandoned, a concrete bridge
spanned a West Mayfield stream.*
photo by Chris Coyle

We saw a wide and flat gravel bank to the north of the highway, and then we went up a slight rise of land to bypass an older and longer dirt section of highway prior to descending a short hill. An ancient, abandoned car sat on the left corner of the dirt road to the north of Highway 16. That road led up to Whitman Bog and Weeks Basin. I think Dad had hiked up in there years before.

We then drove through mostly deciduous woods for a bit. I remember a sunny afternoon in 1964 on our way back to the cabin from Bingham. I looked up through the back window of the car and studied beautiful cumulus clouds set against the Kodachrome blue sky. I can still picture it more than half a century later.

Eventually, we reached Cook Hill where the old road departed to our left for its descent down a steep hill and past the access road to the slate quarry. Dad shifted to low gear, and we saw Kingsbury and Mayfield ponds ahead of us. Most big hills had a pair of yellow highway signs spaced a short distance apart. One read HILL and the other read TRUCKS USE LOW GEAR. In the distance, we could see the stark blueberry barrens of East Kingsbury.

After the steep descent down the hill, Route 151 departed Route 16 to our right at Mayfield Corner. Day lilies grew in profusion at the southeast corner of the intersection. We sometimes picked the blossoms to make day lily macaroni for lunch—delicious hot the first day and cold as a leftover. My mother wanted to learn how to use wild edibles and ways of living off the land.

A steep grade down Cook Hill offers a 1977 view of Kingsbury and Mayfield ponds.
photo by Bob Coyle

Next, we went across Bigelow Brook by means of a large culvert that had been a narrow concrete bridge marked with striped white and red signs until that part of the road was rebuilt around 1967. As we drove over Bigelow Brook, we could see stone abutments of an earlier bridge to our right. I recall a bent over birch tree over one of them. The old Pooler farmhouse stood to our left in early years. On our right between Route 16 and Mayfield Pond was what we called the new gravel pit.

Long abandoned in August 1963, the Pooler house stood near Bigelow Brook.

photo by Bob Coyle

Then we stopped at the top of the quarter-mile driveway to the cabin. One of us unlocked the chain from the gate posts, and we started down the driveway. The gate chain was attached to wooden posts painted with the same red as was the trim on the cabin.

Once through the gate, we drove beneath some stately white pine trees and then past a somewhat more open area where a few blueberries once grew on the left side. After a few more feet, the brook ran very close to the left side of the driveway. Just upstream from that part of the brook, a yellow birch tree and some beech trees grew over the waterway. Then came a small overgrown grassy area to the left where an old and dying elm tree stood at the back.

We made a sharp curve to the right and crossed a culvert that provided drainage to the area. The brook had once run in a dry stream bed to the left. After the road straightened, there was a clearing with several small evergreen trees to our left.

One morning in July of 1964, Dad and I were driving in to the cabin and we spotted several small fawns still sporting white spots on their coats. They fed on browse. Next on the left grew higher evergreen trees without much foliage on the lower branches. A few white birch trees stood there as well and on the right, mixed deciduous and evergreen trees. A number of evergreen trees had snapped over a little across from the overgrown, grassy area. They had likely snapped over during a winter storm. We brought a few picnic lunches up there once in a while and sat on the snapped trees to eat.

Just into the low woods in the midst of some small evergreen trees were a couple of red boundary markers. At last, we reached a long curve to the left and could set our eyes upon the cabin and the blue water of Kingsbury Pond. Just into the woods on our right rested a completely moss-covered boulder we called Moss Rock. In a few moments, we stopped the car outside the back door, unlocked it, and stepped inside. It was always a treat to be back for another summer. Each year, I looked forward for weeks if not months to the day we would go to Maine, about the happiest day of each year for me.

Looking out at the pond to the left, we saw a cove leading out to Birch Point, a delta formed by the brook carrying debris down to the pond. Across Kingsbury Pond a mile or more away in front of Foss Hill, a few camps ranged to our left. A lower peak of Foss Mountain, the hill directly across from the cabin had no name on maps. I nicknamed it Skunk's Hill. When I was very young, I thought a couple of odd-shaped conifer trees at the summit were wings from a downed airplane.

The shoreline of Kingsbury Pond made a right angle at its southeast corner. A number of large rocks on the shoreline gave rise to our naming the area Stone Cove. Several large white pine trees at the next right angle of the pond just north of what we called the Isthmus of Mayfield gave reason to the name of Pine Point. Pine Cove comprised the little area just west of Tom Farrin's cabin a short distance from our camp.

Barbara watches over one-year-old Chris on a 1961 August day at Mayfield Pond.

photo by Bob Coyle

To reduce the high step up to the cabin's back door, we had a small wooden porch we could spike on to the sill below the doorway. In the next order of business, Dad lit the gas for the refrigerator. In order to do it, he removed the cover from the lower front of the refrigerator, lay down on the floor, and lit the pilot light. Initially, he used a regular wooden match, and it often took longer for the pilot light to light and sound its reassuring loud click than there was wood in the matchstick. The match usually burned down to Dad's fingers before the pilot light lit. Much to my mother's dismay, I acquired several interesting additions to my growing vocabulary at a young age during those episodes. Later, Dad placed the match in a straw and used it to hold the lighted match so he would not end up burning his fingers since the straw increased the length of the match.

Once the refrigerator was running, we unloaded the car and brought everything in. Usually, Mother took charge of unpacking kitchen items and putting things where they belonged. Lots of luggage had to be carried in and unpacked. We had to make the beds. Then we had a light, makeshift supper and retired early for the night, often to the pleasant calls of loons in the background. As darkness fell, we could see a few lights twinkling in camps that happened to be occupied that night way down toward the dam on the far shoreline of Foss Hill.

In the morning, Dad and I put the mailbox in the trunk of the car and brought it up to Route 16 where we planted it at the end of the driveway. Attached to its long wooden post, the mailbox stayed in my bedroom behind the clothes rod during the winter months when we didn't live at the cabin. We stored some cardboard castle models Dad had built inside the mailbox.

After we set up the mailbox, we usually drove in to Bingham and did our grocery shopping at Preble and Robinson, an old time rural grocery store.

Decades after we spent our last night at the cabin, I can picture every square inch of our beloved summer home. We entered the cabin from the back door into the small but efficient kitchen. On the right wall, a dining table folded down from built-in shelves. A built-in bench stood to the left of the shelves, and another freestanding bench normally sat against the wall beneath the shelves. The gas stove came next along and on the right of the doorway into the living room. Just in from the back door we had a gas refrigerator to the left with the kitchen counter and dry sink. The counter had cabinets and drawers beneath. A push broom and mop hung on the wall above the doorway.

A window behind the sink always had something interesting to look at outside while washing dishes. We could hang a mirror during shaving on a nail above the window. We had six plastic cups of varying colors that I distinctly remember. The upper part of each cup was fluted to the outside. We had three cups set aside for tooth brushing purposes—green for me—Go, yellow for Mother—Caution, and red for Dad—Stop! Three shelves for food items somewhat angled to meet the doorway to the living room. The living room had only a doorway but no door.

The kitchen in the cabin featured a gas stove along with any number of pots, pans, kettles, and implements.
photo by Chris Coyle

The cabin consisted of four rooms—the large, commodious living room area that measured thirteen by twenty-four feet along with two bedrooms and the kitchen. Wall partitions extended upward only some eight feet.

The two bedrooms had doors. All the doors at the cabin had latches rather than door-knobs. After Mrs. Omar Sawyer's passing in 1969, her son Donald brought some of her furniture to the cabin to replace older, less comfortable pieces. We moved some furniture around the living room from year to year and several times during our stay each summer. Some pieces of furniture remained in the same location. Lengthwise near the left wall of the living room stood the beautiful long maple table and benches Omar had built. A green-and-white checked tablecloth covered the table.

Just inside of the doorway from the kitchen before reaching the table, a beautiful mahogany chest had come out from Bingham. Interesting contents of the chest included a box of black and white photos Don had taken when he worked as a photographer for the *Waterville Morning Sentinel.*

Beyond the table and in the corner of the living room, a small but efficient built-in desk folded down once we turned a turn hook. Small gold chains held it in place in the down position. A very old wind-up clock sitting atop the desk provided us with the time of day, not that it mattered all that much for us at the cabin. The front of the clock had a beautiful heron painted in gold upon the glass.

A four-piece black wicker set with red trim came out from Bingham in 1969. It included a love seat, two rocking chairs with slightly different arms, and a chair with flat legs. A fold-out cot usually stood in the southwest corner of the living room, with the long way perhaps along one wall at one point and then along the other wall at another time. A small shelf made of small birch logs was on the wall in that corner of the cabin. Usually, we had a card table set up, often to the right of the front door in the center of the front wall. A single gaslight above that area complemented another one on the wall facing Tom's cabin. Double gaslights were in the kitchen and above the long table in the living room.

The venerable old Victrola took different places in the living room depending on how we arranged the furniture. Omar's heavy wood and leather rocker sat between the doorway to the kitchen and that to my bedroom. Above his chair, a large frame contained black and white photos from his logging days. To the left of the doorway into the folks' bedroom, a stacking bookshelf unit with glass doors contained a number of old and very interesting copies of *Down East Magazine*. Old copies of *Atlantic Monthly* stacked up next to Lincoln Logs, little wooden toys for building, on the shelf over my bed. I found *Atlantic Monthly* far less interesting than *Down East*. However, back issues of *Atlantic Monthly* proved quite useful when pressing wildflowers we tried to preserve.

We had a few publications of our own that we kept at the cabin as well, and we reread them each summer. We had a set of Sunday comics that were fun, especially *Peanuts* and *Blondie*. We also had a few copies of *Mad* magazine Dad had confiscated from students in his classroom reading the magazines rather than listening to him. The unsuspecting students did not realize how much he enjoyed reading *Mad*, and because of the confiscated issues, I don't think he ever bought any of his own copies!

My bedroom was in the middle of the cabin and the folks used the bedroom in the northwest corner of the building. Before 1969, they had a double bed. Then, a beautiful set of maple twin beds and wardrobe replaced the earlier furniture. They kept two large duffle bags in the corner for dirty laundry with a chamber pot kept along the wall facing Tom's cabin. When I was a little boy, Dad and I lay on our backs on one of the beds and put our feet together to play bicycle, pedaling away.

In my bedroom, I had a built-in bed with two drawers beneath on the long side and one drawer on the end. Over the bed, an L-shaped shelf stored Lincoln Logs and other items, including a small bowling set I played with from time to time. It had pins only about eight inches high and a small wooden ball painted red, if I remember right. I also remember a little souvenir ornament from one of the world fairs. One side had a yellow obelisk about three inches high.

My bedroom also had a small three-drawer pink wardrobe, an ancient crank telephone, and a large trunk belonging to the folks where they stored a few clothes and other items over the winter. Both rooms had hooks on the walls and pipes with clothes hangers. After 1969, I had a cedar chest at the foot of my bed to store blankets and other bed linen.

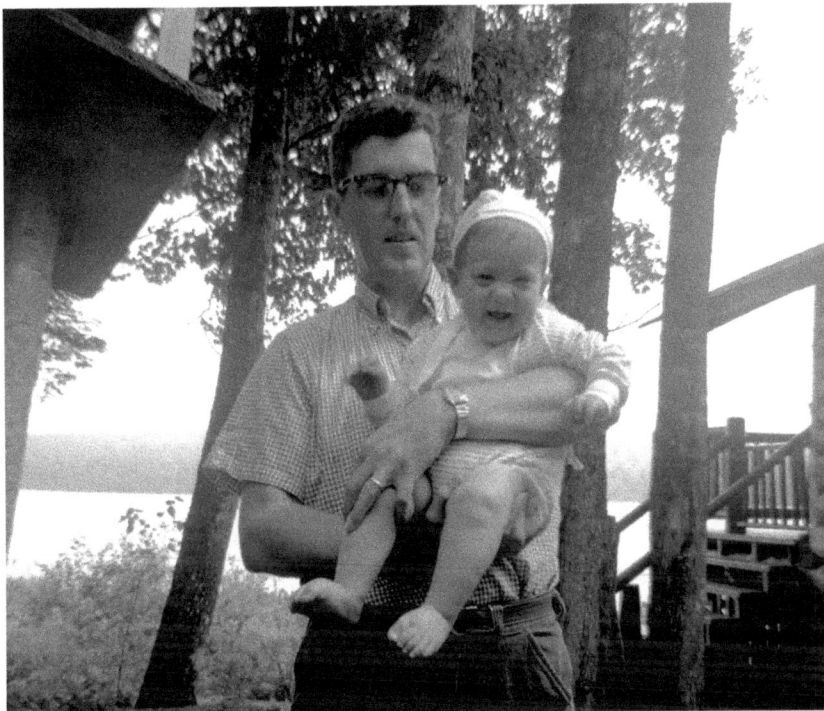

Bob Coyle holds one-year-old Chris outside the cabin in 1961.
photo by Barbara Coyle

The bedrooms were quite cozy and very comfortable. When lying in my bed, I could look up at the ceiling where boards beneath the roof lay across the logs that supported it. Familiar knotholes resembled bats, animals, and faces. On our final morning at the cabin in 1981, I woke up and could hear the folks packing items in the kitchen. Before getting up, I took a few minutes and looked up at those familiar knotholes one last time, because I was uncertain if I would ever sleep there again. As of this writing, I have not.

An old but highly dependable Household 250 cast-iron wood stove kept us warm on cold days and nights with the stove centrally located in the cabin between the two bedroom doors. A front door on the stove contained windows made of muscovite mica. We kept some wood in a box near the stove along with an old metal pail where we always had some kindling on hand—small sticks, pine cones, and the like. Old newspapers, usually the *Morning Sentinel*, *Bangor Daily News*, or the *Christian Science Monitor* helped to get a fire started. Later, near the end of our years in Mayfield, a huge tree crashed through the roof and destroyed the wonderful Household 250 during a storm, fortunately not when anyone was in residence.

A ritual on cold nights involved going out to the woodshed before dusk and bringing in a couple armfuls of wood for the night. Dad often set everything up so when it got cold in the night, we would only have to strike a match on the side of the stove and light the fire. During some cold summers, we used the wood stove every night. Other years, we used the stove only a few times.

The top of the stove had a flat cooking surface capable of producing *the* best toast ever! Donuts, usually Harris's, tasted great if sliced in two and heated on the wood stove. I can also remember heating water on the stove as well as cooking items such as French toast or eggs. We could use the wood stove for cooking if we ran out of gas for the kitchen stove. When we did run out of gas, we went beneath the cabin, closed the valve on the tank in use, switched the junction valve to the other tank, and then opened its valve. As we did not have a telephone, we had to literally go to whoever sold the gas. At one time, it was Tozier's service station on Route 201 across Austin Stream that handled gas. I think that Robie Howes also did bottled gas at one time. Later, it was a man across the Kennebec River bridge in Concord.

I believe the final gas man we had was Harold York. He lived in a bungalow just north of Tozier's in the town of Moscow. He worked nights at a mill in Solon and sometimes slept in the daytime when we looked for him. Whenever he came out to the cabin to change out a propane tank, the folks invited him in for a slice of pie, which he seemed to enjoy. The propane tanks came from several different companies over the years. I think Dead River Propane was the last one and that Harold York carried those tanks.

One evening when I was younger, I asked Dad to let me set up the woodstove with newspapers and kindling. I always wondered why Dad never filled the stove completely to the top with newspapers, so I proceeded to do so and shoved as many as I could right up to the top of the stove and on up the flue pipe. Then I lit a match on the edge of the stove and tossed it in. The stove's contents ignited and nearly blew the stove apart before calming down after a few minutes. I then understood why *not* to fill the stove with newspapers.

Dad did not look amused but didn't say much as he could see I had learned a valuable lesson from that mistake.

Periodically, we had to clean out the ashes from the stove. We used a small coal scoop and put the ashes in a metal pail, taking care to leave a layer of ashes in the stove where we would lay the next fire.

We used wood ashes along with lime and occasionally coffee grounds to put down in the hole in the outhouse. Indeed, we did strive to maintain a nice facility—one where it didn't bother us to linger. We usually had a can of Glade air freshener on hand and sometimes a vase of flowers in the outhouse, too. Visitors complimented us on having one of the cleanest and best smelling outhouses around.

At some point in the summer of 1960 before I made my appearance in the world on August 29, the folks somehow locked themselves out of the log cabin. For whatever reason, my mother, eight months with child, was elected to scale the logs up one wall to a window near the ridgepole, remove the screen, crawl through the opening, and lower herself to the floor whereupon she could open the main door. A similar incident occurred in the late 1970s and I was elected to enter the cabin in a similar fashion. We then made a trip to Andrews Hardware in Bingham and had a spare key made to keep in the car should it ever be needed.

I should mention more about those windows below the ridgepole at either end of the cabin. Each measured more than two feet wide and high, hinged at the bottom. A length of clothesline rope from the top went through several pulleys and down into the cabin for convenient opening and closing. A tie-back on the wall tied the window open, and screens on the outside of the cabin helped prevent unwanteds from getting inside. With the windows open, air could circulate through the upper part of the cabin where warm air tended to collect. We had nicknamed the windows Arctic Window for the one

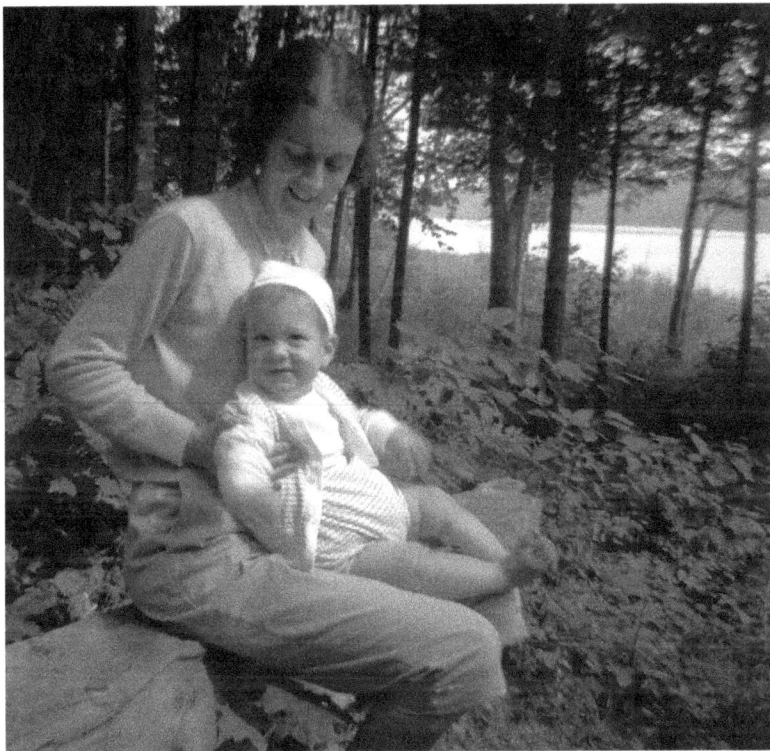

Barbara braces one-year-old Chris on her lap in August 1961.
photo by Bob Coyle

on the north or woods side and Antarctic Window for the one on the pond side. We usually opened Antarctic Window a few inches whenever we used the wood stove.

On the outside wall of the cabin in the early years, a black PVC tube carried anything poured down the kitchen sink to empty outside a few inches off the ground. Later, the discharge pipe plumbed to a dry well. As a youngster, I was thrilled by the sight of sudsy dish water spewing out of the pipe onto the ground. I remember dragging poor Cousin Muriel outside in the early 1960s when Mother got ready to empty the dish water so that Muriel could experience the sight as well—what a good sport!

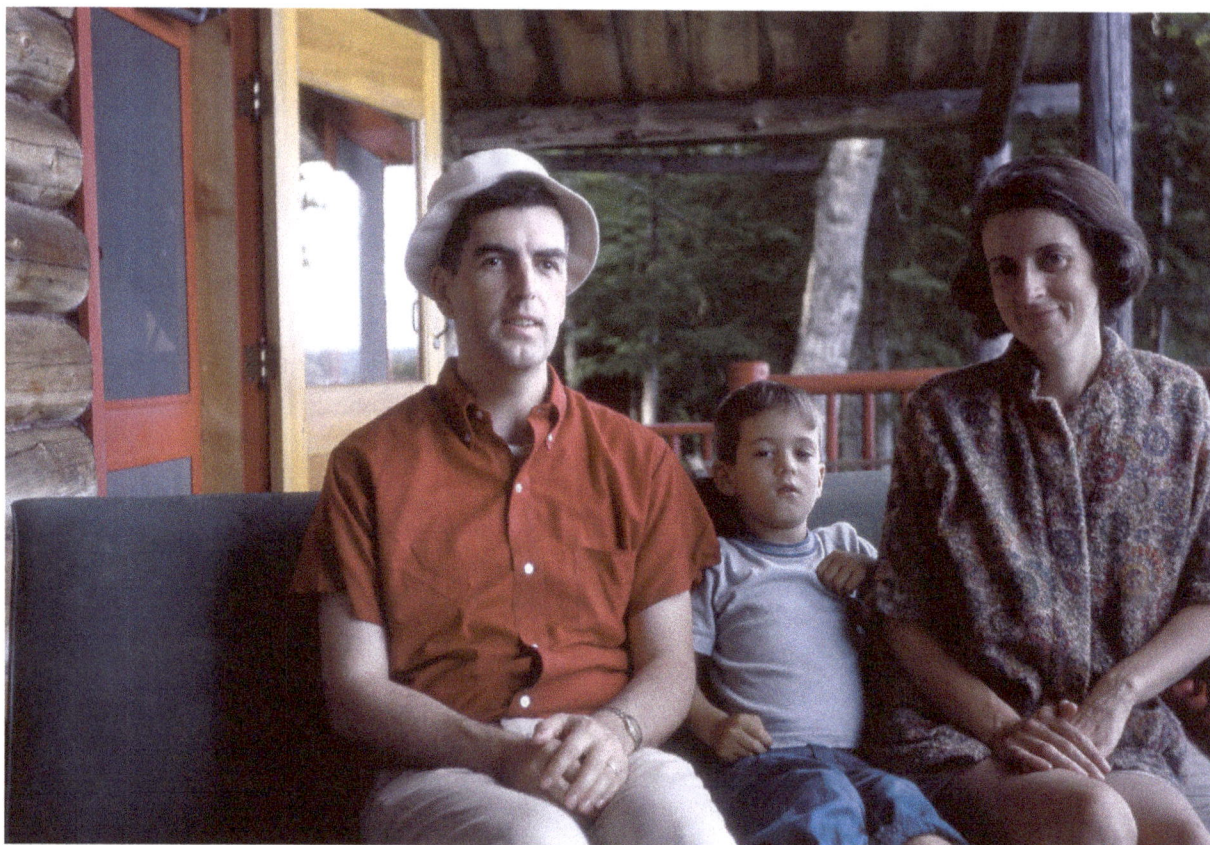

Bob, Chris, and Barbara relax on the cabin front porch in July 1966.

timed photo by Bob Coyle

We often had my dad's one-dish camp supper at the Maine cabin after a day out in the field.

Bob Coyle's One-Dish Camp Supper

Ingredients:

1 pound ground beef

1 can beef broth

1 can water

1 cup uncooked brown rice

1 to 2 tablespoons dried parsley or herb mix

Procedure:

Brown ground beef in large (iron if you have one) frying pan.

Add beef broth, water, and rice.

When rice is almost cooked, add parsley and/or herb mix.

drawing water

The cabin never had running water during our time. We had two types of water—wash water and drinking water. Kingsbury Pond provided all the wash water we needed. We lugged water from the pond nearly daily. We kept three pails—two yellow plastic and one galvanized steel—on the kitchen counter for washing hands and dishes. A two-quart enameled white dipper hung from a nail to the left of the sink, and we used it for washing our hands. We also used pond water to wash dishes after heating it in a large metal kettle over the gas stove.

We occasionally washed small amounts of laundry at the sink with heated pond water. The folks tied clothesline rope to trees and secured the laundry with wooden clothespins to dry. For some reason, laundry equipment fascinated me when I was a youngster, and I enjoyed peering behind the rows of washing machines at the Bingham Laundromat to see myriad sets of hoses, sometimes watching the exhaust spew out of the large dryer vents outside the building. Back at Mayfield, I would invert my tricycle and turn the wheel as I imagined it a washing machine.

Local springs and old wells provided our drinking water before our nearby neighbor Tom Farrin ran a pipe from a mountain spring to his camp, Pine Cove. He offered us all the water we needed from his outside sillcock.

In my earliest memories, we hauled drinking water in the trunk of the car from the well some two miles away behind the old store at Kingsbury Mills, probably at the suggestion of Don Sawyer. The long closed store had once operated in an old house with unpainted, graying clapboards. We never saw anyone at the building, but it may have seen seasonal use from time to time, perhaps during the fall hunting season. Vegetation crowded the structure, but it appeared the grass got cut down once a year or so. An unscreened porch spanned the front of the building. I also recall an old, very large thermometer on the door frame by the main door. I also seem to remember a Moxie insignia on the thermometer. Moxie, still popular today in central Maine, was the most popular soft drink in New England around 1900.

A grass-covered driveway ran to the right of the building. Dad parked the car in the driveway and unloaded the vessels to fill with water. The quintessential country well had an opening accessed by standing on a wooden platform that encircled the shaft up from the water source below. A roof covered the entire apparatus. We could lower the well's pail attached to a rope into the well by cranking a drum-shaped pulley. After filling, we raised the pail by pulling on the rope. It was slow work, and often, woody bits floated in the water.

*Bob draws water from a well outside old
Kingsbury Store around 1958.*
photo by Barbara Coyle

Next, we poured the water into our vessels from the pail for transport back to the cabin. In the earliest days, we used large, narrow-mouthed glass jars that possibly once held apple cider. Unfortunately, much of the water poured into the jars spilled on account of the jars' narrow necks. A funnel might have been useful but to the best of my knowledge none was ever used. Later, Dad used four-quart mayonnaise jars, first made of glass but later of plastic discarded from the Athol Junior High School cafeteria. The jars had large, wide screw caps and were considerably easier to fill than the previously used type, and we lost very little water.

Sometime in the mid 1960s, Dad became concerned about the amount of rotted wood that seemed to crumble from the well structure into the water we drank. For the next several years, we kept empty containers for water storage in the trunk of the car. If we happened by a place where we knew of water good for drinking purposes, we stopped and filled whatever vessels we had in the trunk. If we didn't have much drinking water, we would made a dedicated trip to a trusted source to fill jugs.

When the Omar Sawyers were still alive, we often stopped at their home on Preble Street in Bingham and filled jugs from their outside faucet. It gave them a chance to catch up with us as to what was going on out at the cabin. On the other side of Bingham across the bridge over the Kennebec River to Concord and up the hill next to the road running north toward Carrying Place, a pipe ran out from the hillside near the trail up to Old Bluff. Very cold water ran fast out of that pipe. Hence, it provided a great place to fill jugs. Sometimes, while doing laundry in Bingham, we filled our jugs at that pipe, and occasionally we hiked up Old Bluff as well to be treated to the lovely view toward the Kennebec River valley looking north toward Wyman Lake in Moscow.

The Coyles sometimes collected drinking water at a pipe in Old Bluff, part of Concord.

photo by Chris Coyle

I can still remember many other locations where we drew water. Up the dirt Campbell Hill Road to East Kingsbury, there was an abandoned old house we called the witch's house. Downhill and west of the witch's house, a semi-abandoned farmhouse had a large cast iron kettle next to the road that was about a yard wide and two feet deep. Former residents probably used the kettle to make potash. A wooden trough from some-where up on the hill supplied cold water to the kettle. We could fill our vessels with drinking water from the fresh water running out of the trough, not the water sitting in the kettle. As the kettle filled, the overflow ran over the edge and down the ditch by the side of the road. At times, grass around the house had been cut, but we never saw anyone when we filled our jugs with the clear, cold water.

Also in Kingsbury, we used a spring from time to time up the dirt road by Titcomb Cemetery on Route 16 going east toward Abbot Village. Back in Mayfield, we knew of a small spring on the old road going up Cook Hill a short distance into the woods off the old road between it and the new road. Before the old road became overgrown and dark, we found it a good area to pick blueberries.

We often stopped at the spring after a picking session. A couple of old clothing items tied to a tree branch marked the start of the short trail to the spring. Someone had provided the spring with an old-fashioned dipper to help people get a drink. Although the water seemed

The Coyles sometimes collected water from a tub on Campbell Hill Road in East Kingsbury.
photo by Jane O'Regan

fine, people had difficulty filling jugs at that spring, so we did not use it very much. There were other places where we would stop to fill water jugs if we happened upon them but those are the regular places which I can remember now.

Then, one summer in the mid 1970s, our neighbor Tom Farrin had quite a surprise for us. Tom greeted us back at camp and told us that his contracting crew had installed a very long length of black PVC piping up through the woods under Route 16 to a hillside spring and, so, Tom's cabin had running water! He invited us to come over after our supper to see his new flush toilet. So, we trotted over to Tom and Arlene's cabin, Pine Cove. They greeted us warmly and invited us in.

Tom showed us the kitchen sink recently equipped with a faucet and running water. But the piece-de-resistance was his new flush toilet installed in a small room off the kitchen. Tom proudly flushed the fixture several times for us to admire. Owning a large contracting firm certainly had its advantages for Tom as a camp owner.

Back outside, Tom showed us his outdoor sillcock and offered its use to us anytime to fill our water jugs, thus ushering in a new era of water acquisition for us. From that point on through our final summer at the cabin, we availed ourselves of Tom's kind offer of water.

Our camp had an old wooden wheelbarrow with a metal wheel. I would place empty mayo jars—four to six of them by then all plastic—into the wheelbarrow and head over for refilling at Tom's sillcock. I'd park the wheelbarrow on the grass and fill the jars one by one with cool, fresh mountain spring water. Then I slowly wheeled everything back to our cabin. In my mind, I can hear the sound of the wheelbarrow's steel wheel running over rocks and rough gravel back and forth on the water runs.

We kept jugs in the gas refrigerator. The old refrigerator kept everything very cold. There was nothing more refreshing than a glass of that cold water on a hot day. When I was very young, the electric light bulb inside the refrigerator fascinated me. For some reason, no one ever removed the bulb, but of course it never provided any illumination in electricity-free Mayfield!

After filling the drinking water jugs, I fetched water in pails from the pond. Sometimes I made more than one trip for pond water if we were washing dishes. Although the wheelbarrow could transport the pails, I found that I lost too much water from spillage when wheeling it back up the hill from the pond. It turned out better for me to fill two pails and carry them as such. During the two summers after Kingsbury Dam broke and the water level was very low while the new dam was being built, we had to lug water from much farther away.

In later years after we stopped going to the cabin, we used the old plastic mayo jars at home for sunflower seed storage and transport. A few of them still kick around my house. Some years, I kept one of those jars filled with sand in the trunk of my car in case my or someone else's car became stuck in the snow. Every time I handled one of those jars, my mind went back to years ago at Kingsbury Pond.

going north

During our early years in Mayfield, we had a rather traditional unpainted wooden outhouse located on a woodland trail some hundred feet or so from the back door of the cabin. We referred to trips to the outhouse as "Going North." One year upon our arrival at the cabin in the mid 1960s, I was surprised to find a newly constructed wooden A-frame outhouse painted the same shade of red as the cabin's trim color, the interior painted white, and the floor gray. Omar Sawyer built the structure at his home in Bingham and then moved it to Mayfield.

Omar Sawyer built the A-frame outhouse in the 1960s.
photo by Chris Coyle

For a few summers, we were afforded the luxury of two outhouses. We had pictures up inside them, and they really felt quite homey. The old outhouse had a couple of shelves in the corners covered with contact paper. We could often see birds and other animals if we kept the door open while using the facility. The new outhouse not only sported a window with screen above the seat but also a flue pipe and chimney from underneath to provide good ventilation. Eventually, the Sawyers used the old outhouse to store items from Bingham after Don Sawyer's parents passed on, and we reverted to one outhouse, albeit a "nice" outhouse.

The Sawyers brought lots of items from Omar and Josephine's home on Preble Street in Bingham to store in the main cabin following Josephine's demise in 1969. They placed many books atop the partition between the living and bedrooms. Old and very interesting copies of Maine's *Down East Magazine* came out from Bingham as well. For some reason, the Sawyers had acquired dozens and dozens of candles. A nice chest of drawers came out from the

Sawyers' home and held a lot of the candles. Don's wife, Norma, said to my mother, "Don't be sparing with the candles!"

We often found small clumps of Indian pipe or ghost plant growing near the path to the outhouses. Indian pipe is an interesting translucent ghostly white plant which does not contain chlorophyll and is parasitic rather than generating its food energy from sunlight. It grows on dark forest floors with rich soils and decaying plant material. The legend of Indian pipe is that quarreling chiefs did not smoke the peace pipe and that the Great Spirit turned them into plants.

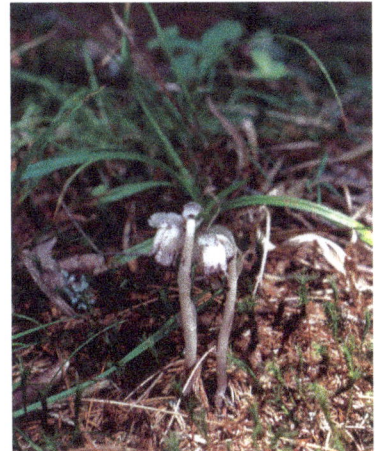

Indian pipe grew along the trails to the outhouse near the cabin.

photo by Chris Coyle

One time in later years, my mother went up to use the outhouse one morning and closed the door. The wooden knob on the outside of the door somehow turned and locked Mother inside. My father and I had gone somewhere, and she didn't expect us back for several hours. Mother chose wisely, as would I, to exit the building by climbing up and out the only window in the building rather than down through the cellar.

On stormy nights, we used a chamber pot with a rickety wooden seat we could set upon the pot as we used it. In the morning, we emptied the unit in the outhouse and rinsed it out with pond water. One time, we caught a pickerel in the chamber pot, but of course let it go back in the pond, as none of us had a valid Maine fishing license.

We saw many fish in the shore waters of Kingsbury Pond—mostly kivvies, which I am told are not too good eating as they are very bony. Better fish swam out in the pond as evidenced by many folks we could see fishing from boats. The kivvies, ranging from about eleven to fifteen inches long, had nests near our dock—sort of rounded, somewhat depressed affairs on the bottom of the pond. When we waded in the water or dangled our feet from the dock, the curious fish often bumped against us and sort of nibbled our feet and legs. Denny Monaghan, one of my father's students from Athol and his mother visited my folks at the cabin in 1958. Denny fished and caught some kivvies and trout that everybody enjoyed for lunch.

One evening around the last year we summered in Mayfield, we made our final trip Up North to the outhouse before retiring to bed. While waiting for the folks, I casually shone my flashlight up in the trees and evidently disturbed a sleeping robin. There was quite a commotion up in the tree branches and leaves and I thought I heard Dad holler "Run!" I took off for the cabin like a soaked cat. I could really run in those days. I thought sure a Nazgul or some similar creature from J.R.R. Tolkien's "Lord of the Rings" was bearing down on us for sure.

I don't think I ever ran so fast! My legs were moving so rapidly that I was actually kicking the top of the back of my legs with my toes. When I reached the cabin screen door I opened and closed it so fast several times that I failed to get inside before slamming it closed again. It then occurred to me that perhaps I should check on the folks' well-being and whereabouts. They soon sauntered down the path from the outhouse and wondered why I had taken off so fast. Apparently, all returned to quiet once the robin had settled elsewhere.

Another evening as we returned to the cabin from the outhouse, we spotted the orange glow of a fire down toward the dam. We all got in the car and headed east. Route 16 got closer to the pond, and we could see high flames leaping up toward the sky. At first, I thought it might be the little camp I so admired between the highway and Kingsbury Pond because of the hand pump in the yard. But as we got closer, we could see that the inferno raged on the opposite shore. We drove into the rest area and stopped the car. The Andrews family, who ran the hardware store in Bingham, owned the camp on fire.

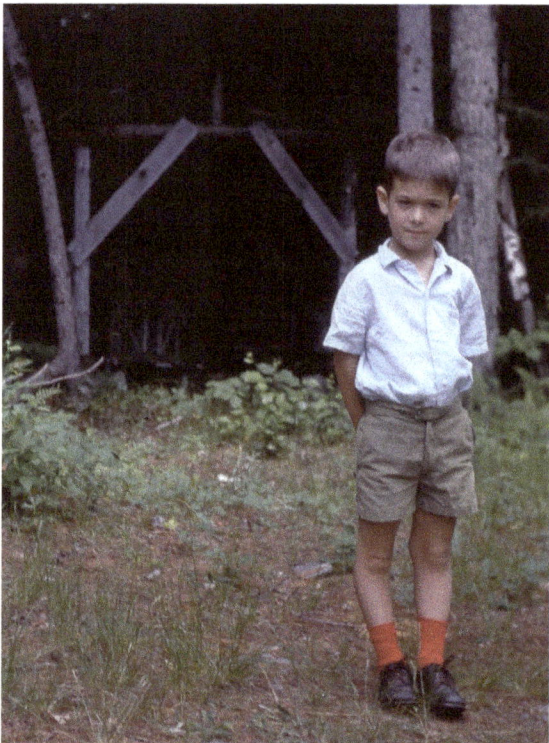

Seven-year-old Chris took a stand in front of the woodshed on the North Trail leading to the outhouse.
photo by Bob Coyle

We saw no fire trucks nor anyone fighting the fire, but people gathered around near the burning camp so we assumed that help had been summoned. I don't know where fire trucks were summoned from—perhaps Abbot Village. It would have taken some time to round up call firemen there and then make the trip out to Kingsbury.

A new camp replaced the burned one by our next summer at Kingsbury Pond. In fact, the new camp looked much nicer and built with better quality materials. Of course, the fact that the owners ran a hardware store with building materials at their disposal must have helped.

We kept an old beige raincoat at the cabin year-round. We called it the outhouse coat. We used it along with a 1940s era dark red umbrella with wooden handle to venture up to the outhouse on rainy days. On mornings after a good rain, we often found slugs on the path to go North. They seemed to disappear about the time surface moisture dried up.

more life at the cabin

We did not often close the chain to the driveway at night but occasionally we did. The folks told me that one summer evening before I was born, my grandparents Sherman walked down the driveway barking like foxes. My parents hadn't expected them until the next morning, so Dad had put up the chain for the night. As it turned out, they arrived in Bingham early, an unusual happening for them, and after checking into their lodging, they decided to go out and see the folks.

Part way down the driveway and on the out-

Bob and Barbara relax on the front porch of the cabin in July, 1963.

timed photo by Bob Coyle

side of a big curve, an old bed spring propped up against it, an old elm tree stood at the back of a clearing. I am told that the Sawyers had a little trailer set up in the clearing while they built the cabin. The Sawyers called the camp PaMaSonSis, which drew its name from the four members of their family and had the slight ring of a Native American name. After the Donald Sawyers retired and spent most of the warm months at the cabin, they referred to the cabin as Fur Enuff.

A brook ran along the upper part of the driveway and then disappeared into the woods behind the clearing for its last few hundred feet down to Birch Point on Kingsbury Pond. Just north of the clearing, the brook was only about six feet from the edge of the driveway. A moss-covered log installed as a dam stood there for years. It was fun to watch the cold mountain water pour over the log. We found two other log dams in the woods a little above that one.

Dad got his driver's license at the age of twenty-eight and his first car shortly before the folks' first stay at Mayfield in 1958. That car was an early model Chevrolet, brown in color, and lacked a reverse. The transmission had been filled with sawdust or something at the Meadville, Pennsylvania, crooked used car lot where he bought it. Soon after the car's acquisition, Dad found out about its lack of reverse motion, so he made sure to park where he would not need to back up. Otherwise, he drove up an incline to let it roll back.

Bob parked his first car, a Chevy with no reverse gear, near the cabin in 1958.
photo by Bob Coyle

The folks told of an infamous drive along Old Kingsbury Road in Brighton, Maine. South of Foss Mountain, the Old Kingsbury Road seemed to end near Decker Bog, according to the topo map. As the folks drove along the road, it became increasingly narrow, brush-encroached, and likely to peter out. Dad realized he would somehow have to reverse direction. He tried to drive up into an overgrown field in hopes the car would roll backwards toward the road, but high grass dashed any hopes of that happening.

The folks got out of the swamped Chevy to assess the situation. Suddenly a crew of French-Canadian lumberjacks came into sight as they walked down the road and stumbled on the folks and their dilemma. None of the men spoke English, but they understood the problem. One of the men muttered a word that my mother interpreted as chien, the French word for dog. She responded "No woof woof" or something like that. The man was actually asking if they had a chain, but they didn't have either a chain—or a dog, for that matter. Then the men all got in front of the car and simply pushed it backwards so Dad could once again go forward.

Following that hair-raising experience, the folks began keeping a can of beans, can opener, and a couple of spoons in the car should they ever become marooned on a back road. I think he must have been a little more careful going down remote roads after that, and I believe Dad traded the car when he could afford a better one—at least one with working forward and reverse gears!

Travelling through the Mayfield-Kingsbury region, I looked for familiar scenes each year. I knew of half a dozen or more old abandoned cars at various locations that I always looked for. Some were quite old. One ancient car in the old Mayfield gravel pit almost looked as though it had been previously buried and came to light when the gravel pit became active.

We took Route 16 to go anywhere. Our quarter-mile driveway curved to the left as it climbed the slight hill to Route 16. Prior to Tom Farrin's arrival at Pine Cove, the driveway was narrow and tree-lined. Dad had to dodge a couple of rocks when driving to the cabin, and low-hanging branches at times brushed against the car.

The year I turned nine, Dad thought it a good idea for me to learn to drive in case of an emergency so I would be able to get to Bingham for help. So, as he and I headed up the driveway one morning in his blue 1964 Ford Galaxie 500 to fetch the mail, Dad had me squeeze left from the center of the wide front seat and try my hand at driving. I took a liking to it and soon could drive up and back along the driveway with Dad still actually in the driver's seat. With a little stretching, I was able to reach the accelerator pedal with my right foot, I used my left foot on the brake pedal.

In a couple of years, about the time I turned eleven, he trusted me to drive up and down the driveway alone to get the mail. I believe that the Sawyer children, Dan and Pam, also learned how to drive on the long driveway. As I grew older, Dad let me drive from the middle of the front seat on nearby back roads, often dirt surfaced, where we rarely encountered other traffic. If we did meet an oncoming vehicle, Dad took over until the other vehicle was out of sight.

For many years, we patronized the dry-cleaning services of PM Laundry in Greenville. The business had a pickup and drop-off service. When we wanted the driver to stop at the cabin, we posted a sign on the mailbox. The original sign carried the words PM Laundry in large black letters on a white background and later, a green sign said the same thing. I think one or both signs may still be around somewhere.

At any rate, the driver had a long route. He left Greenville and drove west close to fifty miles to Jackman. As I recall, he drove south on Route 201 from Jackman forty-nine miles to Bingham and then out Route 16 past our driveway twenty-five miles to Abbot Village. From there, he returned to Greenville twenty-two miles on Route 15, possibly going through Blanchard or Shirley on the way back which added nine or one and a half miles, respectively. I'm not sure how many days each week he drove the route.

I believe that PM Laundry also took clothes to wash and dry in addition to dry-cleaning. The always friendly driver visited for a short while before continuing along the route in his van. I remember him telling us one time that Maine only has two seasons—winter and August!

For several years starting about the time I was fifteen in the mid/late 1970s, Dad and I brought our bicycles to Maine. He had an orange Columbia ten-speed, and I had a green three-speed Raleigh. We had a bike carrier that fastened quite easily to the car trunk. We enjoyed riding the bikes up and down the quarter-mile driveway. Sometimes we rode the easy two-mile trip to Kingsbury Dam or down Route 151 and back. We had fun having the bikes up there, and I often went up and down the driveway a few times before supper.

Thinking about bicycles, I remember one involving my father and me that took place in the mid 1970s. A Taylor Rental store had opened in Athol on the corner of Main Street and North Orange Road. On a pleasant summer morning, Dad and I rented a tandem bicycle. We started up North Orange Road, Dad on the front seat and me on the rear seat. We found it difficult pedaling up the steep incline at the start of North Orange Road, so I thought it easiest if I let Dad do the work while I just sat there for the ride. The strategy would have worked to my advantage had the sun not been out. As Dad pedaled feverishly up the hill, he happened to look down to see the shadow of my legs dangling there doing nothing. I need not elaborate further.

We most fortunately stayed in good health over our years at Mayfield. One of the very few injuries incurred at the

From the cabin front porch, Bob surveyed the surroundings in July, 1963.
photo by Barbara Coyle

cabin happened one night when I rolled out of my bed and onto the floor. which resulted in a concussion. Every so often we saw Dr. Robert Golden, who practiced next door to Riverside Lodge. We procured any necessary prescriptions from Moore's Rexall Drugstore in Bingham. Speaking of prescriptions, I remember one time when I had a prescription for something or other when we were home on Riverbend Street in Athol. I think it was before

I entered first grade. Mother couldn't open the childproof cap. I said, "Let me do it, Mama." So, she handed me the bottle, and I opened it quick as can be.

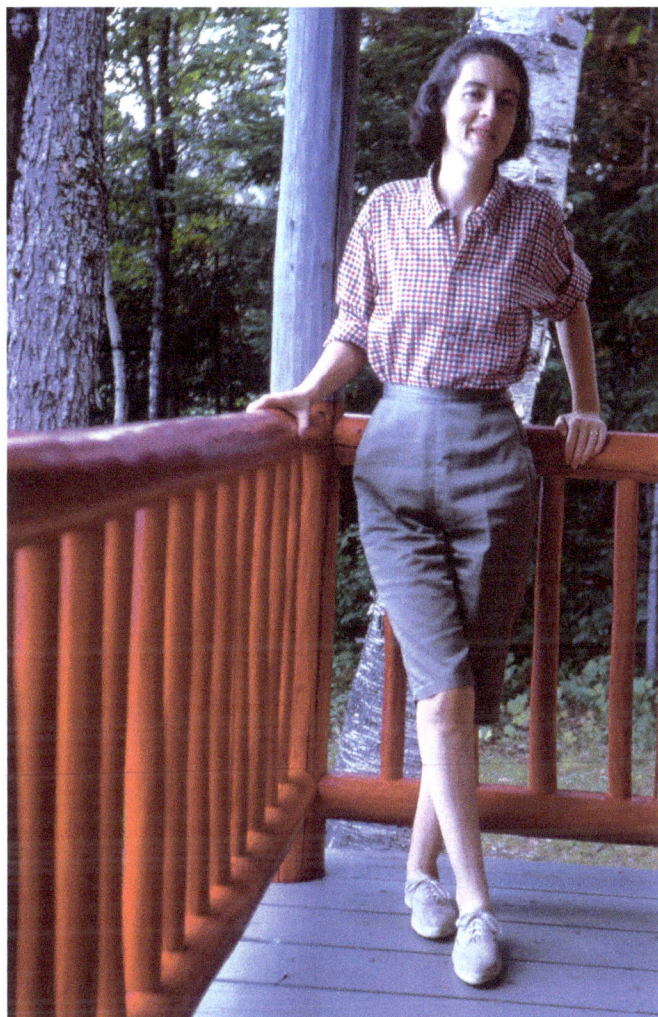

After consulting the chart of our Mayfield residency assembled from Mother's diaries that I relied on for details in this memoir and which appear at the conclusion of the main narrative, I find that I celebrated seven birthdays at the cabin. We returned home on my birthday in 1968 when I was eight years old. It's funny, but fifty-odd years later, I can remember one of the gifts I received on that birthday was Matchbox Number 13, a Dodge Wreck Truck painted yellow and green with a BP label. I think my parents may have purchased it at the Rexall drug store in Guilford. I remember we enjoyed my tenth birthday at the cabin, and Dad let me know that I was now "two digits" old and I needed to start helping around the place more than I had. My parents gave me the tasks of setting the table and sweeping the floor, neither of them especially difficult.

Barbara rests for a moment on the cabin front porch in July, 1963.

photo by Bob Coyle

Without the distraction of television and such, we read aloud in the evenings and at other times. When I was around eight years of age, we read aloud the J.R.R. Tolkien book *The Hobbit* as well as the companion three-book series, *The Lord of the Rings*. We read the books at home as well as at the cabin.

Later when we went out on hikes and other explorations through the Maine woods, we named areas that resembled, at least in our minds, places described in Tolkien's books about Middle Earth such as Rivendell, Lothlorien, and Mordor. At times in the evening, we heard strange, unfamiliar sounds from deep in the woods and envisioned them made by some of Tolkien's sinister characters such as Orcs, Nazguls, or Black Riders.

We read by candlelight into the evening but usually retired early so we could rise soon after daybreak as the early morning sun shone from across Kingsbury Pond on the front of

Every evening, Bob and Barbara used a candle to illuminate the cabin with enough light to allow reading.

photo by David Cass

the cabin. We kept one or two candles lit on the living room table when we made our final trip North for the night as we referred to going to the outhouse. When we looked back from the outhouse to the cabin, the interior seemed all aglow even with the illumination of only a single candle.

Growing up summers at the cabin, I adjusted well to the lack of electricity, running water, or a telephone. An old wind-up Victrola contained equally old records that I loved to listen to from time to time. Before listening to records, I had to wind up the Victrola with the big handle on the right-hand side. It then played several records I chose before the music slowed down and the machine needed rewinding. The record collection included two small records for children. A yellow vinyl Little Golden Record had "Brave Cowboy Bill" on one side and "The Ballad of Davy Crockett" on the other. I think the musicians were the Sandpipers with the Mitch Miller Orchestra. A red record had "Home on the Range" on one side and something else I don't remember on the back.

My favorite 78s were recordings made in the early twentieth century by the well-known Scottish singer Sir Harry Lauder. He sang "I Love a Lassie" and "Roamin' in the Gloamin'" on very old recordings pressed on only one side. That side had a red label with the name Victor, "His Master's Voice," and a sitting dog listening to a small phonograph containing a large horn to amplify sound. A newer two-sided record release with blue labels featured "Ta, Ta, My Bonnie Maggie Darling," my all-time favorite Harry Lauder song on one side and "I Think I'll Get Wed in the Summertime" on the reverse.

Another great two-sided record with black labels had "O, Little Town of Bethlehem" on one side and "Angels from the Realms of Glory" on the back. I think the labels indicated that Trinity Choir recorded both classic Christmas carols in 1903. The cabinet held dozens of other records, but those mentioned were my favorites. We listened to one other somewhat humorous record from time to time. It had the song "Chicken Gumbo" pressed on one side and "Fry Me Cookie in a Can of Lard" on the other.

Besides the Victrola, the cabin had other antique furnishings. We had to wind the old clock above the wall desk by the front windows periodically to provide the correct time. It chimed on the hour in a very characteristic tone. The folks usually brought their battery-powered Zenith radio but, as the batteries ran down, did not use it a lot except to hear the news and weather.

The Sawyers had constructed a kitchen table that folded up against shelves built against the cabin wall. These shelves primarily stored dishes, glasses, mugs and room for some food. I particularly remember a huge coffee mug with the face of a hound dog on the side. Writing on the mug identified it as Coffee Hound.

A set of four instruments sat on two nails on the logs just inside the living room area from the kitchen. The set included a bottle opener, corkscrew, and two other implements, the set of four presented as a barbershop quartet with jolly faces shaped on each tool.

In the mid 1960s, Dad purchased a small green canvas tent, possibly at Grant's in Gardner, Massachusetts. It slept two people. Initially, he pitched it on the slope near the tree inhabited by ichneumon wasps. I think he and I may have slept in it a night or two before a torrential rain raised havoc. Then he moved it to the front porch in front of the large window by the dinner table. From then on, he or I set the tent up there for part of each summer's stay at the cabin. I often took a nap out there after lunch. It typically felt nice and warm inside with the tent facing the sun.

The inside of the tent had a characteristic odor I cannot quite describe. For one of our last summers in Mayfield, Dad set the tent up behind the cabin near the path that led North. He and Mom slept out there a couple of nights and seemed to enjoy it.

There were many interesting things to do around the cabin. Jewelweed or touch-me-nots grew in profusion on the side of the driveway into Tom's cabin area. I enjoyed popping them and watching seeds fly. Ruby-throated hummingbirds fed on them and other flowers.

Other plants of interest I remember include asters, bracken ferns, daisies, goldenrod, Indian pipe, trillium, and wintergreen. We often picked wintergreen and chewed on it for a while. We sometimes made tea from wintergreen leaves.

The folks sometimes collected pearly everlasting and dried it for winter arrangements. We saw a lot of bunchberries when we walked in the woods. We found

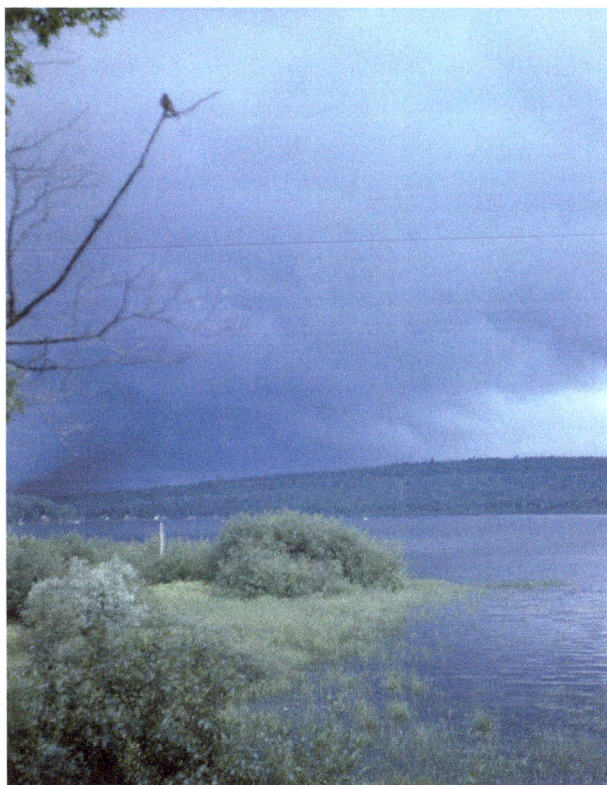

A barn swallow perches on a branch, upper left, as a cumulonimbus cloud gathers over Kingsbury Pond in July, 1964.
photo by Bob Coyle

*In July, 1964, bunchberries grew
in profusion near the cabin.*

photo by Bob Coyle

the pretty bright red berries on the forest floor, sometimes in a bed of moss. Although we saw deciduous trees around such as maples and beechs, Maine is truly the country of the pointed firs as suggested by the title of the well-known book by Sarah Orne Jewett who lived the summer of 1896 in the cottage later owned by my friend Bob Buck in Martinsville, Maine. Spruce, firs, pines, cedars, and tamaracks—also called hackmatack trees by Mainers—are predominant evergreens. Both white birch and yellow birch grew near the cabin.

I enjoyed many hours on my yellow swing Dad had set up suspended from two eyehooks secured to a large plank nailed across two trees by the front porch steps. I sang Harry Lauder songs on the swing and pretended I was the engineer of a train or some other imaginary vehicle. The swing set came with hand rings and a trapeze bar, but I never used either.

*During childhood summers in Maine,
Chris enjoyed the ladder and swing outside the cabin.*

photo by Chris Coyle

I associate certain foods with summers in Mayfield, some available only in Maine in those days. I particularly remember Humpty Dumpty potato chips. Maine stores also carried Old King Cole potato chips. In the kitchen, we had a very large red tin lettered for the latter company. It provided the ideal container to keep cookies, candy, and the like. The tin helped keep food fresh and precluded anything from getting into it. Oh, potato salad is another dish I seem to associate with Maine summers. And summer cold cuts stand out—like olive loaf, macaroni loaf, and sliced cheese—yum!

In thinking back to our summers at the cabin in Maine, I realize now how adept my mother became at preparing and cleaning up meals in a kitchen without electricity or running water. Although her meals were not elaborate, they were satisfying and delicious. She often opened canned foods to heat up but sometimes made meals such as soups and pastry or items such as biscuits and pies from scratch.

On a few occasions, we took overnight trips from the cabin. We went two consecutive years for a couple of nights to Bar Harbor. We went once and stayed a night or two at Quebec City but it was close enough to the cabin that we could go up and back in the same day. Our 1968 summer began with a few days in New Brunswick, especially near the Bay of Fundy.

We drove to Nova Scotia in 1972 to view the total eclipse of the sun on July 10. Then we took the ferry out to visit Prince Edward Island for a couple of days. We arrived at the cabin on July 14 for the duration of the summer.

A path led north from the cabin past the old and new outhouses and up the hill to meet the driveway as it curved above the two cabins. We called the path North Trail. Another path ran about seventy-five feet in the woods parallel to North Trail which intersected the driveway a few dozen feet beyond the junction of North Trail with the driveway on a straight stretch before it curved by the culvert. The woodland path joined North Trail between the new outhouse and the cabin, and we called it Birch Trail because of quite a few fallen white birch trees along it. Yet another trail, one rarely used, went up the hill to Route 16 from the west side of the driveway near Moss Rock, a large moss-covered rock a short distance into the woods. Dad had used the trail as a shortcut back to the cabin years before when he did a lot of hiking.

Dad and I made an annual tradition of going up to Mayfield Corner at the intersection of Routes 16 and 151. Route 16 crossed Bigelow Brook about fifty feet east of the intersection by means of a very large culvert, perhaps twenty-five feet in diameter. That culvert replaced an earlier, small concrete bridge when the road was done over around 1967. Dad and I carefully made our way down the embankment to the edge of the brook. Then, if the water were low, we could walk through the culvert on one side of the stream water. Yelling, singing, and throwing rocks or pebbles against the corrugated metal culvert all produced interesting sound effects.

We occasionally went out for some entertainment. Lake Wesserunsett in Madison had Lakewood Theatre, one of America's oldest and most famous summer theaters. Somerset Traction Company developed the property, once a religious camp sanctuary and one of the last surviving trolley parks. We saw some big names there like Mickey Rooney, Robert Stack, Lana Turner, and Vivian Vance. On the walls, photographs galore showed famous actors who had graced the stage over the years. When I was young, my folks took me there to see a marionette show.

The Strand in Skowhegan was in the 1960s one of the only downtown movie theatres still in operation that I had been to. I saw *Mary Poppins,* which I didn't like too well. We also went to the Strand to see *Dr. Zhivago,* which I liked better. One odd thing during the film there was a woman sitting near us with a white rabbit on her lap. The rabbit stayed with her throughout the rather long movie.

Across the river on Route 201 was the Skowhegan drive-in theatre. It was fun to go there, park the car, and watch the beautiful sunset along the Kennebec River. The concessions stand had lots of snacks available to munch on. We returned to the cabin much after dark about only when coming back from a movie. As we descended Cook Hill to Mayfield Corner, the entire area seemed to come to life from the reflections of headlights from the many signs along the road and guardrails. My mother often referred to it as The Great White Way.

Sometimes, the Coyles saw plays at the Gilbert and Sullivan Festival Theatre in Monmouth.
late 1950s photo by Bob Coyle

Once we went to the theater in Greenville to see one of the Superman movies. We went one other time to the Theatre at Monmouth where we saw George Bernard Shaw's *Caesar and Cleopatra.* What I remember more than the play is running as fast as I could to the nearby railroad crossing during intermission to see the train I had been hearing in the distance. A very long freight train soon came into view running south on Maine Central's Back Road. Especially interesting to me was a maroon and gold EMD GP7 locomotive at the front of the train. As I recall, the locomotives really worked to move the heavy train south toward Rigby Yard.

We usually went more or less straight home to Athol after leaving Mayfield. Occasionally, we went west to Rangeley and drove home through the White

Mountains, a much longer trip than down the Maine Turnpike. In 1973, we stopped to see the famous Poland Spring Resort where Mother had worked as a waitress in the summer of 1944. Then we made our first visit to the Sabbathday Lake Shaker community a couple of miles south of Poland Spring in the town of New Gloucester. When we visited, Sabbathday Lake Shaker was one of only two remaining active Shaker communities in the world. The other, since closed, had flourished for years in Canterbury, New Hampshire.

When we got home, we had to unpack everything, deal with piles of mail, and wash a lot of laundry. For many years we tried to see how long we could go without turning on the television set. I think I was eight before we even had a TV set, so I never became addicted to watching it.

Bob Coyle's Snappy Rice Cakes
Ingredients:
1 cup cooked brown rice
2 to 4 scallions
1 carrot
1 stalk celery with leaves
2 to 4 radishes
1 tablespoon Shaker dried parsley
2 eggs
1 to 2 tablespoons soy sauce
vegetable oil

Procedure:
Cut vegetables into small cubes.
In a large bowl, beat eggs and add vegetables and soy sauce. Mix well.
Heat frying pan to medium.
Add vegetable oil.
Drop mixture by tablespoon into pan.
Turn when cakes are crisp.
Serve hot and add more soy sauce if desired.

loons, raccoons, and bears

With their mournful yet exuberant calls, loons seemingly beckoned us back to Kingsbury Pond year after year. It was indeed a wonderful night when the loons provided a symphony after we settled into bed.

Mom told about the first time they moved into the cabin in 1958. A loon began to call as the folks got settled in. She asked my father to identify the bird call, as she had not heard it before. At first, she didn't quite believe him when he told her it was the call of the common loon. But soon she agreed, and they grew accustomed to the frequent serenade of loons on the pond.

Loons require a substantial runway of water to take off. They are completely dependent on water and can not take off from land. Wind helps them to get airborne. When they taxied across the pond and became airborne, it was a sight to see! The loons often became very vocal while taking off, much to our delight.

We experienced a very close encounter with loons many years later during the era we stayed at Echo Valley Lodge in Phillips. By then, I had graduated from college.

We drove into town to purchase groceries the morning after our arrival. We drove back by way of Toothaker Pond Road. As we started down the hill from the pond, we drove toward a boggy area with high grass and reeds to our left. We saw a woman standing next to the road and a loon marooned on the grass area next to her, a scant ten feet from the roadway. We stopped and inquired as to what went on. The woman had spotted the loon which, perhaps due to foggy conditions, had thought it landed on water. But after the loon touched down on the grass, it could not, of course, take flight and was in a bit of a predicament.

The kind woman had called the game warden, who responded that he might be able to stop by on Tuesday. My father and I took control of the situation. Dad emptied out one of the cardboard boxes of groceries in the trunk. Meanwhile I approached the helpless bird. I worked at the University of Massachusetts, Amherst, Poultry Farm and had grown quite accustomed to catching large birds.

I gently reached down with my right hand and took hold of both the loon's legs while restraining its wings with my left hand. Dad put the box under it, and together we walked several hundred feet back up the hill to the little fishing area at Toothaker Pond right next to the abandoned grade of the Phillips and Rangeley Railroad, eventually Toothaker Pond Road. Dad removed the box, and I set the bird down on the water. The loon set its sights toward the pond's center and began swimming away from us but not before turning its head back toward us with a gesture that said "Thank you so much for saving my life!"

Loons nest on dry land but only a few feet from water's edge, as that is about as far as they can walk on land. At the cabin, we rarely saw loons come closer than about fifty feet from the shoreline. We always presumed they built their nests on the far shore against Skunk's Hill, with the shoreline over there devoid of any cabins or human activity.

Loon chicks ride on Mother Loon's back, left, on Kingsbury Pond in July, 1966.
photo by Bob Coyle

If we arrived early enough in the summer, we saw loon chicks, usually two of them, riding on their parents' backs. Occasionally, the parent loon dove below the surface to capture an unsuspecting fish. Devoid of their "boat," the chicks bobbed up and down in the water until the parent returned.

Maine's state bird is the black-capped chickadee. That year-round resident has the honor of also being the state bird of Massachusetts—perhaps not surprising, since the District of Maine belonged to Massachusetts until 1820. The little chickadees are friendly, gregarious birds. Many of those birds who live in the deep woods rarely see people and are quite curious over the occasional human visitor to their habitat.

I secretly wished that their cousins, the brown-capped (later renamed boreal) chickadees, had been selected as Maine's state bird. We saw them once in a great while. Those pretty little birds are slightly larger than black caps and have an abbreviated, slower, and buzzier chick-dee call.

One afternoon in the mid 1970s, we climbed the trail to the Attean Lookout on the road to Jackman. A rare sight and a real treat indeed to add to our bird lists, a flock of boreals fed in high spruces and firs. Another time, we spotted a small flock of the secretive birds while we blueberried up an old farm road that led to Coburn Ridge at West Mayfield on the north side of Route 16.

Another bird species of the north is the gray jay or Canada jay. Those birds also go by the nickname Whisky Jack. As sightings were not very frequent for us, it was always a treat to see one. One year, we saw a small flock of them at Lily Bay north of Greenville on the road to Kokadjo. Dad tossed some Cheez-Its to the birds in an effort to draw them closer so he could take some photographs.

Besides the loons, there are two other bird species I always associate with the cabin, I enjoy hearing their songs as much as I enjoy hearing the loons. From the deep woods, we often heard the wood thrush with its ee-oh-lay call and the white-throated sparrow with its Old-Sam-Peabody-Peabody calling from the deep woods outside the cabin. Both have beautiful songs, and I can hear them now in my mind as I write.

We heard frequently the call a raven with its nasal, gurgling croak that sounds sort of like a hoarse crow. The first time Dad heard a raven, he thought it was a man calling for help. He took off through the woods for the old gravel pit in Mayfield whereupon he discovered a raven as the source of the vocal calling.

From time to time, song sparrows visited us at the cabin. One summer, Dad taught a song sparrow to whistle the opening bars of Beethoven's *Fifth Symphony*—the bird was indeed a good learner! Winter wren infrequently visited the cabin. It has the longest song of any bird in New England. The only wren outside of the Americas, it is called the Jenny Wren in Britain.

Sometimes, we saw belted kingfishers sitting on a nearby branch between flying expeditions over the pond to catch food. The birds are unusual with females more colorful than males. The females have a chestnut-colored belly band and flanks, while males only sport white plumage on these areas.

Less thrilling barn swallows nested at the ridgepole over the front door. The log cabin made a good place to build a nest, and they usually were well along with their activities by the time we arrived, so it was too late to move them along to another location. Dad often constructed a canopy of cardboard over the doorway to keep waste from landing on the porch where we walked.

More annoying were bird lice from the barn swallows, as they sometimes got into the cabin and onto us. One time when I was very young, we were in a store somewhere likely in Bingham, when I exclaimed in a loud voice "Look, Mama. There is one of those lice like we have at home going up my arm!" The folks managed to shut me up and whisk me out the door before anyone may have figured out who we were.

Barn swallows built nests every year over the front door to the cabin.

photo by Bob Coyle

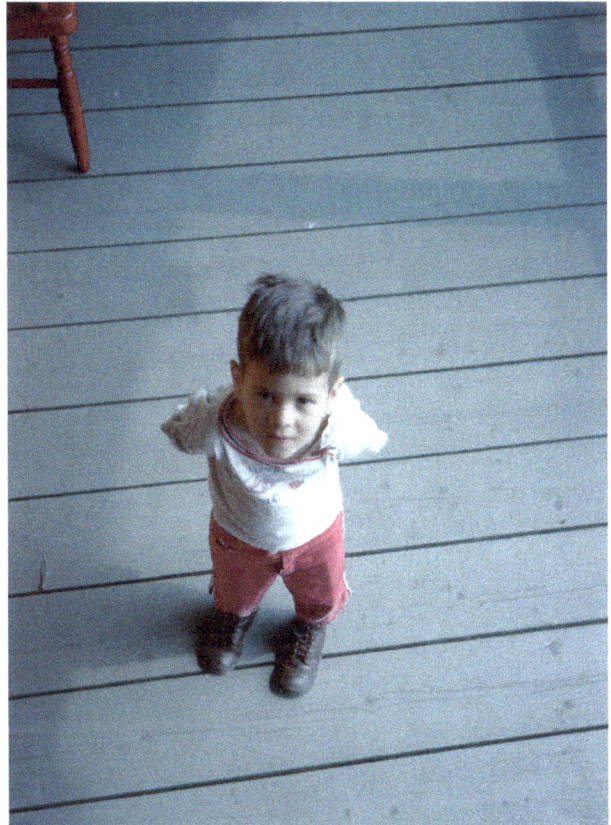

Three-year-old Chris studies the nest of barn swallows over the front door of the cabin.

photo by Bob Coyle

Bats built a den in a crack below the ridgepole at the other end of the building. Occasionally, a bat managed to squeeze all the way into the cabin and then dart about trying to figure out where to go. Usually, Dad and I got the Sawyer's fish net with a very long handle. We could usually catch a bat against a corner with the net and then let it go outside. One year, Dad bought a little bag of mortar at Andrews Hardware in Bingham. He mixed the mortar with water and went up the ladder to the hole the bats used for a den. He banged on the logs until eventually five bats flew out and all was quiet. Then, he thoroughly plugged the hole with the mortar he had mixed up. But apparently not all the bats exited, for that night we heard one scratching from within the wall.

Toward dusk and into the evening, bullfrogs along the shore between our cabin and Birch Point began their characteristic "chug-a-rum." In recent years, I found out that Mother did not like their sound and complained that they kept her awake. In the daytime, we saw many leopard frogs in the grass between the cabin and the pond.

Gram Coyle had a lifelong fear and dislike of frogs and toads. Whenever she visited us, we saw her jumping in the air each time she spotted a frog as she sauntered down to the dock. Apparently her younger brother, Uncle Walter, had put them down her back when they were youngsters!

There was a raccoon feeder on the maple tree outside the kitchen. Although we intended it as a bird feeder, we had more success feeding raccoons. Bold visiting raccoons were

In July, 1966, a nocturnal raccoon made its way to the feeder outside the cabin.
photo by Bob Coyle

unafraid of humans. It was always exciting at night to shine a flashlight out the kitchen window and see a raccoon up in the feeder eating the various delights we had put there. When I was very young, Dad took some slides of my mother and me feeding slices of bread to a raccoon nicknamed Racky. One afternoon, a mother raccoon with two small babies visited, and they took cookies from our hands.

Barbara feeds Racky a slice of bread.
photo by Bob Coyle

When we arrived at the cabin one summer in the early 1970s, we found a very large nest paper wasps had attached to the logs just under the roof near the kitchen window. The hardworking wasps kept adding to the nest until one night we heard a great deal of commotion outside the cabin. In the morning, we found that a raccoon had knocked most of the nest down to the ground, leaving only a small amount of the hive still attached to the cabin. Raccoons and other mammals find sustenance by eating the larvae in paper wasp nests.

The wasps were "mad as hornets," and we decided it would be best not to use the back door for a few days until things calmed down. To go North, we went out the front door and took a rather circuitous route

44

to the outhouse. After the raccoon had taken what it wanted, a red squirrel came by and fed on some of it, also. Eventually, the wasps sealed over the remaining part of the hive in an effort to protect the remaining larvae, and that was that.

The small maple tree with Racky's feeder attached grew each year. I remember one summer seeing a small twig with two or three leaves protruding from the trunk about ten feet above the feeder. By the time of our final stay at the cabin, that twig had become a five-foot branch with many leaves. As our stays at the cabin occurred mostly in August, we often saw some leaves on nearby trees start to change to their brilliant fall colors. Racky's tree was no exception.

Near the shore of Kingsbury Pond right by our dock grew a small evergreen tree. I remember it a scant two feet in height. Like the branch from Racky's tree, I watched it grow up over the years. I think it may have measured between ten and twelve feet in height the last time I saw it.

We saw snowshoe hares from time to time. Much larger than cottontail rabbits, they can really move if they feel it necessary to do so. One of the summers, our cat Wee Gillis was out and about in the early evening while we sat on the front porch reading and taking in the evening air. Suddenly, a snowshoe hare shot across the area in front of the porch and headed toward Pine Cove, hoofing it for all he was worth. Immediately behind the hare sped our cat going full speed. Both disappeared in a cloud of dust heading toward Tom Farrin's cabin. Wee Gillis returned after a while, and we surmised that the hare had evaded capture but had quite a workout.

Snowshoe hares forage in front of the cabin.
photo by Bob Coyle

We could see a large growth in plain sight of my swing high up in a spruce tree between our cabin and Tom Farrin's. We often saw small birds using the well-protected area. We saw red-breasted nuthatches there from time to time. Their presence by their characteristic beeping, a sound like the horn on a tricycle, alerted us to their presence there.

Besides raccoons and snowshoe hares, the cabin grounds had a lot of fierce red or "king" squirrels around. One often climbed the lofty hundred-foot white pine behind the cabin early on summer mornings and proceeded to drop pine cones on the roof of the car to open them up. The little beings seemed also to delight in knowing that they woke us up. The squirrels seemed to object to our very presence at the cabin, and when we walked up the driveway, they chattered incessantly and followed us along from thirty or fifty feet away in the woods.

The summer of 1959 when the folks stayed at the Tibbetts cabin down by the picnic ground, Dad had an all-out war with a diabolical red squirrel. The Tibbetts cabin had an attic. The squirrel spent nights up there rolling nuts back and forth across the floor and scampering about, thus keeping the folks awake much of the night.

Dad found that the squirrel slept in the woodshed during the day. He started making all sorts of noise around the woodshed in an effort to tire the squirrel out in hopes its nighttime activities might lessen. I'm not sure if it worked or not, but Dad enjoyed "giving it back" to the small rodent.

Chris and the cat Wee Gillis loll on the shore of Kingsbury Pond as Chris takes a break in 1970 from playing with the miniature boat built for him by Al Gallup.

photo by Bob Coyle

One day—I'm not sure where Dad and I were or perhaps I was not yet born—Mother decided to walk up our long dirt driveway to fetch the mail. As she rounded the big curve approaching the brook, she met a red fox trotting toward her. Mother didn't quite know what to do, so she just kept walking along. The fox simply trotted right past her and paid her no attention at all. Mother said it felt just like meeting someone on a city sidewalk during our time living in Boston.

Porcupines lived near the cabin, although we rarely saw them. For years, there was damage to the green lattice boards that partially camouflaged the area below the cabin. Several boards near the southwest corner of the cabin were chewed on to make an opening just wide enough to permit a porcupine to enter the area beneath the cabin for shelter. It probably occurred as winter approached and the animal sought a good place to make a den for the cold months. It made its hole in the lattice boards near the stairs to the front porch next to my swing.

We spotted white-tailed deer occasionally, but for the most part, they seemed to keep out of our sight. Occasionally we saw a black bear. Joe Bourque, who ran the Bingham A&P, often spoke of seeing black bears at the dump near Moxie Pond. We drove in there every time we were in the area but never did see a bear at that location.

Although we frequently saw their footprints through muddy areas, we rarely saw any moose right at the cabin, but they were nearby. Our friends Lencie Rousell and Gert Dubriske, Athol elementary teachers, visited in 1978. We drove up to Greenville and then up the east side of Moosehead Lake toward Lily Bay. As we rounded a curve, we spotted a moose grazing on vegetation on the side of the road. Dad stopped the car, and we got out. The moose paid little attention to us. Dad took a photograph of Lencie, Mom, and me standing about ten feet from the huge animal while Gert watched us from the car.

The folks liked to go out and look for moose. One spot was Bryant Bog only a mile or two from the cabin. Despite the fact we spent many evenings there fighting off biting bugs, I don't ever recall seeing one of the large, majestic animals at that location. We also looked for moose at Wellington Bog along the dirt road from Kingsbury Dam south to Wellington. We could look out across the bog with binoculars and Dad's telescope toward an interesting peninsula way across the bog with a white pine tree growing on it. I often wished I could get out there and pitch a tent.

The Coyles always found it a treat to see moose, like this one in 1990.
photo by Chris Coyle

When visiting Wellington Bog, we usually drove either clockwise or counter clockwise from the cabin via Wellington. Driving south from Wellington Bog, the road eventually made a sharp turn to the left and crossed the outlet stream from the bog. In later years, the curve had lessened with a new bridge built. A camp constructed south of the bridge had long metal girders protruding from beneath the foundation. I had an idea they had come from the former bridge. If we made our excursion during open hours at the Wellington post office, we usually stopped to get our mail, especially during the days when we did not receive delivery.

Several old farms had large, interesting barns on the road, State Highway 154 between Wellington and Brighton. The Heart of Maine cabins were located at Trout Pond on that road. A beautiful, serene small pond with pond lilies growing in profusion, Trout Pond had a small dam on the north side of the road that kept the water level where the owner desired. I think I remember the words Heart of Maine painted on the roof of one of the buildings. The camps looked like their days of glory had about ended, although people may have stayed in them more during fall hunting season than when we were in the area.

Wellington Bog hosted a number of beaver dams.
photo by Bob Coyle

quarries, fossils, and minerals

One of Monson's deep slate quarries , shown in 1969, provided slate used for sinks, blackboards, shingles, and monuments through the mid twentieth century.

photo by Bob Coyle

Large-scale slate veins run through the part of Maine near the cabin where we stayed. Monson had a great number of commercial quarries that provided slate used for sinks, blackboards, shingles, and cemetery monuments through the mid twentieth century.

I toured the dwelling house at the Canterbury, New Hampshire, Shaker village in 2008. I noticed that the several slate sinks in the kitchen had plates affixed to them calling attention to the fact they had been manufactured by the Monson Slate Company. Those slate sinks certainly shipped out of town on the two-foot gauge Monson Railroad. Slate shingles supply one of the longest lasting materials for roofing. The nails holding slate shingles to a roof tend to wear out long before the slate does.

A small slate quarry accessed from a side road off the old Route 16 operated on Cook Hill in Mayfield. Unlike Monson, which had a railroad to ship heavy slate products, Mayfield had no such luxury, and transportation must have been difficult. The Mayfield quarry has not been used commercially in many years, but people often help themselves to pieces of the hard gray metamorphic rock. The back doorsteps at the cabin came from the Mayfield slate quarry. Slabs of slate from the Mayfield quarry reinforce the Kingsbury Dam since its rebuilding in 1970.

Workers load slate in the 1930s on a two-foot gauge flat car at Monson.
photo in the collection of Chris Coyle

Around 1915, men process slate inside the Monson Pond Quarry slate mill.
postcard from the collection of Chris Coyle

In our familiar part of Maine, we found fossils, particularly brachiopods, among interesting geological features. The glacier deposited them, probably moved from the Jackman region.

We frequently looked for and found fossils at the "new" Mayfield gravel pit. Each summer, we ventured down to the gravel pit to see anything unearthed from excavations since we last visited. We found it worthwhile to look after a rainstorm, too, as sometimes new specimens came to light.

Oxen pulled wagons loaded with slate at the Mayfield quarry in the late 1800s.
stereoscopic view in the collection of Chris Coyle

By November 2009, the Mayfield quarry had been long abandoned.
photo by Chris Coyle

51

After a while, I got to recognize which types of rocks yielded good fossils. One time I took a sledgehammer and broke open a large, likely looking rock—it was gorgeous inside! Silver-colored fossils appeared that had not seen the light of day in millions of years.

Fossil hunters find remains or brachiopods in the Mayfield area.

photo by Chris Coyle

I made a small rock and mineral museum beneath the cabin and put that great fossil there. Later, half of the rock disappeared, so I brought the other half home. I keep it in my rock and mineral collection. I saved most geologic specimens larger than a softball in my museum. I found them during our scouting around outcrops, gravel pits, and quarries. Most were not overly exciting or valuable, but I found them interesting and representative of nearby rock and mineral deposits.

Beneath the front porch next to my museum area, two upright gas tanks supplied propane to the cabin's kitchen area and gaslights. Six-foot green lattice boards provided a finished look to the otherwise bare area beneath the front porch. Two hinged sections opened after we turned a small turn bolt and allowed them to swing open to access the gas tanks and museum. The height from the ground to the porch floor above permitted an adult to stand easily once inside. However, clearance between the ground and the cabin floor decreased to the rear of the cabin with little space. My little rock and mineral museum just behind the porch area allowed me to stand without banging my head.

We found small, flat rocks about two or three inches in diameter along the shoreline of Kingsbury Pond. Dad showed me how to throw them just right to make them skip across the water. We might get four or five skips if we threw them just right. Other rocks we found sometimes had orange oxide powder on them. We could take a dab of that orange powder on our fingers and put it on our faces.

My father's interest in geology and other natural sciences and his desire to impart that interest to his students and others gave rise to the formation of the Athol Bird and Nature Club in late 1963. Dad collected rock and mineral specimens during our long summers in Maine, and many found their way to the classroom and to the Athol Bird and Nature Club Museum, originally located in the Athol Junior High School.

He and others added displays of birds and other animals to the museum. No animal was ever killed to place in the collection. Rather, bird and nature members brought bodies of animals that had lost their lives on the highway, flown into windows, or otherwise accidentally died to local taxidermists for mounting and placement in the museum. At times, individuals or groups donated collections to the museum that included specimens acquired through hunting.

eclipses and meteors

A rare total eclipse of the sun took place in our region of Somerset County in 1963. My mother's parents, Grandpa and Grandma Sherman—Milton Francis Sherman and Laura Virginia Brown Sherman, Aunt Martha, and some of Martha's odd acquaintances from Washington, DC, came up to view the phenomenon. Dad selected a vantage point over in Wellington at King Hill on the old dirt road leading to Burdin Corner and Parkman. King Hill boasted several large open fields in that bygone summer which, half a century and more later, have since all grown in. I can vaguely remember the area and its big stately elm trees, although I had yet to reach my third birthday.

Chris, Barbara, Stanley Weintraub, Martha Sherman, and Barbara's parents,
Milton Francis Sherman and Laura Virginia Brown,
await the total eclipse in Wellington on July 20, 1963.
photo by Bob Coyle

I could write an entire thesis on the subject of my Aunt Martha, my mother's younger sister. She has lived a very unusual life. She had a friend by the name of Stanley Weintraub in the 1960s. Mother referred to Stanley as Martha's "to-do-with." What I called Aunt Martha's Gang arrived in Mayfield in at least two cars, possibly more. G&G Sherman traveled in one car along with Aunt Martha and Stanley. Another car or cars contained Martha's odd friends from the District, as she referred to her home area of Washington, DC.

Martha and Stanley had driven to G&G's home at 413 Conant Road in Weston to stay overnight before driving to Maine, which took another day or two including the stopover. Stanley had red hair

A dramatic sky preceded the total eclipse of the sun on King Hill in Wellington on July 20, 1963.

photo by Bob Coyle

and a red beard. My grandmother did not like beards, especially red ones. When night fell, she banished Stanley to sleep in a hole out in the yard Grandpa had dug to plant a tree. A canvas, a couple of blankets, and a pillow went out with Stanley. I am sure he was glad when dawn broke the next morning.

I remember the events surrounding the eclipse more than I remember the actual eclipse. The adults spread out a large picnic at our viewing area. I recall sneaking off to the car and sitting in the driver's seat before my grandfather put a stop to that and yanked me back out of the vehicle. Dad took a classic photo slide of us all as we awaited the eclipse. I do not think that Martha's friends watched the eclipse from the same area we did.

My parents and I looked forward to the Perseid meteor shower that takes place annually around the second week of August. With favorable viewing conditions, we typically took a drive in the evening to a place with a large expanse of sky. The top of Cook Hill at the start of the old road was a good location. We kept track of all the meteors we saw over the evening.

They appear and disappear so quickly that it is virtually impossible to call each other's attention to them.

Dad and I often carried one of the long benches from the porch down onto the dock before dark as the Perseid night neared. In the middle of the night, we took several warm blankets and went down to the dock to sit gazing skyward for an hour or more. We huddled together under the blankets eagerly awaiting the show. While sitting there, we listened to the sounds of the night—the occasional fish jumping out of the water, bull frogs croaking, a fox barking, an animal walking through the woods, loons calling, or maybe even an owl hooting.

After a time, we retired to the cabin. We frequently made hot tea before snuggling back into bed. How good it felt back under the covers! The nights were often cool at the time of the Perseid showers. One good thing about that was the fact that there were fewer annoying bugs to bother us.

maine folks

As I mentioned, Omar Sawyer and his son Donald built the cabin. When Omar retired as manager of woodlands for Hollingsworth and Whitney Paper Company, he received a parcel of land on the northwest shore of Kingsbury Pond in Mayfield where he could build a camp.

Omar Sawyer was a legend in his own time. One local Mainer explained to us that, "North of Waterville, Omar Sawyer's word is law." That rather summed up the respect he commanded in that neck of the woods.

Walter Macdougall in his book *The Old Somerset Railroad* relates

Omar Sawyer was twenty-six when he became boss of the seven hundred men at work on the Bald Mountain cut. Omar had gone on his first drive when he was seventeen (about 1903), and he had gone with a bad head cold. His mother was worried; there was still ice floating down the river. Riding a log downstream that first morning, Sawyer and a companion were swept under an overhanging tree, which brushed them into freezing water. According to Omar, the shock cured his cold. Sawyer was young, but he had learned how to handle troublemakers early on. When a big bruiser caused a scene in one of Sawyer's camps, Omar held him on the cookstove until the fellow pleaded (to be let go).

On July 10, 1944, a special train carrying German prisoners of war arrived at Bingham station at three o'clock in the morning, the first passenger train in town since 1933. Accompanied by US soldiers, the prisoners were transferred to trucks of the Hollingsworth and Whitney Paper Company for transport to the lumbering operation at Spencer Lake in Hobbstown. Omar Sawyer had responsibility for general supervision of the prisoners while they worked in the woods.

Robert E. Pike writes an anecdote in his book *Tall Trees, Tough Men*:

Omar Sawyer, who for many years was manager of timberlands for Hollingsworth and Whitney, operating on the upper Kennebec...recalled stopping into a camp one afternoon and being offered a dish of tea by the cook. Of course, a tea-pot was always boiling and sizzling on the stove, twenty-four hours a day. But this tea tasted a little strong, even to Omar, who was used to black tea that would float an axe. Finally, he got up and looked into the pot. An old sock, hung up over the stove to dry, had dropped into the pot and had never been fished out.

When Don Sawyer first rented the cabin to my folks in 1958, his father, Omar, was a little nervous about it. But my folks soon earned his respect and confidence in that they were responsible and would take good care of the cabin. Because of Omar's intimate familiarity with much of the area where Dad did his research, the two of them talked at length about different destinations and how best to reach them.

Omar and his friend Pearly reshingled the cabin roof during late July 1960. I believe that the roof only had tar paper on it for the first decade or so. Asphalt shingles replaced it in 1960. The folks said that Omar and Pearly drove out each day and seemed to have a great time working on the roof, stopping each noontime to enjoy the lunches their wives had sent out to camp with them.

A real perfectionist, Omar wanted everything done correctly. He made sure no wood ever sat directly on the ground where it could get wet or pests could get in. He thought everything out before building. A man came out to the cabin to fix or do something one day. The folks explained that Omar wanted it done in a certain way.

"Well, that's Omar Sawyer for you," The man replied. But in his Maine dialect, it sounded more like "Well, that's Omah Sawyah fah yah," with most words sort of rhyming.

I remember Omar Sawyer mostly after a stroke partially incapacitated him. I recall the afternoon of July 27, 1964, when we accompanied the Sawyers up to Rowe Pond to see the cabin he had built about 1957 for their daughter Bea and her family on 1.5-acre Beaver Island. After a 10-mile trip north from the bridge over the Kennebec River to Concord, we climbed into a boat to reach the cabin. I remember that it differed from ours with everything contained in one room for easier heating.

We never met Bea Sawyer. Sadly, she passed away at a relatively young age. Her father, Omar, related a story of years ago when Bea was paddling a canoe out on China Lake at the onset of a surprise storm. Back on shore, someone called out in alarm, "There's a woman out on the lake, and a storm's blowing in."

Another person, recognizing the canoe operator, replied rather nonchalantly, "That's no woman. That's Bea Sawyer." The speaker meant no disprespect, as she was a skilled outdoorsperson.

We did become acquainted with Bea's son Don Nodine, who lived up in Millinocket. Besides being an interesting fellow, Don is a skilled and knowledgeable outdoorsman. One hot summer afternoon while we sat on the porch, we noticed an unusual house-like craft moving toward us across Kingsbury Pond. The atypical vessel tied up at our dock, and we found it piloted by none other than Don Nodine. He had built the one-of-a-kind boat and was taking it out for a voyage.

Don and his wife told us they had a big thunderstorm up their way the night before. When asked how close the storm came to them, Mrs. Nodine replied, "It was handy." Presumably she meant that the storm was very near to them.

We never saw the Sawyers' China Lake camp. (By the way, many places in Maine take their titles from afar—Calais, China, Denmark, Madrid, Moscow, and Naples just to name a few). But when Mrs. Sawyer told us they had recently returned from China, we envisioned them exploring the Great Wall or wandering the streets of Beijing. Later, we realized their trip had been a little less global than we had mistakenly thought.

While exploring the location where a farmhouse had once stood in Kingsbury, we found an old ladder hewn from logs and still in excellent condition. Dad and Mother related the find to the Sawyers, and they all decided that the ladder would serve better use at the cabin than lying in the woods of Kingsbury. So, with Mrs. Sawyer driving her big Buick, we rode over to where we had found it.

We tied the ladder to the roof. Then, through the windows from our places in the car, Dad and I held onto it as Mrs. Sawyer slowly returned to the cabin. We unloaded it and hung it from two large spikes in the logs beneath the cabin's floor. Later, under Omar's direction from the ground, we used the ladder to change out the cap to the flue pipe on the roof. Speaking of Omar and the roof, an interesting photograph in the cabin showed Omar jumping off the roof after having shoveled off a good build-up of snow.

Mrs. Sawyer, nee Josephine Gipson, was no stranger to the wilderness frontier. Her father ran the Lily Bay House north of Greenville on Moosehead Lake. After the Sawyers were married, Josephine joined her husband at the Bald Mountain operation and lived in the lumber camps for several years. Again from Macdougall's book *The Old Somerset Railroad*,

> Life was never boring. Omar's brother-in-law, Leon Bailey, was chief clerk; Mrs. Bailey and Mrs. Sawyer learned code from the station agent at Bald Mountain and kept in touch with all the news on the company telegraph line.

Bingham was home to three siblings among the nicest people I ever met—Annie and Wilder Rollins and their sister Elizabeth Cummings. Annie ran the Yellow Bowl Inn, the enterprise her mother, Grace, had operated before her. Annie's house was the next building north of the Yellow Bowl, and beyond that, her younger brother Wilder ran a Shell service station, all on Main Street where Route 201 makes a broad curve.

In the mid 1960s, Wilder opened a small

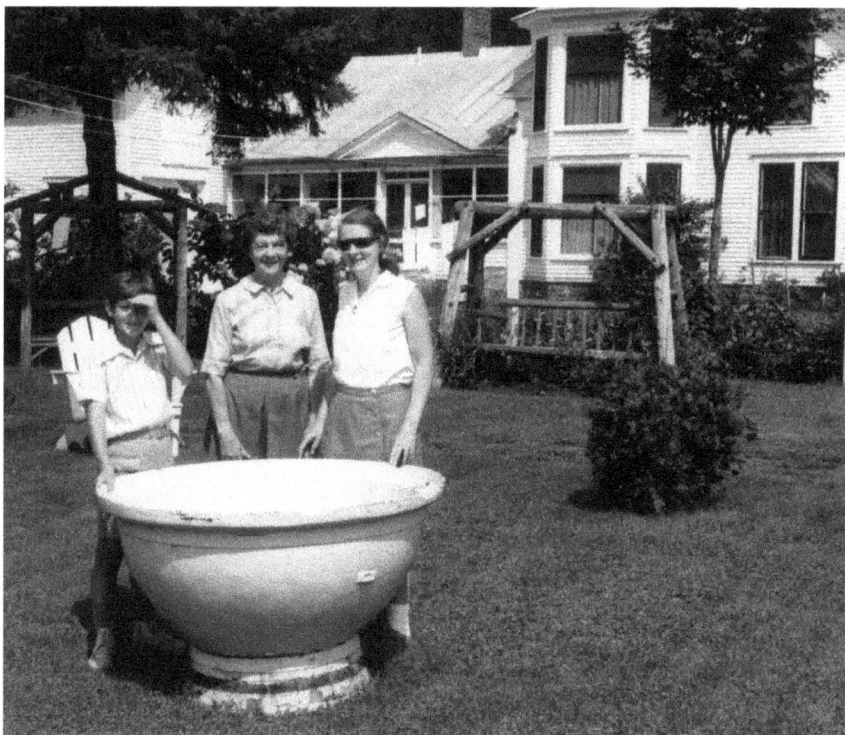

Chris, Elizabeth Cummings, and Barbara pause on the lawn of the Yellow Bowl Inn in Bingham around 1973.

photo by Bob Coyle

convenience store in a small building at the west end of the paved area at his service station. Later, he downsized the operation and moved it inside the main service station leaving a cooler for purchasing milk and such. He later sold the original store to someone who moved it away to make it into a camp.

By ramp on the west side of the service station, users reached restrooms outside Wilder's in the upper story of a barn with the lower part accessed from Dinsmore Street.

The widowed sister Elizabeth lived in her own home in North Anson and, when we first knew her, came up to help Annie when needed. Elizabeth had met her husband, Arthur, at a dance hall on Route 16 across the river from Solon while he was working on the construction of Wyman Dam back in 1932. I believe that Arthur grew up in Madison. During World War II, Elizabeth and her husband served the country as air wardens from the unusual windmill tower by the side of the road next to a cornfield on Route 16 west of North Anson.

An unusual tower in North Anson, photographed in 1977, served as a vantage point for air wardens like Elizabeth and Arthur Cummings during World War II.

photo by Bob Coyle

The windmill was built in 1905 with a well and pump once located on the first floor. They supplied water to a nearby farm, all of which burned in 1915 except the windmill. An interior spiral staircase leads to the balcony. Reportedly, it is one of only a few surviving agricultural windmills in Maine.

My mother was seven-plus months with child when the folks arrived in Bingham in 1960. They stopped at the Yellow Bowl Inn to see Annie, who greeted them with a big smile and said, "Well, I can see you have good news!" Soon after my birth on August 29 at Scott-Webb Hospital in Hartland, the folks went into Bingham with baby Chris. They stopped to see Annie, who presented us with a red rose that Dad later pressed for my baby album. Annie was the first person outside the hospital besides my parents to hold me.

Another interesting fellow, Bill Melcher lived in Moscow on Route 16 in almost the last house on the right going up the steep hill out of the Kennebec River valley on the way to Mayfield. I believe he worked as a forester. My father once bumped into him while hiking over at Harvard Forest in Petersham, Massachusetts, in the 1970s. They were both very surprised to see each other in a place so distant from the Bingham area.

Fire wardens worked in towers on various mountains in the area at one time. Timberland is valuable, and the sooner a forest fire is detected and efforts to extinguish it begin, the better. Airplanes largely carry out forest fire watches in the twenty-first century. But a few decades ago, fire wardens staffed fire towers in warm weather to watch for trouble.

Dad and I visited the tower at Moxie Bald Mountain when we hiked that part of the Appalachian Trail in the summer of 1972. The fire warden lived a solitary life during the summer up there atop the mountain. Therefore, he was only too glad to greet the occasional hiker. He invited us up in the tower to visit and admire the view. He had radio contact with other wardens and the Maine Forest Service.

From Bald Mountain, hikers can see Austin and Bald Mountain ponds as well as timberland.
photo by Bob Coyle

The warden stayed in a small cabin not far from the tower. His cabin had a room where a person or two could sleep if hiking over Bald Mountain toward evening. The occasional visitor to Bald Mountain gets treated to the beautiful sight of nearby Austin and Bald Mountain ponds as well as the vast wilderness timberlands of the entire region. Vegetation grows stunted near the top of the mountain.

Nearer our cabin over the line and into Brighton Plantation, Kelley Mountain, had a staffed fire tower. Sometimes if we had a fire in the wood stove on a cold or rainy day, the fire warden would drive in just to make certain that the smoke he saw from the lookout tower was not the start of a forest fire. I remember signs along Maine roads often featuring Smokey Bear promoting prevention of forest fires.

Driving back from Hartland on June 30, 1966, we noticed heavy smoke to the north as we traveled through Athens, Harmony, and Brighton. It originated with a forest fire up on Cook Hill somewhere along Bigelow Brook beyond the old slate quarry. Fortunately, firefighters brought it under control before it got too serious.

There had been a forest fire in the mid 1960s east of the Mayfield/Moscow line that had jumped Route 16. We could see traces of the burned-over area for several years. A swath fifty feet wide just east and north of the highway cleared of trees provided a view toward Mount Katahdin, highest peak in Maine at 5,267 feet above sea level. Clear-cut logging operations in years following our time at Mayfield have rather ruined the natural beauty of the region.

Occasionally if our gate chain was down at the end of the driveway at night, a car would drive in. We would look out the windows to see who it was. Usually, we saw the lettering Sheriff's Patrol emblazoned on the car's trunk dimly illuminated by the taillights.

The Sheriff's Patrol provided the only presence of law and order we ever saw in those parts except for Don Walker, the local game warden. Don, perhaps part Native American, was skilled at slipping through the woods undetected without making a sound. He drove an old Model A or similar vehicle. It rode high enough off the ground and traversed back roads and went over rocks and ruts without getting bogged down.

We often saw a man, I think from Bingham, and his dog in a boat out on Kingsbury Pond, usually not too far from our dock. The man fished while the dog watched. The dog may have been black, but I have kind of forgotten. We recognized other characters who fished on a regular basis. Usually, an older couple appeared one weeknight each week in a boat out in front of our cabin. The man fished while the woman seemed to be crocheting.

Early on Saturday mornings, we often saw two men fishing from a boat not far from our cabin. We nicknamed them Tweedledee and Tweedledum from their somewhat roly-poly appearance. A ghostly character who looked like Teddy Roosevelt appeared from time to time in a green canoe. Looking back, it seems likely that more people fished in those days. We often saw people fishing in the many nearby brooks and streams. Some wore high hip boots for wading far out in the water.

None of us were swimmers, but we enjoyed splashing around in the pond, especially on hot days. We enjoyed the water and beach at Tom Farrin's dock at his invitation better than our own where algae and kivvy nests covered the pond bottom of Kingsbury Pond, where we predominantly saw kivvies. Occasionally we spotted a larger fish called a pickerel. We also had to watch for blood suckers or leeches in the more plant-filled water at our dock.

Al Gallup, our Athol neighbor and fellow model railroader, gave me a model boat he had built when I was about ten. It ran on three D-cell batteries and had a little outboard motor on the back. A fishing reel brought the vessel back after it had run out a distance. I had a lot of fun with it.

In my younger days at the cabin, I remember the Sawyers had several boats in the yard. A white boat, apparently used when the Sawyers stayed at the cabin, lay inverted on the left side of the walkway down to the dock. Tucked into the woods perpendicular to the path to the pond rested an older red boat that didn't appear to be used any longer. And I seem to remember an even older green boat long out of service, but I cannot remember just where it sat.

The Sawyers had obtained some old beams from an area building dismantled years before. They had intentions of using them for constructing a shed but never did so. The beams, six or eight of them I think, piled up against the woods between the cabin and the outhouse trail.

One summer, Dad got the idea that, if we dragged one or two of the beams down to the water, we could paddle about on them like boats. We tried it, and it worked like a charm. I remember sitting on a beam while Dad navigated it around close to shore. I liked seeing the water fill and empty in the little areas of the beam cut out where connecting pieces of wood had once fit.

Several maple trees around the cabin had wooden plugs in them where holes had been tapped years earlier for harvesting maple sap to make a little northern comfort, as maple syrup is sometimes called. Ichneumon wasps inhabited one old tree a short distance up the hill from my swing set. The wasps fascinated Aunt Martha when she came up to see the total eclipse of the sun in July of 1963. Dad took a slide of Martha and Stanley intently studying the wasps.

A partially disintegrated wigwam stood just into the wooded area between our cabin and Tom Farrin's. Danny Sawyer built it with white birch bark and logs.

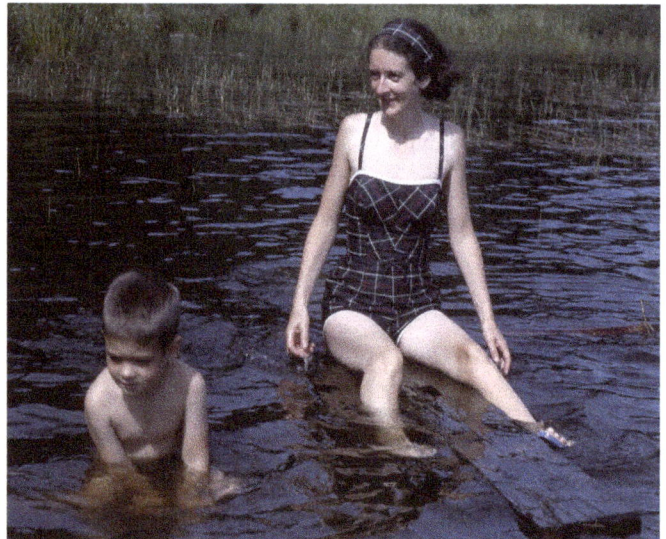

Chris and Barbara float on an old beam on August 15, 1965.
photo by Bob Coyle

A tree house Danny had also built was a short distance behind the new outhouse. He had nailed slats of wood crossways to the front of the tree to make a ladder to where several boards nailed flat made a platform.

Dad and I constructed a tree house in the mid 1970s in the woods not far from the cabin. We built it close to the ground. It had a large platform where we could sit and look out at the pond.

Folks in that part of Maine generally held a rather dim view of people from Massachusetts. It may have been due to Massachusetts people wrecking things in Maine or may have gone back to the days before 1820 when Maine was part of Massachusetts.

For the first few summers in Maine, we lived in Pennsylvania, so Dad drove a car with Pennsylvania license plates. My parents frequently heard tales of someone held in low regard that concluded with the statement, "Well, they are from Massachusetts." Later on, we heard similar stories, especially if folks didn't see our Massachusetts license plates.

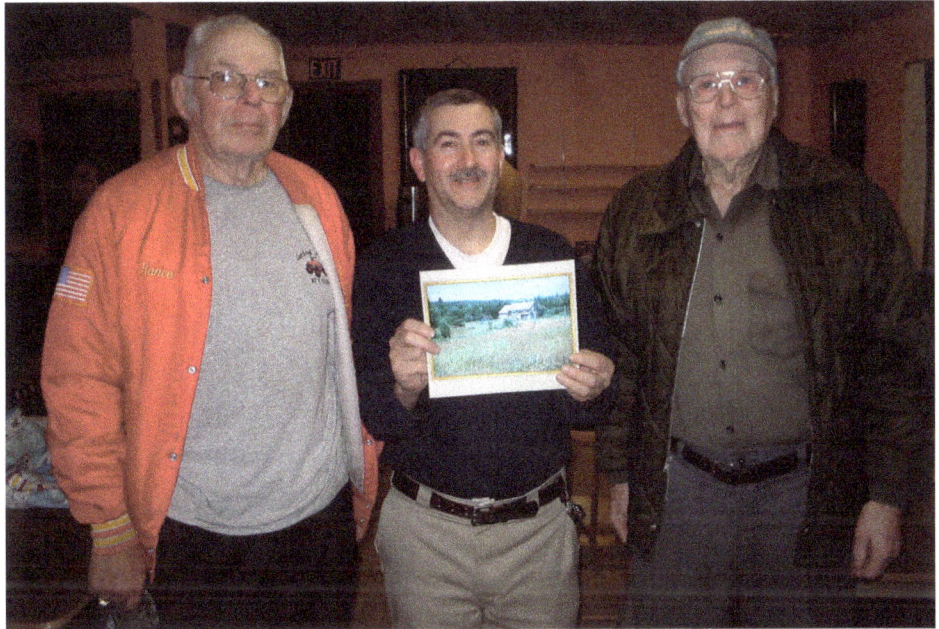

On November 2, 2009, Chris shares a photo of the old Pooler home with the last two Mayfield residents, Rance Pooler, left, and his ninety-three-year-old father, Charlie Pooler, who moved away in 1948.
photo by Douglas Drown

Occasionally, someone would try to make us seem okay by saying, "But you're from Maine originally, aren't you?" Alas, only I could claim Maine as my native state, for both of my folks were born in the Bay State.

dogs and other visitors

I have never really been a dog person. I guess that's just the way I'm built. If I'm standing with a group of people and there's a long-nosed, pointer-type dog nearby, mine is the butt he stuffs his nose up while the owner chimes in, "Don't worry, he doesn't bite."

I will admit that during our summers at Echo Valley Lodge in Phillips after we stopped going to Mayfield, the lodge hosts owned a beautiful golden retriever by the name of Rusty. We were very attached to Rusty. We remembered when he was a puppy. We happened to be there when he had to be put down many years later.

Various dogs come to mind in addition to the many folks in Maine we got to know.

Occasionally the Donald Sawyers came out to camp, although not usually when we were in residence. They owned an active, jumpy sort of dog named Buffa. That canine was sort of golden orange and of medium size. Once out to camp and released, Buffa seemed happier to bound off through the woods than to stick around us. Now and then, someone would call out "Buffa!" in an effort to keep the dog from wandering off too far.

Another canine visitor to Pine Cove from time to time belonged to one of Tom Farrin's boys. That brown stick-figure type of dog was appropriately named Nuisance, and presumably it lived up to its name. Sort of grayish with short hair, it didn't have much of a tail. I do not recall ever being bothered by Nuisance, but if he appeared, I usually made it a point to go inside the cabin.

But by far the most exciting canine stories revolved around Tom Farrin's sister Sally Malloy from Bingham. Sally's husband ran a service station just north of the lower railroad crossing near Austin Junction and almost across the street from the Gadabout Gaddis Airport.

The Malloys sometimes came out to visit when Tom and Arlene were at their camp. However, they also came out Wednesday evenings, I believe, when the Farrins were away working.

Mr. Malloy drove a black pickup truck. Sally rode with him, and in the back of the truck traveled their mean-spirited dog who, when it felt like it, answered to the name of Queenie. We nicknamed the dog Vicious.

As the truck approached, we heard Vicious barking ferociously in the distance. We raced for the safety of the cabin as fast as possible if we were outside. As the truck rounded the last curve of the driveway, the giant dog always launched itself over the sideboards with feet in motion to race ahead of the truck and then fling itself into the pond. Ducks rushed for safety if any still happened to be on Tom's lawn. After a great deal of splashing and yelping, the dog bounded back up on dry land, shook off the excess water, and turned its attention to threatening whatever living being it could find on land.

Sally came over to call on us one day early on during the dog's performances. A very pleasant and friendly woman, she warned us to stay away from her dog and not to come out of the cabin when they were there or the dog might go after us. We definitely took her warning to heart!

I think we saw that dog a couple of summers. One day Tom asked me, "Well, how do you like my sister's dog?"

I sort of hemmed and hawed and finally said something non-committal like, "Well, it has four legs (pause) and a tail . . . ."

Tom then bellowed out at the top of his lungs, "I HATE the damned thing!!" Nobody ever accused Tom of bottling himself up.

Another summer arrived, and one night the Malloys drove in but no barking and yelping from the Hound of the Baskervilles. Instead, Sally stepped out of the truck with a little black toy poodle whose name was Lucy, pronounced Lu-say. Lucy did not seem to have any out-standing habits or do much that stands out in my mind now, but she certainly contrasted with her predecessor.

Of course, not only canines visited the cabin. In later years, we recalled all the visitors we had at the cabin. Not too many of them stayed overnight due to limited sleeping space. We had a cot and at different times various sofas where someone could sleep. Both Keith McGuirk and Dave Cass from Athol used the cot during their visits. Cousins Jimmy and Steven McCastor from Quincy, Massachusetts stayed over in 1965. One slept on the cot, and the other slept on pillows on the floor. Others who slept over before I was born,

Grandma Sherman enjoys an afternoon on the dock in August 1965.
photo by Bob Coyle

according to my mother's journals, included Gram and Gramp Coyle, Uncle Ronald, Uncle Wilson, Denny Monaghan and his mother Marilyn, Grandma and Grandpa Sherman and lastly, some fellows from the BU geology camp.

Gram and Gramp Coyle visited several times that I can remember back in the 1960s. The folks told G&G Coyle about the primitiveness of the cabin prior to their first visit before I was born. They especially stressed the lack of electricity. Nevertheless, on their first morning, Gramp came into the kitchen carrying his electric razor asking "Where's the plug?" Dad lent him his safety razor.

Gram enjoyed visiting but had a few reservations and said "It's nice, but I would go crazy after three days." She also seemed bored by the sight of "nothing but trees." Gram sometimes walked down to the dock. Gramp carried a large stick when he walked up the driveway to fight off any wild animals that might choose to attack—none did. Gramp enjoyed sitting on a plank nailed across two stumps in front of the cabin and looking out across Kingsbury Pond.

Grandma and Grandpa Sherman also visited us and enjoyed the surroundings. As I recall, G&G Sherman's last visit to Mayfield was in 1965. I remember having the task of going around behind the cabin and picking up any pine cones or small sticks on the ground so Grandma would not slip on them. I put them all in a metal pail that we kept near the wood stove to hold kindling.

G&G Sherman stayed at the Yellow Bowl the last several times they visited but had previously stayed at Folsom's Cottages. Folsom's was located just west of the Yellow Bowl. Two of the Folsom cabins became part of the Yellow Bowl. G&G Coyle stayed in one in 1965. Some of our other visitors over the years stayed at the Bingham Motor Inn just south of town.

Jane O'Regan of Baldwinville, Massachusetts, came up for a few days back in 1980. She pulled a trailer behind her car and set it up outside the cabin near the raccoon feeder. She really enjoyed her stay, looking at nature, and doing photography. Cindy, her very well-behaved little pit bull, rode up with her and spent the bulk of its time in the trailer.

Other people who visited (listed more or less chronologically by their first visit, according to the journals) included Dad's college friends Reverend Ernie and Diana Geigis; Dad's sister, Aunt Carleen; Robin McCastor, Maddie McNeice, various folks from the BU geology camp, Aunt Martha and Stanley, Aunt Martha's Gang including a Mormon bishop and his entourage, Muriel and Don Pope, Ken and Maxine Wilcox, Paul Prokopas, Eleanor Jennings, Sarah Planting and Myrtle Modzeleski.

More recent visitors included Evelyn Merrifield and Norman Frigon, the Campbells—Elwood, Mrs. Lorna and Brent; Mrs. Jordan, Annie Rollins and her sister Elizabeth Cummings, Wilder and Lephie Rollins, and the Beers—Brian, May, and Homer. Oh, and the hitchhiker came with the G&G Coyle group and stayed awhile before Dad drove him over to Abbot Village where he could more easily catch a ride on Route 15. Gary Kohler spent a night in the back of his truck behind the cabin following a day of exploring the abandoned Monson Railroad.

I remember one year that the folks went up to Mayfield and I stayed at home to work a little while longer on Mrs. Merrifield's farm down the road from us in Athol to earn money for college. Dave Cass and I took a bus or series of several buses north to Waterville where we disembarked and my folks met us.

I took my mother's old suitcase, purchased in the 1940s and no longer in prime condition. It was a brown suitcase and Mother's initials of BJC were emblazoned in gold letters near the handle. I took some rope and tied it shut, as I had difficulty getting it to stay closed. I did not want it to open while on the bus.

After Dave and I got off the bus and into Dad's car, the folks told us what they had seen just before we got there. Another bus stopped prior to ours. A man got off the bus with a suitcase tied up in rope. As soon as he took a few steps away from the bus, two men approached him, then handcuffed him and led him away. I was rather glad that my bus was the second to arrive and

Stanley and Martha study ichneumon wasps outside the cabin on July 20, 1963.
photo by Bob Coyle

67

not the first, as law enforcement was evidently on the lookout for a man with a suitcase held together by a rope!

We took Dave to Rummel's Ice Cream in Waterville, famous for its many homemade flavors and make your own sundaes. It also had a nice mini golf course.

The family sometimes went to Waterville for the day. Dad bought Hathaway shirts. The company made high quality shirts, and when their Waterville factory closed in 2002, it was the next to the last shirt factory in the United States. The company had a long history and had made shirts for Union soldiers during the Civil War.

In the plaza near Hathaway in Waterville, I knew of a small store that sold model railroad equipment, and the store was always worth a visit.

We often went to Rummel's and sometimes the cinema. We saw several good movies at the Waterville cinema including *Tom Sawyer* and *The Three Musketeers*. On one occasion, we stopped and photographed the Maine Central steam locomotive 470 next to Waterville yard. After the 470 pulled Maine Central's final steam-powered passenger train in 1954, she went on display for the public to enjoy. In the 2020s, the locomotive was being rebuilt for eventual return to service.

We visited the Taconic Foot Bridge in Waterville once. The four-hundred-foot suspension bridge, built in 1902, provided pedestrian access to the Hollingsworth and Whitney Company, a paper mill in Winslow. The bridge earned the nickname Two-Cent Bridge after the toll charged to pedestrians to cross it. The structure was not in the greatest condition when we walked across it in the 1970s and has since been rebuilt. I was rather astonished to find the tollkeeper woman smoking not one but two cigarettes at the same time.

neighbor tom farrin

It is now time for a little more about our colorful neighbor Tom Farrin. Tom's camp, Pine Cove, pre-dated the Sawyers' cabin, perhaps dating to the 1920s, but I am not sure. Overgrown woods surrounded Pine Cove cabin, painted brown during my earliest years in Mayfield, could not be seen from the pond because overgrown woods surrounded it. Lea Smith, Tom and his brother Lyman's business partner, owned Pine Cove then. I am not entirely certain of the spelling of Mr. Smith's first name. I have seen it spelled as Lea as well as Lee. Mr. Smith lived in a large white house with green shutters, the nicest looking home in the Plantation of Brighton. The large, palatial home stood only a short distance from the Farrin Brothers and Smith general headquarters.

Summertime neighbor Tom Farrin shared proprietorship of Farrin Bros and Smith, a business housed in headquarters at Brighton Plantation shown in 2003.

photo by Chris Coyle

A few times each summer, we walked over to the Smith camp and waded through the underbrush. At my young age, I was fascinated by the sink pipe terminating a foot or so out from the exterior wall of the kitchen. A large white pine tree stood adjacent to the camp. Occasionally in the evening during our early summers at the cabin, a car slowly drifted down the driveway without benefit of lights and rolled to a stop at the Smith cabin. Later, the car started and quietly disappeared up the driveway and on out of sight. We never saw any other activity at the cabin.

Everything changed drastically in the summer of 1966. Ownership of the cabin transferred from Lea Smith to Tom Farrin starting about midway through our summer in Mayfield.

One day, large pieces of equipment belonging to Farrin Brothers and Smith arrived. Trees came down. The driveway was widened and graded. Noise filled the air. Truckload after truckload of gravel dumped into the shore of Kingsbury Pond to create a beach, muddying the pond water and rendering it unfit for washing purposes. We packed up and headed to Bar Harbor for a few days.

The changes to our quiet, secluded area appalled us. But in time, we accepted the changes and saw that Tom appreciated Kingsbury Pond as much as we did although perhaps in a different way. Tom liked the woods pushed back. The cabin was repainted bright yellow with white trim. Plastic flamingos appeared at the edge of his new beach.

I don't recall we had much contact with Tom during the first few years. Then, one summer on the evening of our arrival and we may have even still been unloading the car, Tom strode down the driveway and inquired, "Does Donald know you're here?"

Well, yes, Donald and Norma Sawyer did indeed know of our presence and may have even cashed the rent check by then. We told Tom, and off he went.

We maintained a cordial acquaintance with Tom and Arlene. Tom was a very colorful but good man. His weekend visits to Pine Cove usually involved arrival on Friday evening followed by some initial relaxing. Sometimes on Saturday mornings, he went down to his office in Brighton for a little while.

After his return to Pine Cove, the libation would begin, at times providing us with some real entertainment. To the best of our knowledge Tom never touched a drop of alcohol during the week, but the beer sure flowed on Saturday afternoons! He normally arose very early on Sunday followed by hard physical work such as splitting wood. Later in the day, Tom and Arlene left in their separate cars. If Tom's work for the summer happened to be nearby, he might stay at Pine Cove all week and rise early to head to their job site. He drove a large diesel-powered car, a Ford product, I think, for several years.

Tom had his men construct an attractive fireplace and chimney utilizing local rocks. Dad and I happened to be over there one day, and Dad started identifying the rocks. Tom was very interested and asked Dad to come over and sketch out a diagram describing each rock on a large piece of paper. Tom tried several times to interest Dad in a cold beer, perhaps so he wouldn't feel guilty having one himself, but Dad, a life-long teetotaler, declined.

We were sitting down at our dock one evening. With corn on the cob in season, Tom called over to us in a very loud voice, "How'd you folks like some cawn (corn)?"

The folks responded in the affirmative and dispatched me to go over and fetch it. Then, in an even louder voice, Tom bellowed out, "Well, that got him up off his ass!! Har, har, har."

One summer in the late 1960s as we drove into Somerset County, we saw lots of large signs with black letters on white proclaiming T.J. FARRIN for STATE REPRESENTATIVE. We never heard how the election turned out, but Tom did not seem to be in the state legislature down to Augusta when we returned the following summer.

Tom, his brother Lyman. and Lea Smith owned Farrin Brothers and Smith. They had also run the Norridgewock Race Track for stock car racing back in 1951 but closed it to concentrate on their road construction business. Razor Crossman, well-known announcer and auctioneer, was in on the race track as well. I don't know that we ever saw Lyman or Lea Smith.

My mother often mentioned "hot Saturday," August 2, 1975, a day of record temperatures for inland Maine. As outside temperatures reached three digits, Arlene constructed a tent of sorts over Tom, who lay sound asleep on the lawn. As I recall, even the water in Kingsbury Pond was almost hot that day culminating in one of the very few nights we left the windows of our cabin open all night.

Various and sundry other characters visited Pine Cove from time to time. I think some of them may have been Farrin Brothers and Smith employees in search of free cold beer.

Behind Tom's kitchen, a nice woodshed connected to the house by an overhead roof. Besides wood, the shed housed an old-fashioned soda cooler that cooled by circulating cold water when powered up. Tom had a loud generator that ran in the evenings until he retired for the night. After the generator was shut off, silence reigned once again, only broken by the call of loons or croaking of bullfrogs.

One of Tom Farrin's many trucks parked in Brighton Plantation on August 14, 1987.
photo by Chris Coyle

At any rate, the soda cooler was well-stocked with beer, and I think many of Tom's friends and employees knew. One Saturday evening with already great carrying-on over at Pine Cove, a vehicle without headlights quietly slipped down the driveway. It drew to a stop near the point where our two driveways joined to become one. Several men got out and tiptoed down to the front porch, which seemed to be the center of commotion. Suddenly, a gunshot rang out followed by great hollering within and laughter from outside. The party poopers were admitted, but after that night, we noticed that Tom locked the gate chain at the head of the driveway as darkness approached.

A few nights later, we spotted a boat slowly navigating toward Pine Cove with what looked like the same hooligans onboard. It began the "one if by land, two if by sea commentary," the one and two referring to gunshots, although I don't recall any firearms being discharged from the boat.

Tom had a small vegetable garden in the latter years of our summers in Mayfield. He asked us to harvest vegetables for ourselves during the week while he was away, as some of them wouldn't keep until his next weekend visit. I picked Swiss chard, lettuce, tomatoes, and perhaps carrots. They always tasted nice and fresh.

The camps of the Poolers and Waughs were on Mayfield Pond. Those cabins stood maybe half to three-quarters of a mile from us on their own shared driveway from Route 16. The Pooler and Waugh names were painted in black letters on silver boards cut out in the shape of fish and nailed to trees at the head of the driveway.

We occasionally hiked to another cabin to the east of us. It was not on the shore and had no view of the pond. The cabin did not appear to have been used recently, and the driveway to it grew up to brush.

A cabin I liked was between Route 16 and the pond near the Kingsbury dump. Mainly, I liked the hand pump out in the yard. Hand pumps fascinated me when I was young, and I wished we had one at the sink in our cabin so I could pump it all day long to my heart's content. Maine has many beautiful rest areas, some graced with hand pumps, a feature I just became ecstatic over if we stopped at one of them.

A sign proclaiming the Do-Drop-Inn identified a small group of cabins near the camp with a hand pump. The folks had inquired years before about renting a cabin. The woman owner

Chris pumps water at Katahdin Campground in August, 1968.

photo by Bob Coyle

exclaimed, "Why, yes we do have a toilet. All we need to do is to hook it up." The folks decided not to stay there.

One other cabin I remember sat a little bit into the woods near the top of Cook Hill on the old road just east of where it joins the new road. We gathered it was probably used as a hunting cabin in the fall, for we never saw anyone there. Eventually it showed signs of disuse and likely disintegrated.

wellington and the united states mail

We had all our mail forwarded to Wellington for the duration of our Maine stay. Our address was simply Wellington, Maine 04990 with never a street or road added to the address. Unfortunately, I never knew the name of the fellow who delivered our mail in a pickup truck. Tuesdays, Thursdays, and Saturdays, he drove the route around Kingsbury Pond. He covered what was called the Star Route over Parkman way the other three days of the week. He usually stopped at our mailbox, a little after 10 a.m., although there may have been a time or two that he drove down the driveway with a package.

Going up to fetch the mail was an exciting event for us. Sometimes, we walked up the long driveway to the mailbox at the end of the driveway on Route 16. Other times, we drove up in the car, and during the summers Dad and I brought our bicycles to Mayfield, we sometimes rode them up for the mail. From time to time during the winter, we received an item of mail forwarded from Wellington.

The small town of Wellington did not have many paved roads when I was a boy in the 1960s. Later, more of the roads received macadam pavement. The small center of Wellington had a general store, post office, grange hall, and a church. The McCue family ran the general store and post office.

In the early days of our Mayfield summers, Mrs. Rose McCue was postmaster of the post office located in one side of her large kitchen. We entered through a door that led only to

Mail arrived three times a week in the mailbox at the head of our driveway, shown in August, 1963.

photo by Bob Coyle

the post office section of the house. Looking through the service window, we could see Mrs. McCue cooking at her stove. After she gave things a good stir, she would come over to the window to wait on us. Unpainted clapboards covered the exterior of the house as with most homes in the area.

*McCue's General Store, which served as the post office in later years,
was housed around 1900 in the white house, right, near the road in Wellington.*

postcard from the collection of Chris Coyle

The Sawyers stayed all summer at the cabin in 1959. Therefore, the folks needed to find alternative lodging. They stayed at the Yellow Bowl, the inn in Bingham, while they looked for a cabin or camp for the rest of the summer. They had many adventures tracking down camps and then trying to locate owners, who always seemed reluctant to rent or sell places they obviously had not used in a long time. The folks found several that had passed the point of saving due to lack of use and care.

They tried to get leads from people they had met the summer before. They stopped to see Mrs. McCue. She mentioned a house on the road to Burdin Corner. They were not too sure about the location, and when they asked her about the color of the building as a means to help identify it, she paused a moment and said, "Wood color." That meant it had lost all its paint from weathering, if in fact it was ever painted at all.

Around 1970, the older Mrs. McCue retired and the post office relocated next door to the general store operated by the younger Mrs. Greta McCue. Mr. John McCue drove a delivery truck for Humpty Dumpty Potato Chips and parked it on the gravel area next to the store at times.

On hot days, we went into the store and purchased Hoodsies, little ice-cream cups with a cardboard cap produced by HP Hood, which issued a small wooden spoon to buyers of the desserts. Then we ventured outside to consume them prior to shopping or heading elsewhere. The store closed a few years later, but the post office remained. A retired general moved to Wellington and built a nice home and property along the dirt road that led to Huff Corner. He was spoken of often at the Wellington Post Office and likely lived at an income level much higher than that of the rest of the small town's residents.

I consulted the book *Maine Postal History and Postmarks*, 1943, by Sterling T. Dow for postal history of the area. The Fordstown (original name of Mayfield) Post Office opened in 1832 and became Mayfield in 1836 with change of town name. The Mayfield Post Office closed in 1844 but reopened in 1886 and then closed again in 1931 with duties moved to the Kingsbury Post Office.

The Kingsbury Post Office opened in 1838. It

The Wellington post office, previously McCue's General Store, served the public for many years.

postcard from the collection of Chris Coyle

closed in 1917 with duties moved to the Mayfield Post Office. The Kingsbury Post Office reopened in 1931 and closed after Dow compiled data for the book, but I believe the last year of operation was around 1957 based on what my folks told me. By then, it operated only seasonally, mainly serving the people who stayed at area camps in the summer. The folks said the Kingsbury postmaster's name was Effie Bean Nugent. I think the folks told me that they got their mail for the first year or two at the old Justin Worcester private home at Kingsbury Mills, once the location of the Kingsbury Post Office. A row of mail-boxes was set up for camps in the area. During my time in Mayfield, several mailboxes remained at the Worcester home.

My article "The Post Offices and Mail Delivery to Mayfield and Kingsbury, Maine" in the *Maine Philatelist*, July 2023, included some of the information shared here.

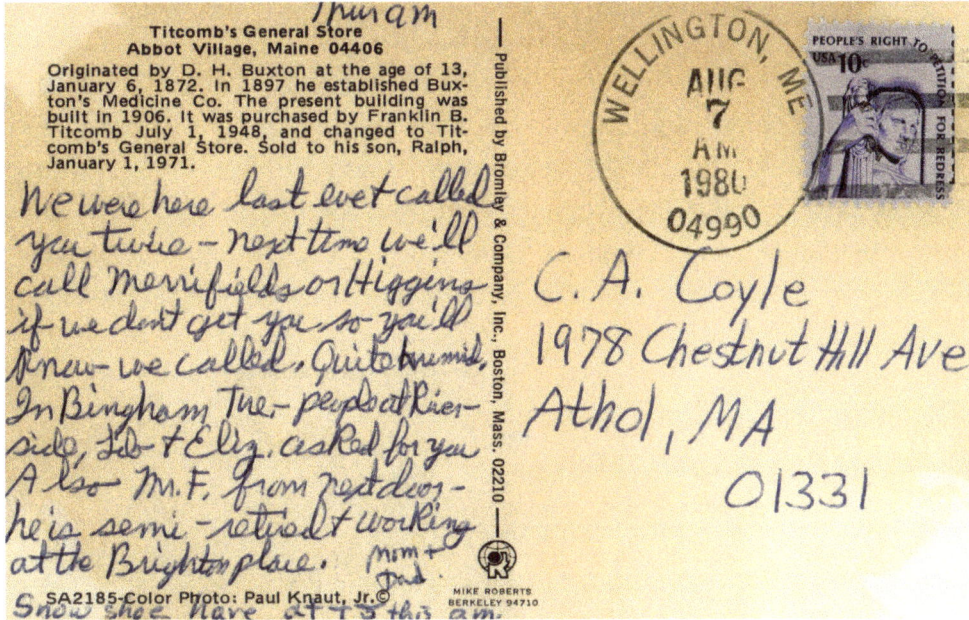

A postcard sent to Chris Coyle in 1980 bears the Wellington, ME postmark.

bingham

The closest center of civilization for us to transact business was Bingham some twelve miles west on Route 16, most of which was paved by the time our family began staying in Mayfield. Bingham, a quiet little village, sits alongside the Kennebec River on Route 201, also called Arnold Trail through the Bingham area, which leads north to Quebec. Known as the Gateway to the Maine Forest, Bingham is halfway between the Equator and the North Pole by latitude. It is the last stopping-off point for supplies before hitting the North Woods of Maine.

A lot of beautiful trees were cut down and many front lawns shortened when the state did Main Street over around 1970. Whitney and Baker streets previously connected to Main Street changed with the do-over so that they fed instead into Preble Street where Omar and Josephine Sawyer lived. We used to get the key to the cabin from them and sometimes get drinking water there as well.

We enjoyed a close friendship with the longtime proprietor of the Yellow Bowl Inn, Annie Rollins and with her sister Elizabeth Cummings. The Yellow Bowl, formerly a home, had been converted for use as an inn. The actual yellow bowl was a large iron kettle painted yellow and standing in a prominent place in the front yard of the inn. As I understand it, Annie's mother, Grace, had brought the bowl from

Bingham's site is halfway between the North Pole and the equator.
photo by Chris Coyle

the farm in Concord, Maine, where she grew up. Grace's grandfather Daniel Robinson had made potash or lye in the bowl. After the inn closed in 1973 when Annie sold the property to the Skowhegan Savings Bank, she had the bowl moved to the lawn at her house directly east of the inn.

Flowers, shrubs, a wishing well, and seating adorned the front yard of Bingham's Yellow Bowl in July, 1960.

photo by Bob Coyle

Beautiful antique furniture furnished the inn, originally purchased new and aging in place at the inn. I remember marble-topped tables next to the beds. Annie invited us to see the tea room near the end of our 1973 summer in Maine. Located in the right

Before it was painted yellow, the bowl outside the Yellow Bowl Inn was used at a nearby farm for making potash.

photo by Chris Coyle

front of the house, the tea room had always been closed since the folks first visited the Yellow Bowl in 1958.

Errold and Harriet Hilton had once leased that portion, the oldest part of the building, for a number of years and operated the tearoom. When Annie showed it to us, I gathered it had not been used for many years. We were fascinated to see tables and chairs and imagined what it had been like decades before in operation. Some of the tables and chairs from the tearoom ended up at the little restaurant at the Gadabout Gaddis Airport in Bingham after an auction of the contents of the inn. Gadabout Gaddis

*During the summer of 1961,
Barbara holds one-year-old Chris
at the Yellow Bowl in Bingham.*
photo by Bob Coyle

himself, the airport's namesake, hosted television programs about fishing in Maine.

The Yellow Bowl grounds had several attractive seats with canopies over them and logs for walls. Well-tended and beautiful flower beds surrounded the buildings. There were also two cabins situated on the broad lawns to the rear and another smaller house across the main street used for overflow at the height of the season.

After the Yellow Bowl closed, part of the main inn was demolished with another part moved north of town just across the bridge over Austin Stream quite close to Tozier's service station. The boarded-up structure sort of languished there for a few years, a sad reminder of what once was such a warm and inviting place. I am not sure just where the building did end up.

Some of Annie's guests had stayed at the Yellow Bowl for years and often came and went without even seeing her. One older salesman stayed in a room in the house that Annie used across the street for overflow. If Annie was not around when he arrived, he let himself in, and since he had to be on the road at an early hour to get to his next stop, he left before Annie was up. He stayed one night every other week, as he had for many years. Annie said sometimes several months would pass before she saw him, and they would know he had been there when they checked the room to make it up the next day. The fellow continued to stay at the overflow house after the Yellow Bowl itself closed, as the overflow house did not sell with the inn.

In the mid 1970s, we often watched the annual bicycle race which took place in early-to-mid August. As I recall, the race course started at the Canadian border in Sandy Bay Township and went south 101 miles to downtown Waterville. The folks of Bingham knew when to expect to see the bicycles arriving in town, and many lined the streets holding bottles of water out for contestants who wished to grab one on the go. We often parked at the Yellow

In the summer 1973, the annual bicycle race passes through Bingham.

photo by Bob Coyle

Bowl to watch the race. Usually, most of the excitement lasted no more than twenty minutes or so. Then it was all over for another year.

Mother telephoned her parents in Weston, Massachusetts, at frequent intervals. Since the cabin had no phone, she often did it from the pay phone beneath the staircase at the Yellow Bowl. If Annie happened to be in the lodge, we visited with her in the lobby for a while. After the Yellow Bowl closed in 1973, Mother usually used the pay phone on the landing at the top of the front steps outside Preble and Robinson's Store. Somerset Telephone Company had ceased to provide phone booths with closing doors by then, so Mother was forced to shriek in a loud voice over the telephone to compete with noisy vehicles driving through town.

I found lamp globes over front door lights an interesting sight at many older Bingham homes. For whatever reason, perhaps from years of exposure to the sun, many of the globes had taken on an attractive purple hue. Colby Movie Theatre on Murray Street behind Preble and Robinson's P & R store remained in operation in 1958, my folks' first summer around Bingham. They did not go to a movie but later regretted the decision as it closed soon after.

Andrews Hardware used the building for storage for a number of years. Attorney Walter Harwood's home and office with a small fenced-in area facing Murray Street stood on the opposite corner from P&R. I think he kept a tame pet red fox in the enclosure. The animal had a little doghouse in one corner.

Bingham Union Library was and is a real gem. Originally a house built, I believe, in the early 1800s. During our era, the library was open three afternoons a week—Tuesday, Thursday, and Saturday—but the small, varied, and interesting collection has a lot of good material on Maine history. One enters through the front door in front of a spiral staircase that leads to the second story. Elizabeth Goodrich Jordan, the elderly, mostly retired librarian, lived in a small apartment through a door to the right. The door to the left led into the main library room and had likely been a living room at one time. The librarian had a large wooden desk on the east side of the room where she checked out our books.

The next room back was the children's room. In addition to new books to read, there I had a few favorites I checked out each summer. They included the well-known Robert Mc-Closkey books, *One Morning in Maine, Blueberries for Sal,* and *Make Way for Ducklings.*

During open hours at the library, Mrs. Jordan often sat with Grace Rollins, the active librarian. Mrs. Jordan had lived a fascinating life. She taught school and roomed out to Mayfield in the early years of the twentieth century.

As I became more interested in the history of Mayfield, I corresponded with Mrs. Jordan during the winter. What she did not know she asked Charlie Pooler to answer. Charlie had grown up in Mayfield and resided in Bingham. Charlie attended the program I presented on the history of Mayfield in 2009 for the Old Canada Road Historical Society at Bingham Grange Hall. Charlie passed away in 2017 at the ripe old age of 101 having been active to the end of his days still chopping wood and cutting hay.

Elizabeth Cummings who with her sister operated the Yellow Bowl Inn, Barbara, and Bob chat outside Wilder Rollins's former service station on August 20, 1984.
photo by Chris Coyle

The extended Rollins family of Bingham was rather large. Grace Rollins was a cousin of our friends Annie and Wilder Rollins and their sister Elizabeth Cummings. Wilder's service station was diagonally across the street from the Bingham Union Library.

Mrs. Jordan went to live in a nursing home in Skowhegan in the early 1970s. Then she moved to a new facility in Bingham and remained there through the rest of her life. She was in reasonably good health but unable to live alone.

Several times we got the okay from each of those facilities to take her out for a drive for a few hours. One time, we took her for ice cream in Skowhegan. On another occasion after she was living back in Bingham, we brought her out to the cabin for tea, probably her first visit to Mayfield in many years. She passed away in late 1976 at a ripe old age. The rooms where Mrs. Jordan had lived on the west side of the library building were renovated for library expansion after she moved out.

A huge wood frame structure, home to several fraternal organizations, sat east of the library on Main Street. I wish I had photographed the sign Moxie Lodge prior to its removal from the building. The name Moxie applies to many things in the area. When I was young, I became familiar with what was in the nineteenth century New England's favorite soft drink, Moxie. I mistakenly thought it was bottled using water from Maine's Moxie Stream.

An interesting coincidence from our winter home in Athol, Massachusetts to our summer home in central Maine involved the move in late 1976 of the Reverend Douglas W. Drown from the Congregational churches of South Royalston and Royalston, the next town north of our winter home in Athol, to Bingham's First Congregational Church. The move helped facilitate his completion of coursework at Bangor Theological Seminary.

Our family knew Doug somewhat although not well when he lived in Royalston. Doug shared and shares an interest in railroads with me. One Sunday afternoon in August of 1977 when I worked as engineer at the Sandy River Railroad Park in Phillips, Maine, my mother called my attention to the fact that Doug and his mother had just purchased tickets to ride my train. I climbed out of the locomotive cab and went back, found Doug, and invited him up into the cab. Doug remained in Bingham as minister for thirty-two years.

Still a narrow road, Route 16 in 1958 offered a view of Wyman Dam in the distance.
photo by Bob Coyle

stores and restaurants

I remember the Preble and Robinson store in Bingham as if only yesterday. Upon entering the store, it felt like stepping back in time several decades and seeing what stores had looked like years earlier. Multi-storied, and was painted light yellow. Later, the owners removed the top stories and repainted the building mint green. They installed new concrete steps with handrails, too. Previously, there had been steps as wide as the building. Ruby Robinson told us once that every time the Bingham fire alarm sounded, she always looked out the window to see if the upper stories of the store were on fire. So evidently, the family worried about extra unneeded stories.

I remember the sound of old-style grocery carts rolling along the four aisles of heavily oiled wooden floors in the store. Allan Robinson, proprietor, was a kind and friendly man. When customers brought groceries to the counter, he read prices of items while Ruby, his wife, entered them on the cash register. Sometimes she read the prices and Allan entered them. The groceries were usually packed in boxes and carried down the stairs and out to the car. Allan used to give me one of those great big pretzels out of the circular glass pretzel jar when I was a small boy. We often saw him smoking a cigar at the same time, and I thought the pretzel to be an imitation cigar!

Years later, long after we stopped summering in Mayfield and even longer since Allan Robinson retired, we happened to be driving west along Bingham's Main Street one afternoon when we spotted him walking up the sidewalk near Wes Baker's home. Dad pulled over, and we all got out. Allan recognized us immediately, and we had a great visit. Sadly, that was the last time we saw him. Allan's father, Walter, a well-known lumberman, worked in the woods north of Bingham.

The meat counter was at the back center of the store, and to the left, an additional room contained other merchandise. No one could top Preble and Robinson's meats. Wes Baker ran the meat counter. I can remember seeing hanging beef out back with Wes getting ready to break it down.

Wes made great barbequed chicken, but the *best* were his spare ribs. I do not know what Wes used for a sauce to coat the meat, but it tasted absolutely delicious. You had to order those delicacies in advance to be sure you got them. When we wanted spareribs, my father asked Wes when he would be making them and then placed an order. Customers could see spareribs or barbequed chicken cooking and turning inside a small glass-walled oven atop the meat counter.

When done, the meat got packaged in paper bags with aluminum foil outer wrapping. After we picked them up, we usually went up to one of the picnic areas on Route 201 north of town. On more than one occasion, people saw and smelled the spareribs and inquired where to purchase them. They were heartbroken to find out they would have to order the delicacy well in advance.

Phyllis Huggins, who lived in Concord, worked at the store. A very friendly woman, she took quite a liking to me when I was young. One day, she came out from a back room and presented me with a nice yellow plastic pail. I found it very useful out at the cabin for hauling pond water up to the kitchen for washing.

We usually shopped at Preble and Robinson's particularly for the outstanding fresh meat but did go to A&P sometimes. Like most stores in Bingham, the A&P, had a couple of steps leading up into the building. I think A&P may have stayed open later in the day than P&R. Like most older A&P stores, the one in Bingham had a coffee grinder on each of the two checkout counters. Although not a large store by today's standards, it carried all the necessary items. I remember the three people—a woman, Charlene Hunnewell and two men, Jim Richard and a French-Canadian fellow by the name of Joe Bourque—who ran the store. After A&P closed in 1975, the store re-opened as J&L under the ownership of Joe Bourque and Leslie Martin. Joe retired in 1981 and passed away in 2012 at the age of ninety-two. Joe served as town moderator for years and, proudly wearing his World War II uniform, participated in the annual Memorial Day program.

Diagonally across the street from A&P stood Hill's Variety, where we purchased newspapers, usually the *Waterville Morning Sentinel,* and occasionally film or a few other items. Hill's also sold topographic maps and hunting/fishing licenses. Hill's had a luncheonette and soda fountain years before, according to an old advertisement.

Bushey and Sterling's large store was a couple of storefronts west from Hill's Variety on the corner of Preble Street. Bushey and Sterling offered clothing, furniture, and I think appliances as well.

Moore's Rexall Drugstore just west of A&P in the adjoining storefront consisted of two stores in our early days in the area. The one on the right housed the drugstore section which besides the pharmacy had postcards, film, and a few gift items for sale. A large sheet of green plastic over the west-facing window could be rolled down to provide relief from hot afternoon sun.

A separate store to the left of the drug store section featured their toy department, I think opened mainly at Christmas. Although the toy department had a door to the outside, customers normally accessed it from the drugstore section through a connecting door. Normally closed in summer, it would be opened for us once in a while. Later on, the toy section stayed open every business day. Eventually with removal of the wall, it all became one large store.

Often on days we went into town to do laundry, shop, and perhaps visit the Bingham Union Library, we ate at a couple of restaurants. We liked Bemis's Restaurant located a little west of Preble and Robinson's store on the same side of the street. Diners had to ascend a short flight of stairs at the front of the building to enter the small restaurant. It had a counter with stools to the left and a few booths or tables to the right just past the entrance. Single-serving cereal boxes sat on a shelf against the wall on the counter side of the restaurant. Below that was a working surface with equipment such as a frappe machine.

I enjoyed my first frappes and ice cream sundaes at Bemis's. Mother related the story of the summer Bemis's introduced Key Lime pie to the menu. Local people were not familiar with the tasty dessert and did not purchase it, so the owners dropped it from the menu.

After Bemis's closed in 1968, a new owner reopened under the name the Habitant. The building burned a short time later and the owner rebuilt, but on the ground level. I don't recall that we ever ate at the Habitant. Our friend Elizabeth Cummings commented on the restaurant "You need to take your pocketbook in there!" she said. Evidently it soon priced itself out of business.

Across the street from the Bingham Laundromat on the north side of Route 201, venerable Thompson's Restaurant has been in business since 1929. We enjoyed the food, although more expensive than Bemis's. I think that Thompson's may have wanted to cater a little more toward tourists than local folks. My parents became incensed that Thompson's charged more for toasted homemade bread than for commercial bread. Quebec buses stopped at Thompson's for passengers to buy a meal.

One interesting feature, at least to me as a youngster, was the presence of gaslights throughout the establishment that could provide illumination during an electrical outage. Also, I noticed that every year, a large calendar hung on the wall behind the counter. I believe Lidstone Insurance provided the calendars, which always featured black bears engaged in antics such as raiding camps, picnics, vehicles, and boats.

And, of course, Bingham had Riverside Dairy Bar, part of the Riverside Inn, just south of town on Route 201. We enjoyed peacefully watching logs silently floating down the Kennebec River to mills as we ate our meal. Sometimes we enjoyed a pizza at Riverside.

We visited Pooler's each summer in Skowhegan until it closed. There, we purchased new handmade moccasins each year to carry us through to the next summer.

We ate at the little restaurant at the Gadabout Gaddis Airport a few times, too. A few miles north of Skowhegan, another place, O Sole Mio, featured pizza and Italian food. I don't recall that we ever ate inside but, rather, we preferred to take the meal out, usually a supper. We might enjoy it in Coburn Park, sometimes before seeing a movie at the Strand or the drive-in theatre. Sadly, O Sole Mio is long gone. One place in Skowhegan still in business, though, is Island Dairy Treat, a frequent stop on our trip from Athol to the cabin. We often enjoyed a Creamie and went out on the nearby swinging pedestrian foot bridge which Dad would always get moving back and forth, much to my distress.

Swinging Bridge, Skowhegan, Me.

When Chris was small, Bob always got the Skowhegan swinging foot bridge to get moving back and forth—much to Chris's distress.

postcard from the collection of Chris Coyle

Canadians traveled Route 201 south through Bingham, Skowhegan, and other towns as a popular route to areas along the south coast of Maine, especially Old Orchard Beach, for vacations. Many businesses displayed Bienvenue signs to welcome tourists from Quebec.

Small signs displayed near cash registers in the area noted that the establishment would discount Canadian money by a certain amount, depending on the current exchange rate. We often picked up Canadian coins in change.

The restaurant at Martin Pond north of Bingham on the road to Jackman was about the only place one could

MARTIN POND DINING ROOM -- THE FORKS, MAINE

On Route 201 between Bingham and Jackman, Martin Pond Dining Room offered good food.

postcard from the collection of Chris Coyle

eat between those two towns. One time, we had a supper there years ago. The proprietor announced during our meal that he was sick of cooking so went over and locked the door and flipped the open sign to closed. The next would-be customers who came to the door and found it closed yet saw us eating supper through the window were not amused.

After an unusual 1972 storm,
Chris makes balls of hail
at Don's drive-in in Cornville.

photo by Bob Coyle

A favorite drive-in for several years, Don's at Cass Corner in Cornville famously served pies that drew customers from far and wide. Don bought the pies from local people and in turn sold slices to the public. Don's had great cheeseburgers too! A strong thunder and hailstorm blew in one day in 1972 when we stopped at Don's for lunch. Dad took photos of me making hail balls, a rather unusual opportunity. One summer probably about 1975, Dad and I frequently drove down to Don's to bring slices of pie back for dessert after supper. We usually listened to a radio station on the way. It always seemed to play Gordon Lightfoot's "Sundown" at least once during our trek. Dad and I sang along. I remember those pie runs whenever I hear the song.

We might stop at other stores and restaurants in Piscataquis County if we happened to be east of Mayfield. Titcomb's General Store operated in a large white, three-story wood frame building at the junction of Routes 16 and 15 in Abbot Village. After climbing the half dozen heavily oiled wooden steps that ran most of the width of the building on the Route 15 side, we lifted the latch on the old wooden door to enter the store, packed with considerable merchandise. Large glass windows helped light the interior including an old, water-cooled soda machine during the first years we stopped there. Upon sliding the doors on the top of the unit open, you retrieved your soda bottle from cold water always circulating around the bottles.

An icehouse behind the building supplied ice well into the 1970s and perhaps later mainly for camps in the area. The folks bought ice at Titcomb's for refrigeration in the summer of 1959 when they stayed at the Tibbetts camp on the east end of Kingsbury Pond. An article in the March, 1975 *Down East Magazine* talks about the annual ice harvest on Piper Pond. The stored ice kept all summer packed in sawdust which provided insulation.

Bingham is in Somerset County, but Abbot Village belongs to Piscataquis County. We saw that, although separated by scarcely twenty-five miles, each store carried a slightly different product line. We found Pleasant Hill Dairy milk cartons from Bangor at Titcomb's, while we usually bought Hunt's milk from Skowhegan at stores in Bingham. With a play on their initials, Pleasant Hill Dairy promoted their product as the Milk with the PhD. When I was very young, I didn't understand why we could not buy milk from Peterson's Dairy of Royalston, Massachusetts, in Bingham as we did at home with Peterson's just up the road over the town line. Of course, Peterson's certainly did not have that large a distribution area. Years before we stayed in the Bingham area, the town had its own milk plant—Austin Dairy. EBay frequently has bottles and caps from that company.

The *Bangor Daily News*, from a larger city than the *Morning Sentinel* in Waterville, was the newspaper available at Titcomb's. The *Morning Sentinel* was the usual newspaper at Bingham stores.

Piscataquis County stores carried Pleasant Hill milk.
photo by Chris Coyle

Titcomb's General Store in Abbot Village carried different items than the Bingham stores.
postcard from the collection of Chris Coyle

We stopped at Titcomb's one day back in the 1960s. A car from "away" stopped, and the people came into the store to inquire as to where they might find a meal. Not revealing the fact that a little drive-in restaurant existed scarcely a mile farther down the road, the woman behind the counter proclaimed, "We have the Italian (pronounced eye-talian) sandwiches." The hungry folks purchased several and returned to their car. We wondered what they thought when they found the little drive-in a short distance away.

Titcomb's closed soon after we stopped staying at Mayfield and surprisingly only a short time after they remodeled and expanded the store.

Pat's was east from Abbot Village on Route 15 and a good place for fried chicken until one day the cooking fat caught fire and the place burned down! Prior to that fateful day, we sometimes had supper there and then have dessert at the little drive-in Creemee place on the way back to Abbot Village.

The Gold Nugget Restaurant in Guilford offered nice meals, although had much more appeal prior to its remodeling. Then one could sit at the back of the restaurant by the windows over the Piscataquis River before it was modernized and they removed windows with a great view.

An embarrassing incident in Piscataquis County concerned the infamous Swedish meatball supper at Guilford Universalist Church when young Chris spilled his meatballs that

Bob and Boston University students enjoyed suppers at North Anson Methodist Church, shown in 1959.

photo by Bob Coyle

proceeded to roll in all directions, much to the amusement of local folks watching Dad crawl around on his hands and knees picking up meatballs from beneath the tables! Other church suppers we enjoyed took place in Abbot Village, Greenville, and years before at North Anson Methodist Church.

A large brick nineteenth-century Masonic hall dominated the center of Guilford across the street from the Gold Nugget. Route 15, the main road through town, made a couple of ninety-degree curves as it crossed the Piscataquis River. Guilford of Maine, a textile manufacturer, was the largest employer in town. The company had a small factory outlet store where we purchased a couple of good quality blankets decades ago. We still use them.

Another area industry located east of Guilford, the Puritan plant manufactured wooden tongue depressors among other products. In the yard, we sometimes saw large piles of logs constantly doused with water from sprinklers to prevent checking and decay.

Many homes and other wooden structures in Guilford were painted a characteristic orange yellow color back in the 1960s. We referred it as Guilford yellow. Perhaps the paint had a good price at the local hardware store or maybe someone

Guilford of Maine, one of the last area textile mills, produced plaid blankets.

photo by David Cass

popular had his house painted this color, but at any rate, the color prevailed in town then. Sometimes we saw a structure elsewhere painted that color and remarked that it was Guilford yellow.

Another very common circumstance not just in Guilford but in that entire region of Maine involved the fact that virtually all homes and many other buildings sported tin roofs rather than asphalt shingles. Tin roofing greatly helps reduce problems from ice dams and such during Maine's long winter months. In fact, when we started having bad problems with ice dams along our north roof at our home on Chestnut Hill in Athol, we decided to have a metal roof put on that side of the house and have had no problems since.

West of Guilford village stood a small group of buildings built in the 1960s, perhaps for senior housing, at Riverbend Drive. A parade float made to look like a narrow gauge Monson Railroad steam locomotive often parked there.

Known for food with a Finnish flair the Kavilia, a delightful restaurant, operated on the shore of Lake Hebron on the main street in Monson. Sometimes we did our laundry in Monson and usually had a meal or at least a snack at the Kavilia. Like many older stores and restaurants we visited in that part of Maine, the Kavilia had a tin ceiling.

I believe that the man who owned the Kavilia but did not actually take part in its daily operations also owned a large tract of largely forested land, including Borestone Mountain, its territory later conserved as an Audubon sanctuary. Artwork by Thurley Knowles adorned the walls. She may have also worked in the restaurant, but I cannot remember for sure.

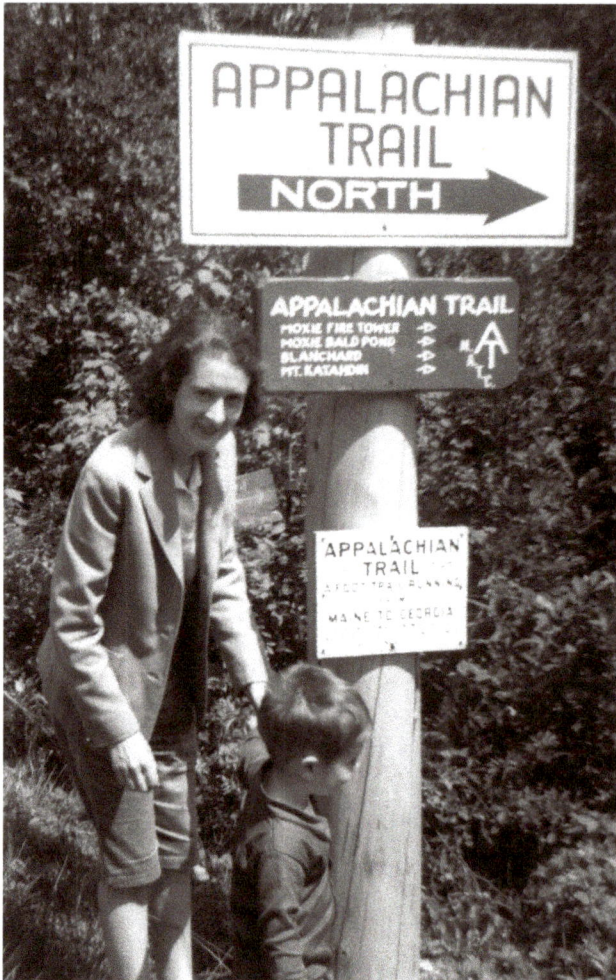

Barbara and Chris take a moment on the Appalachian Trail near Joe's Hole in 1964.
photo by Bob Coyle

Many Maine folk prefer red snapper hot dogs.
photo by Chris Coyle

Uniquely, the twenty-two-hundred-mile Appalachian Trail from Mount Katahdin, Maine, to Georgia runs down Monson's Main Street. We often saw hikers doing laundry and having a meal at the Kavilia. As we had walked up and down Main Street in Monson many times, we have indeed hiked that portion of the Appalachian Trail. We hiked another more significant part of the trail east a few miles from the old Somerset Railroad grade near Joe's Hole, a fishing pond at the south end of Moxie Pond. Dad and I did go all the way up Bald Mountain on that stretch in 1972. Incidentally, Maine has several Bald Mountains. I refer here to Moxie Bald Mountain. North of Jackman, Boundary Bald Mountain rises near the border with Canada. In 1993 Mom, Dad, and I climbed yet another Bald Mountain in Perkins Plantation overlooking Webb Lake.

Life in the United States means the popularity of foods in only certain regions. Boston is a brown egg market while New York prefers white eggs. Maine folks seem to like red hot dogs. A few years back, I was at the visitors' center at the Sandy River Railroad Park in Phillips, Maine, during Old Home Days when a fellow asked for a hot dog from the grill. The cook asked if he wanted a brown or a red hot dog. The customer responded rather matter-of-factly, "Why red, of course, (pronounced coss)!" After years of wondering what they tasted like, I finally tried one and found it to taste about the same as brown ones. The only real difference seems to be a red coating on the outside.

Years ago, we often saw and purchased little boxes of spruce gum in various Maine shops and gift stores. The green and red on white boxes advertised the product "from the forests of Maine." C. A. McMahan Company of Five Islands, Maine, put up the products "made of gum base, edible softening agents, rolled in corn starch." Other companies had marketed spruce gum over the years as well, but I remember C. A. McMahan gum available during our time in Maine. There is nothing sweet about spruce gum, and it does not resemble teaberry or spearmint gum. Dad equated it to dried turpentine. The gum is collected from spruce trees damaged from a broken limb, woodpecker attack, or a lightning strike. Lumberjacks of old enjoyed spruce gum, always a curiosity to chew on.

Speaking of spruce trees, I should mention the eastern spruce budworm, reputedly the most damaging forest insect in the state of Maine. Outbreaks of the insect occur from every forty to sixty years and lead to severe defoliation and ultimately death of spruce and balsam fir trees. I can remember hearing a lot about the problem when we stayed in Maine. Such outbreaks could devastate Maine's paper company woodlands.

Back on the subject of foods, every now and then we got some green sticks and roasted marshmallows through the side door of the wood stove. We had to keep the door closed as much as possible or smoke would come out into the room. Occasionally we bought a container of Jiffy Pop popcorn and prepared it on the surface of the wood stove. I was fascinated by the way the top grew in size as the popcorn popped. By the time it was full, the aluminum foil top resembled a magician's head covering.

Moxie, the leading soft drink in America at the end of the nineteenth century, is now found primarily on the grocery store shelves of northern New England. Certain foods we could purchase at home we couldn't find in Maine. We couldn't find peppermint stick ice cream, the flavor known for its small red and green candies throughout the mix. That flavor was not available in Maine stores in the 1960s and has not been too prevalent in the two thousands in Massachusetts, either.

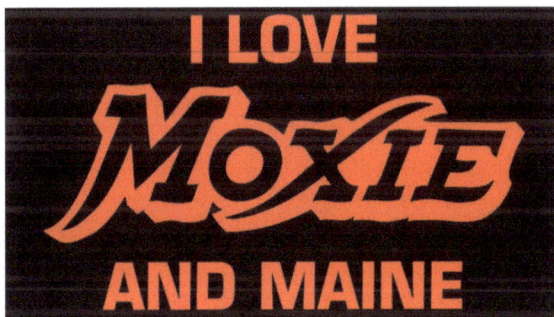

The soft drink Moxie remains popular in Maine.
photo by Chris Coyle

One day back in the mid 1960s, we took a long drive over around Bangor way. Among other sights, I remember stopping to see the statue of Paul Bunyan, the giant lumberjack of American folklore. At some point, I got a hankering for peppermint or, as I called it, candy ice cream. We stopped at quite a few stores, but we found none. Nothing else would do, for I was set on that flavor. As Dad drove along, I kept wailing, "Candy ice cream!"

After I kept it up for quite a while, Dad pulled into a gas station. He came out with a grape popsicle, tore off the wrapping paper, pried my mouth open, and inserted the popsicle. That shut me up. Even at my young age, I realized it best not to mention candy ice cream again that day.

dirt roads and covered bridges

We never minded rainy days, for it was always cozy in the cabin hearing the pitter-patter of rain drops on the roof. We would get the wood stove going if it got chilly. How snug and nice it was to curl up on the cot or sofa with a nice book! We went for a ride or perhaps into Bingham sometimes on rainy days. The folks and I loved to drive on back roads. One time, we thought it would be fun to take a drive and each time we reached an intersection take turns deciding which way we would go. I am not sure now just where we did end up.

Whenever we had the option to drive on some replaced or bypassed section of road, I would always exclaim, "Take the old road!" I particularly enjoyed taking the old road up or down Cook Hill until the lower section finally became impassible in the late 1970s. Once in a great while we might even take the old, *old* road at some location. In thinking back to my childhood, I suppose that the appeal of old roads fell to my growing love of the past, of history, and of imagining we were perhaps reliving past times.

We often found highway signs announcing Pavement Ends on our various travels. Our journey continued on a dirt road—something far more common in rural Maine in the 1960s than in Massachusetts, although not very common at all today. The dirt sections of roads might be short, just a few hundred or few thousand feet in length.

State Route 151 remained a dirt road at Mayfield in 1960.
photo by Bob Coyle

A stretch of Route 16 between Kingsbury and Abbot Village was dirt during our early years in Mayfield. I remember it was paved one afternoon when we went to Greenville with my paternal grandparents. An old moss-covered split rail fence ran next to the southeast side of the road. Thick woods grew behind the fence that hadn't held back any animals in many years.

Another short section of dirt road ran along Route

151 on the way to Brighton on the first hill south of Bryant Bog. Much of Route 15 between Greenville Junction and Jackman remained dirt until the 1970s. I also remember Route 16 between Concord and Embden largely dirt during that time. My folks remembered when part of Route 16 between Moscow and Mayfield was dirt, but I do not remember it. I think Dad may have told me that for the first year or two, Route 16 was dirt at the end of the driveway to the cabin.

When traveling back roads, we always kept the presence of electric and telephone wires in mind. If wires continued, we figured it a good chance that the road was maintained and went somewhere inhabited. But if wires ended, then the road might peter out.

Speaking of electric wires, occasionally on our travels we saw places with four electric wires bundled together on the highest point on the utility poles. When we spotted that uncommon situation, Dad and I played a game, and one of us shouted out "I've got the wires!" Then, if the pole line crossed to the opposite side of the road, the other person called out in similar fashion. I generally sat in the back seat behind my mother. The game was to keep me amused so I wouldn't get bored while riding. As my mother was sitting in front of me on the passenger side of the car, she likely would have spotted the wires first and I would have lost interest in looking for them if she always saw them first, so she did not take part in the game. Come to think of it, I have not seen that type of electric wire in quite some time.

Although many roads had been paved by the 1960s, a lot of them were not very wide. Crews had simply macadamized a dirt or crushed-stone surface with tar to make the initial paved road. Secondary state-numbered highways such as Route 16 never had dividing lines painted in their centers in our early years in the area. Trees lined most of the roads and provided shade in the summertime.

Dad and I went on a hike about seven miles in length one pleasant day in the summer of 1973. We walked down to Mayfield Corner and then through Charlie Pooler's overgrown field for access to the Lake Road. We hiked eastward passing overgrown Flanders Cemetery on our left and the foundation to old Mayfield School on our right. There, a very steep climb confronted us for about

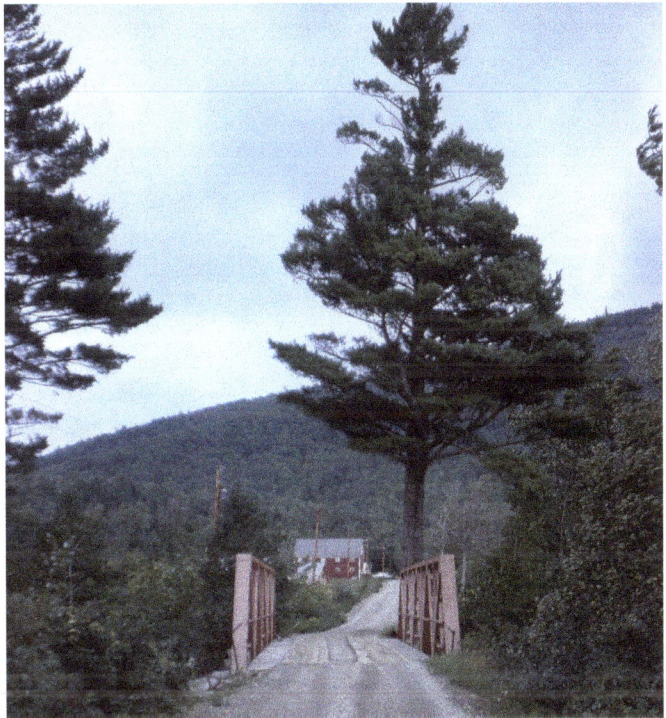

A narrow highway bridge on a dirt road crossed the Carrabassett River in the 1960s.
photo by Bob Coyle

a mile as we climbed nearly three hundred feet. The first section seemed for the most part impassable to vehicles, although we had from time to time seen a Jeep exiting the road near the old school.

Then the road leveled out for a bit, and the surface seemed quite good, in fact with three-wheel ruts in places. The hike was long but very interesting. I wondered what the area had looked like a century earlier when with subsistence farms where people attempted to eke out a living from the land.

Finally, we turned right down a road for another mile and a half toward Kingsbury Mills and an old graveyard called the Hilton Cemetery a few hundred feet after we turned off from the Lake Road. This cemetery is in Mayfield but very close to the Kingsbury line. Fifty years later, aerial views of the area show the cemetery on the east side of the road. I still have vivid memories of much of the hike but sadly, I don't remember seeing the Hilton Cemetery.

We hiked back down off the high terrain but more gradually than during our ascent upward from Mayfield Corner. The large white home of the Worcesters at Kingsbury Mills loomed ahead of us. Although tired, we plodded west along well-paved Route 16, which after several miles of hiking on abandoned dirt roads seemed quite the super highway. After the final two-mile hike from Kingsbury Mills back to our driveway, the cabin seemed so nice to get back to, but Dad and I had a great hike, one that neither of us ever forgot.

Lowes Covered Bridge has spanned the Piscataquis River between Guilford and Sangerville since 1857. We visited in the 1960s.

photo by Bob Coyle

We often enjoyed driving over Lowes Covered Bridge in Guilford, just off Route 15. The bridge spans the Piscataquis River and carries a side road to Sangerville. Built in 1857, it was sadly destroyed in the April 1, 1987 flood. A replacement covered bridge, patterned after the original, was built on the original abutments in 1990.

The Bangor and Aroostook Railroad Greenville branch crossed the highway near Lowes Bridge. A by then unusual wigwag crossing signal with a pendulum protected the highway grade crossing. Evidently, nineteenth-century crossings often had wigwags. I remember a large barn with a gambrel roof nearby. I think it had a sign about seed potatoes.

We picked up several abandoned highway signs and put them up on the woods path Up North toward the outhouse. We found an S sign lying in the trees along Route 16 east of Kingsbury. We also retrieved an old yellow curve sign from encroaching brush along the abandoned former road on Cook Hill. Newer curve signs were more orange. Unusual yellow stop signs on some of Bingham's side streets, particularly around Milford Avenue, harkened back to another era. Fade-resistant red paint was not available until 1954, when white letters on red stop signs became the norm. I photographed one of the last yellow stop signs I knew of years later over in Phillips.

Some secondary roads sported yellow stop signs into the 1990s.

photo by Chris Coyle

We often came to right angles on back roads. Sometimes they had been three-way intersections or crossroads years before with one or more of the roads discontinued. Arrow signs marked some such ninety-degree turns but not others, especially the less-travelled ones. Many older, smaller bridges were narrow. Diagonally painted red and white vertical signs marked some of them in the early years, and then yellow and black signs replaced most of them.

Along about 1970, small green signs with four-digit numbers started appearing along highways at odd places like culverts or bridges, or a place of seemingly no importance at all. We mentioned it to the man who drove the PM Laundry van. He told us that the signs had been set up in case a motorist should break down. The driver could then report being near a particular numbered sign and request help. That sounded good, except there was no telephone service at all in the area and the introduction of cell phones was several decades away. Even today, I question whether cell phones have much of any signal in such remote areas.

We found many interesting roads in the area to explore, many of them passable by auto and some not. We occasionally hiked parts of them. When he was in graduate school doing his field work in the Kingsbury quadrangle Dad made a large wall hanging of nine United States Geological Service, USGS, topographical maps with the Kingsbury map in the middle. He had glued the maps onto what looked like cheesecloth, and two holes at the top allowed hanging it on the wall of the cabin each summer.

The composite map always fascinated me, and I studied it at length to learn about back roads and railroads as well as the locations of houses, farms, and one-room schools, many of them long gone. We sometimes ventured out to see how far along a particular back road we could make it by car before it petered out so we had to turn around. Some of the roads led past abandoned farms and unused houses and barns. I wish that I had photographed more of them. We stopped from time to time on Highway 15 west of Abbot Village to look at a post with a pair of moose horns affixed to the top.

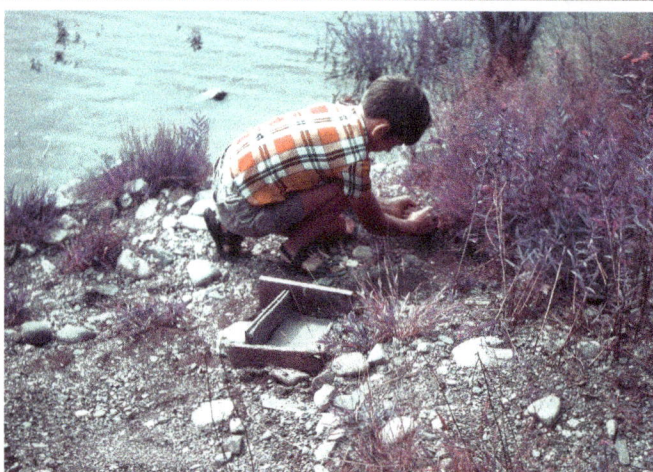

Chris squints, top, near the moose horn post near Highway 15. He built his own roads by the pond shore in 1973.

photos by Bob Coyle

For years, I had my own set of "roads" for toy cars on the gravel bank along the shore in front of the cabin. I had two main roads—one I called Cook Hill and the other Campbell Hill. We eventually paved most of Cook Hill with cement mix Dad purchased from Andrews Hardware in Bingham or from Titcomb's General Store in Abbot Village. I made it an early priority to get the roads back into shape each summer after we got to the cabin.

I used Tonka Toys and other similar vehicles on the outdoor roads. Inside, I frequently laid out roads using Lincoln Logs along lines on the cabin floor lino-leum on the cabin floor. Particularly on rainy days, I played with my Matchbox collection on the imaginary roads. Dad and I made cardboard road signs to use on my roads. I never brought my Match-box models outside, as I reserved them strictly for indoor use.

Although I sometimes built cabins with the Lincoln logs, I used them just as often if not more for my roads on the large living room floor. I always kept myself amused. It was fun to use the old crank telephone to use to talk with some imaginary party. At times, I pretended to run a hotel and assigned numbers to the two bedrooms and used the telephone for incoming calls to reserve rooms.

A large wooden trunk belonging to the Sawyers sat across the partition separating the two bedrooms. Among other items, it contained an assortment of interesting hats. One day when I was quite young, I tried on all the hats, and Dad photographed me several times wearing different ones.

Another fun thing to do in the cabin involved taking the two long benches in the living room and the single movable bench from the kitchen to set up grocery store shelves. Dad made a nice collection of make-believe goods on cardboard cutouts for me to sell at my store. I had a toy cash register with play money I used to ring up purchases.

We also had a cribbage board and several sets of old playing cards in the little wall desk we used to either play card games or solitaire. Dad could frequently be found playing Spiderette Solitaire. Mom and Dad and sometimes the three of us, enjoyed such games as Crazy Eights, Michigan, Hearts, or perhaps Go Fish. No doubt there were other games we played, but time has erased what they were from my mind.

My mother became increasingly concerned that I had yet to learn the alphabet in 1966 just before I started first grade, so Dad made flash cards out of construction paper one morning and drew one letter in magic marker on each card. We both got down on the floor and started arranging the letters as he taught me the alphabet. I had it memorized by lunchtime and don't seem to have forgotten it since.

Each summer, I set up a card table to the right of the front door and proceeded to make the Mayfield Library. I had our favorite books set up there and made cards to check out the books. No wonder I went to library school when I was older.

I really enjoyed my collection of Matchbox die-cast cars, trucks and equipment manufactured in England by Lesney. I soon learned good places where I could purchase the best ones. Beyond the weekly allowance my folks gave me, I worked hard for extra money doing yardwork, washing the car, cleaning projects, and so forth. I saved my money for times when I could purchase Matchbox models and other such items that appealed to me at my young age.

At the Indian Store in Greenville, we bought Matchbox models for me.

photo by David Cass

Among other stores in Maine we might just happen upon, there was Moore's Rexall in Bingham and the Rexall or LaVerdiere Drug Store in Guilford across the street from the old Universalist church. Also, in Guilford across the street from the Gold Nugget Restaurant, the new Treworgy's Department Store later became the Ben Franklin store. All of them sometimes had appealing Matchbox toys.

I could also depend on the little general store at the foot of the hill on Route 150 in Athens to yield some desirable Matchboxes.

My favorite Matchboxes were those produced in the 1950s and 1960s prior to the line's conversion to Superfast models. My all-time favorite place to acquire them was the wonderful Indian Store in Greenville on the shore of Moosehead Lake. Not only a great place to find long-discontinued models with all sorts of sought-after variations, the Indian Store sold them at the old price of forty-nine cents instead of the fifty-five or fifty-seven cents I was accustomed to paying elsewhere. We visited the Indian Store each summer at least once, and I had a list of variations and discontinued models to look for. Eventually, the clerks invited me behind the counter to check through all the stored boxes for whatever I wanted.

While I was busy unearthing interesting Matchbox models, Dad kept busy in a separate room that held rocks and minerals. I am not sure what Mother did then, but when she was with us, I don't recall her complaining about the long stops at the Indian Store.

Many times, we visited the Indian Store, shown in the 1930s.
from the postcard collection of Christopher Coyle

The Wabanaki Nations, specifically the Abenaki, Maliseet, Passamaquoddy, and the Penobscot tribes, held a large presence in the Moosehead Lake area when the first European settlers arrived. Their population gradually declined, although some families still persisted well into the twentieth century. Two well respected Abenaki residents of Greenville, Francis Faye and his wife, Mary Tomer Faye, opened the Indian Store in 1927 in the prominent Shaw Block in Greenville where Route 15 today makes a ninety-degree turn west to Greenville Junction.

The Fayes sold many baskets and other wares made by Greenville Abenakis, including many items made by their own relatives. They made annual trips to reservations in the West where they made friends with the Navajo and other Indigenous Peoples. They purchased and were given items that could not be found in the Greenville area. They displayed many such articles in the store without offering them for sale. The store contained many rare pieces forming perhaps the most complete and beautiful collection of such articles in the state. Besides selling goods to the public, the Indian Store was a great place to learn about Wabanaki and other Indigenous Peoples. A large sign painted on the exterior wall proudly advertised *Buy from Indians.*

Indian Hill in Greenville offers a good view of Moosehead Lake, like this 1965 vista.
photo by Bob Coyle

On Moosehead Lake behind the Indian Store, seaplanes belonging to Folsom's Air Service landed and departed. A long spur track belonging to the Canadian Pacific Railway crossed Route 15 and ran immediately behind the Shaw Block. I never saw a train on that track and do not know where it led, but the track appeared to be in good condition.

Sometimes, we drove west from Greenville through Greenville Junction and all the way to the border town of Jackman where we intersected Route 201 and took the long, scenic, and interesting drive south to Bingham and then out Route 16 to the cabin. Until the early 1970s, a large part of Route 15 between Greenville Junction and Jackman remained a dirt road. The road crossed the Canadian Pacific Railway's Moosehead Subdivision at the small railroad hamlet known as Tarratine.

I have photos of the little group of buildings, section houses, and sheds, including one with a train order board. In the days before the use of two-way radios in railroad operations, dispatchers contacted train operators, clerical workers usually located at stations

Inside one of the buildings above, a train order board used before two-way radios to issue special orders by telegraph or telephone to railroad workers, who received payment in cash until 1960.

photo by Chris Coyle

along the route by telegraph or telephone to issue special train orders to supersede the timetable to establish a meeting point for trains, advance an inferior train against a superior one, create a route for an extra train, warn of track conditions, and or provide other important information for governing a train. Train operators manually signaled train crews to receive orders according to the position of the train order board. Depending on the position of the order board, trains either had to stop to sign and receive train orders or receive them while in motion.

Route 15 was rerouted later, and most of the buildings as well as traces of the former grade crossing have disappeared over the ensuing years.

Route 15 runs alongside Brassua Lake and Long Pond west of Rockwood. My father collected a large piece of driftwood there one year and brought it back to the cabin. He tied it to the roof of the car when it came time to return to Athol. Despite traveling at high speeds, it did not blow off as we sped homeward bound down the Maine Turnpike. He fastened it to the living room wall in Athol along about the middle of the following December and hung a portion of our Christmas ornaments from the upside-down roots to provide our Christmas tree that year.

Visitors sort of shook their heads when they saw it and seemed to feel sorry for me, although I got used to it and no traditional evergreen Christmas tree before long. We had a normal Christmas tree the next year. I got the idea in the 1990s to use the driftwood for something or other. I asked my father where it was, and he replied that he dumped it out in the woods as no one seemed to appreciate it. Perhaps I would have had more appreciation of the driftwood in 1998 than I did in 1968.

Most years, we took another scenic ride over Mahoney Hill Road off Route 201 south of Bingham east to Route 151 just south of the village of Brighton. Sometimes, we took a side road and ended up at South Solon before making our way north back to the cabin. When they visited us in 1977, we brought Evelyn Merrifield and Norman Frigon, our Chestnut Hill Avenue, Athol, neighbors, down the scenic road to see the South Solon meetinghouse. The following morning, Elvis Presley's passing was all over the news. He had an upcoming concert scheduled at the Augusta Civic Center in Maine, but of course, it never happened.

Through 1983, at least, not much changed over the years at Huff Corner in Wellington.
photo by Bob Coyle

We often stopped at farm stands at the side of the road to purchase fresh vegetables while out on our sojourns through the Maine countryside. Dunlap's Vegetable Farm on Route 16 between Concord and North Anson was a particularly nice one. Another time, we stopped at a small stand on the outskirts of Dover-Foxcroft and ended up talking with the couple who ran it for an hour or more after they invited us into their house to sit a spell. Memorable also was the organic vegetable farm stand between Monson and Greenville. I think Mother enjoyed the organic freshness of the produce while Dad and I were more interested in the braless young women with their low-cut T-shirts who ran the place and were eager to wait on us.

A real treat was picking up a dozen ears of fresh butter-and-sugar corn and bringing it back to the cabin for cooking. My job was to husk the corn out on the front porch. After completing the task, I brought the ready-to-cook ears into the kitchen and then grabbed the paper bag of leaves and silk from the porch to dump at the edge of the woods toward Birch Point. We always hoped to see wildlife poke through the woods, but I don't think we ever did.

Another food treat was fresh apple sauce. We ventured in around Charlie Pooler's old farm at Mayfield Corner at least once each summer to pick apples from long abandoned trees. We brought the apples back to the cabin, and usually Dad spent quite a deal of time cutting out bad parts and worms before preparing apple sauce over the gas stove. We enjoyed a wonderful treat upon completion.

Yet another summertime treat was cooked fresh beet greens. Dad made a tea with the juice. The addition of a little butter and salt made a delicious warm beverage.

At times we packed picnic lunches to bring on our rambles along the back roads of Maine. Once in a while we had our picnics just a couple miles away at the picnic ground at the other end of Kingsbury Pond near the dam. Some maps showed a public picnic ground between Mayfield and Otter Ponds, but the dirt driveway into the area from Route 151 always seemed to be marked with signs indicating that visitors were unwelcome.

I always wanted to have a better look at Otter Pond but never had the opportunity. Otter Pond did not connect to Mayfield and Kingsbury ponds, although the two ponds were only about a quarter mile apart. A small area of stagnant water in the woods, Black Pool was to the west of Otter Pond alongside the east side of Route 151. Black Pool contained little if any water during dry summers, and in recent years it seems to have dried up all together.

Water from the Bryant Bog—Otter Pond area and Mayfield and Kingsbury ponds flows through Kingsbury Dam into Kingsbury Stream and the Piscataquis River southeast of Abbot Village. Route 151 crosses a stream a mile or so south of the Mayfield—Brighton town line. That stream flows into a boggy area on the west side of the highway into small Parlin Pond, through another boggy area and then into Smith Pond with a small dam at the southern end. Its outlet flows into the east branch of Wesserunsett Stream which runs through the center of Brighton.

Smith Pond had a couple of camps but for the most part was uninhabited. There is a small picnic and recreation area about two thirds of the way south along the eastern shore of the pond. A narrow dirt road leads into the area from Route 151. The road is level for the first section and then begins a slight downgrade toward the pond past a number of raspberry bushes where we used to stop to harvest a few berries. Then the road makes a sharp left-hand curve and descends a steep grade eventually paved to prevent washouts.

The road crosses a stream and then levels out in front of a sandy beach with a few picnic tables and a beautiful view out across the pond. Quite a few cedar trees there included many growing with crooked trunks that made good seats. The beach area usually was devoid of other visitors. Sometimes, I put on my bathing suit kept in the trunk of the car during our stays in Maine and waded in the warm water. At times, we saw loons out on the water, and if we were fortunate, they might sound forth their resounding calls.

Until the mid 1960s, Dad had two Argus cameras of the same model. He kept slide film, usually Kodachrome 64, in one camera and black and white in the other one for a while. One day as he leaped across a mountain stream, one of the cameras fell from his pocket into the drink. Evidently, he felt the cost to clean and repair it likely too high, so he discarded it. He did take many nice color slides in Maine over the years. Dad often showed slides back at home for an enjoyable afternoon or evening pastime.

My folks gave me their old Kodak Brownie camera when I was eight. I began making my own photos, usually black and white, but once in a very great while color, which in those days cost quite a bit more than black and whites. Once I thought I had a good photo ready I would announce my taking of the image by exclaiming "Tip-see-doo!"

In the days before digital photography, my old Brownie took roll film, and I think I got about twelve images per roll. Film then had to process in a darkroom, often through a pharmacy's service or directly with a representative of Kodak. I always waited excitedly for processed prints to come back, especially when awaiting the images of the day the Kingsbury Dam broke. The folks saw that I had an interest in photography from a young age when as a toddler I pretended my mid twentieth-century stereoscope viewer was a camera.

Besides Kingsbury Dam I took interest in other dams including the large Wyman Dam in Moscow, Harris Dam up

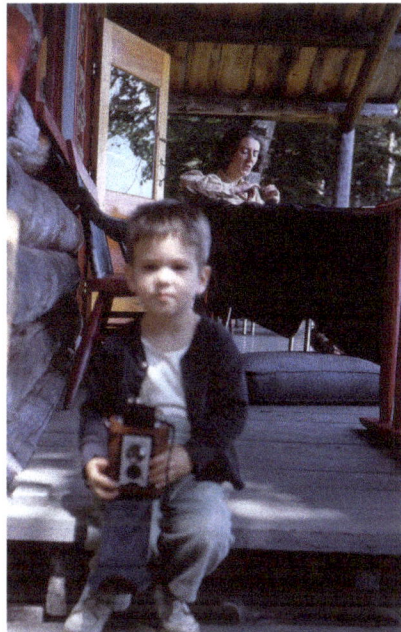

Three-year-old Chris learns about his Brownie camera.
photo by Bob Coyle

Wyman Dam, Moscow's massive hydroelectric project, powered Maine homes and industries.
photo by Chris Coyle

at Indian Pond, and Ripogenus Dam on the Penobscot watershed. The first two dams were built for hydroelectric purposes. Workers gathered logs in groups called booms when they reached still water upstream from dams. Boats towed booms to the sluiceway at the dam where workers manually sent the logs down a sluiceway to the moving water below the dam. I remember watching workers for the Kennebec Log Driving Company sluicing pulpwood over Wyman Dam. I took interest in two sets of rails along the roadway across Ripogenus Dam. They were presumably used for moving equipment along the deck of Ripogenus Dam. They appealed to me at a young age because of my interest in trains. One set of rails looked to be around standard gauge while the other set looked about two-foot gauge, although I cannot remember that I ever measured their widths.

Ripogenus Dam entailed a long drive from our cabin. We drove to Greenville and then up the road along the east shore of Moosehead Lake past Lily Bay and continued northeast along a well-maintained dirt road to reach Rip Dam, as it was nicknamed. I remember the road north of Lily Bay as one of several oiled to keep dust to a minimum. I think workers spread engine oil along the surface from time to time, thus turning the dirt from brown to black.

Beyond Lily Bay, we sometimes stopped at Kokadjo, the next place of interest as one of several farms left from the days of horse-drawn logging operations in the woods. I photographed a large barn there one year.

We reached the Golden Road and Ripogenus Dam after driving quite a distance through the woods. Loggers drove pulpwood down the Penobscot waterway, through the Rip Dam,

Native American Penobscots named Mount Katahdin, Maine's highest peak, "great mountain."
photo by Bob Coyle

until 1970. I have memories of watching logs going down the sluiceway into Ripogenus Gorge. Great numbers of cliff swallows flew up underneath the walkway of the dam where they had quite a nesting colony. After leaving the dam, we normally drove east along the Penobscot River. Soon heading off to the north, we saw Nesowadnehunk Tote Road. This a primitive access road for reaching Mount Katahdin deep within Baxter State Park. Maine's Hundred-Mile Wilderness and the Allagash Wilderness Waterway lay to our northeast. Upon arriving at Millinocket, we returned to the cabin on faster, so-called improved roads.

We liked to bring out-of-town visitors to see Wyman Dam. Before Gramp Coyle's incapacitating strokes necessitating his use of a walker to get around, Dad's parents came up to visit us one summer. On the way up to Maine, Gram thought that Gramp was having a heart attack. She had him lie down on the back seat, opened the windows, and let cool Maine air blow over him. As he seemed okay, we drove them over to see Wyman Dam the next day. Evidently Gram's heart-attack treatment had succeeded, as Gramp charged up the side of the dam to look out over the cool water of Wyman Lake.

Moxie Falls, another great sight, has a vertical drop of close to ninety feet as one of the highest such waterfalls in Maine. The falls are located along Moxie Stream in the township named Moxie Gore. A short hike from the road connecting the village known as The Forks with the old railroad grade at Moxie Pond ends with a view of the geological spectacle of Moxie Falls.

Dad explored much of the region's back country during his era of graduate-school field work. He told of meeting game warden Don Walker the first time. Very adept at slipping through the woods silently, Don searched for poachers or others with ill intent. Mapping an outcrop deep within the woods one day, Dad was astonished suddenly to see a man standing next to him. Don inquired what Dad was doing and became quite interested in Dad's project after he explained it. Don helped Dad by telling him how best to access some of the remote areas in the region.

Moxie Falls, Maine's highest waterfall, tumbles ninety feet.
photo by Bob Coyle

107

Dad often went out in the woods alone, but at times Dr. C. Wroe Wolfe, Dr. Mohamed Gheith, and others from the BU geology camp at North Anson accompanied him. One day with a large contingency of the geology group at the cabin, one of the men, Dr. Gheith, brought along his daughter named Jehanne. Both about three years old, we went into my folks' bedroom and jumped away on their bed. Once he realized what was going on, my father came in and hollered at us to stop our trampoline antics before we broke the inner spring.

We headed our way east along Route 16 toward Abbot Village one afternoon in the mid 1970s a decade or more after Dad ended his graduate work. We saw a man intently studying a rock outcrop beside the highway a few miles east of Kingsbury Mills. Dad stopped to chat with him. Also a student at BU, like Dad he conducted research on the geology of the region. The fellow said he knew of Dad's research project.

Moxie Bald Mountain rises at the horizon as seen from abandoned Somerset Railway on Austin Stream near Deadwater.

photo by Bob Coyle

I can't overstate the remoteness of the region. Dad was brave indeed to venture so many miles alone into the wilderness. He told the spine-tingling tale of one day's solitary adventure many years ago. He had a lot to work on that day and finally started hiking on a long-abandoned road back to the car as he rapidly lost the sun late in the day. As he ventured on, he began to sense that he was being watched. He turned around periodically and glimpsed something he thought may have been a large cat such as a mountain lion just as it disappeared out of sight behind a tree. He felt mighty glad to get back to the car that day and even happier to get back to the coziness and safety of the cabin.

We always made certain to keep the car's fuel tank filled and often stopped to refuel long before the tank got low. We did not want to run out of gasoline many miles from a gas station on any of the many back roads we traveled along.

The road through Athens was paved, but not much else changed from a 1910 postcard view.

from the postcard collection of Chris Coyle

old graveyards, churches, schoolhouses, and farms

Visiting old graveyards in our area of Maine provided connection to past times and people who once lived nearby. Looking at inscriptions on stones commemorating their lives, we could not help but wonder about events that occurred between the day of their birth and the day of their death. I hoped that other people besides us remembered those long-deceased people. Some graves appeared decorated from time to time while, sadly, others appeared totally forgotten.

The old Flanders Cemetery at Mayfield Corner was the closest to us at less than a mile from the cabin. That uncared-for graveyard had vegetation growing all around during our years in Mayfield. Iron fences enclosed the cemetery as well as a plot in the northeast corner. The old Lake Road running in front of the cemetery was a Jeep trail and impossible for regular passenger cars to drive.

I have since located Postmaster Mary E. Flanders's gravestone in Flanders Cemetery, where she was buried near Mayfield Corner in 1924 as the last interment in that cemetery. At ninety-five years old and spryer than I, former Mayfield resident Charlie Pooler brought me around Mayfield to show me various sites in 2011. He told me that he had helped dig the grave for Mrs. Flanders some unbelievably eighty-seven years previous when he would have been eight years old. He said it was difficult digging.

Small Clark Cemetery with only four headstones is up the steep hill on the old Lake Road east of Flanders Cemetery. I never knew about it when we lived in Mayfield. A good friend, the late Robert A. (Bob) Buck of Warren, Massachusetts (former director of the Amherst Railway Society Train Show and proprietor of Tucker's Hobbies in Warren), told me that his grandmother was born a Clark in Mayfield. The graves, he said, are for members of their family.

The only remnants of civilization in West Mayfield I can remember are gravestones at the largely overgrown Ben Adams cemetery. Much gravel has been removed in the vicinity in recent years, and the Concord/Mayfield Cemetery Association takes good care of the cemetery. Signs indicate where to find obscure graveyards. I recently located Kelley-Hall cemetery in Mayfield west of Bryant Bog. We owe our success in finding it in no small part to the new signs.

A small church also served as a school at West Mayfield years ago. No photographs have surfaced to show the building designated on the 1905 Bingham topo map. The Reverend Douglas W. Drown, former minister at the First Congregational Church of Bingham, told me that the church was Freewill Baptist, with at least one elderly person who remembers the building.

During a 2007 exploration of the area, I failed to pinpoint its exact location, but it may have sat on a small rise of land across from the Ben Adams Cemetery on the dirt road to Withee Pond. I remember my folks and I started walking along that road toward the pond late one day in the very early 1970s. As we got farther along, the alder trees grew more and more into the road, and we could see that evening rapidly approached, so we headed back. We never did get all the way in to see what remote Withee Pond looked like.

Don Sawyer wrote in a 2005 letter, "There are several cemeteries in the vicinity of Mayfield. No less than six within a few miles."

Unfortunately, I never got to follow up on that with Don. I am not certain that all the cemeteries were necessarily within the township of Mayfield. When seeing some old cemeteries deep within the Maine forest, it is difficult to imagine today the once cleared farm fields nearby where families lived and eked out their existence.

Well-cared Foss Hill Cemetery on Foss Hill Road in Kingsbury has stones facing ninety degrees from the road. We wondered if they once faced another, long-since abandoned road.

We found that a woodchuck had built a burrow down into one of the Foss Hill graves one summer. I remember trying to peer down the hole. Past residents of Kingsbury had been interred there prior to widespread use of burial vaults that prevent the graves from collapsing over time. There were quite a few hummocks near graves.

In 1961, grass overgrew stones in Kingsbury's Titcomb Cemetery.
photo by Bob Coyle

In Titcomb Cemetery also in Kingsbury between Route 16 and a short section of old road paralleling the current highway on the way to Abbot Village, stones face the old road. The cemetery was fenced and was accessed through a small hinged gate from the old unpaved road. We did not find Titcomb Cemetery as well maintained as Foss Hill. Although not overgrown, it usually had a lot of bracken ferns growing amongst the stones. Another old road veered north from the old section of highway behind the cemetery and connected to the old Moosehead Stage Road. We used to collect water from a spring up there.

At Burdin Corner in the northeast corner of the sparsely populated town of Wellington, we visited another relic, an abandoned church. It stands on the southwest corner of the crossing of two dirt roads. One of the roads leads to Parkman. Before brush grew high and surrounding fields gradually grew back to forest, we could see Mount Katahdin to the north.

I do not know when the building had last been used—perhaps during the years of the Great Depression. Rustic and unpainted, the wooden building had long been devoid of glass in the windows. The front steps had also disappeared. We had to climb from the ground up about four feet to reach a small entryway into the sanctuary. Evidently, there had been two sets of doors at one time. The interior of the building was strewn about with old

In 1963, Barbara wades through an overgrown field outside the abandoned Burdin Corner church in Wellington.
photo by Bob Coyle

boards, pieces of glass, and other debris. It smelled kind of musty. As I recall, there was a raised section of flooring at the front of the building from which the preacher conducted services along with remains of a very old pump organ. That was about it for any signs inside the building that it had once been a church with seating long since removed along with all other tangible items used for worship.

For a few years, the tower retained a bell. You could look up from the entryway into the tower and see it hanging there. Then it was removed and put into a newly-constructed church elsewhere. One day, my father just happened to mention the Burdin Corner church to a local contractor of our acquaintance and asked if he knew the bell was no longer there.

He replied in a loud voice, "Of course I know that—I'm the one who got sued forty-three hundred dollars for taking it out!!"

So, then we knew a little more about the story of the bell. The old church has recently been made into a residence. The building looked rather solid although it lacked a cellar.

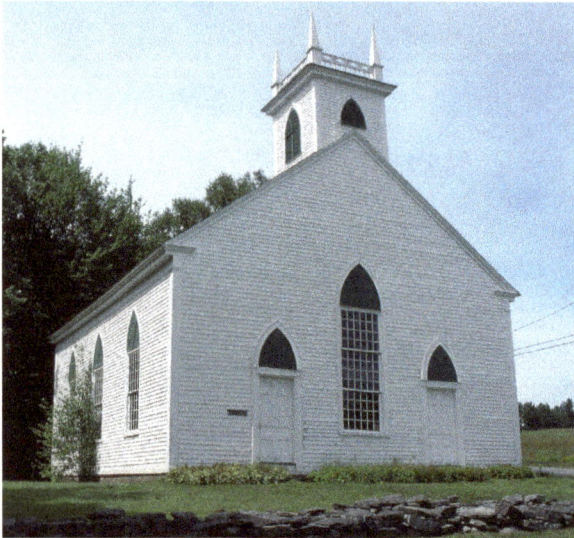

*Last used for regular services in 1893, South Solon Meetinghouse was built in 1842.
Twentieth-century frescoes painted by Skowhegan Art School students depict
Biblical scenes inside the South Solon Meetinghouse.*

photos by Chris Coyle

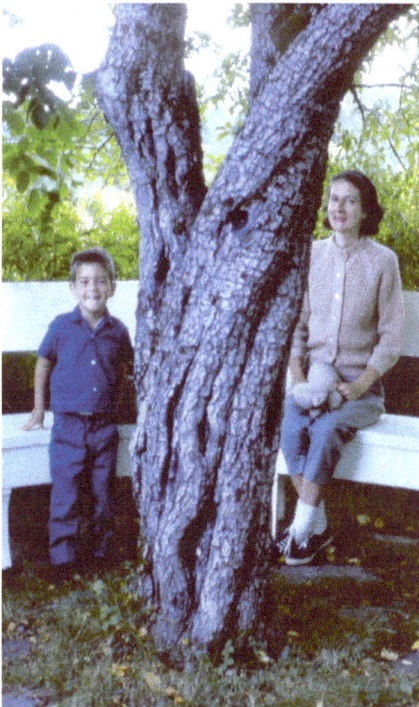

*In 1965, Chris and Barbara
sit outside
South Solon Meetinghouse.*

photo by Bob Coyle

An old, well-maintained meetinghouse at a crossroads in rural South Solon was built in 1842 and last used for regular church services in 1893. A mown yard within stone walls surrounds the attractive building. Years ago, there was a field, now grown to forest, behind the building. A circular bench painted white ringed a little apple tree on the side lawn.

Painted white, the building has a nice little tower with parapets plus two front doors. We usually entered the one on the left. Inside the usually unlocked doors a small entryway curved at the center stretches across the width of the building. At the extreme left, a narrow staircase which provides access to the balcony at the rear of the sanctuary. The occasional visitor is invited to sign a guest book in the entryway.

An unexpected sight greets the visitor stepping into the building. Beautiful frescoes painted by Sidney Hurwitz and students from the Skowhegan Art School in 1956 depict stories from the Bible. With doors and little turn latches to keep them closed, original box pews furnish the hall. Many of the pews have comfortable cushions as well as old hymnals.

A raised platform and pulpit reached by four or five steps is at the front of the sanctuary. Another set of pews to the side of the raised section can house a choir. I often played an old pump organ in the balcony and enjoyed the various sounds by adjusting the stops. The balcony has long wooden benches not fastened to the floor. The building possesses a certain characteristic odor I cannot quite describe but still remember. The meetinghouse remains in use for concerts or an occasional special service.

A small wooden church on the west side of Route 151 in Brighton was painted white on the sides and front. Later, with rebuilding of the highway to bypass the village, we noticed that the back side of the church had never been painted, although later it was painted.

Bingham Free Meetinghouse no longer serves as an active place of worship. It stands as a sentinel on the little hill near the old railroad yard. The building was dedicated on October 30, 1836 and is still used for special services. In the late 1970s, Dad attended a service there conducted by then current and former Bingham Congregational Church pastors Douglas W. Drown and Arthur R. MacDougall. Our friend Wilder Rollins, very active in the town of Bingham, was honored with his funeral in the building. Ironically, we just happened to call on Wilder's sister Elizabeth the day after his funeral in 1990. We always called on Elizabeth in later years when we stayed at Echo Valley Lodge in Phillips.

Guilford Universalist Church on the north side of town from the Piscataquis River had very beautiful frescoes painted on the interior wall. Later, the congregation disbanded, and Methodists moved in and tore down their old building on the other side of the river. Sadly, the frescoes were painted over, and the building no longer has the unique charm it once had.

Guilford Universalist Church once held frescoes of Biblical scenes. An old-style mailbox adorned the lawn in 1964.

photo by Bob Coyle

Sangerville Universalist church still houses an active congregation and has a magnificent interior complete with frescoes. The Victorian style church has pews arranged in a semi-circle. In 1997, we were fortunate to meet the minister, Reverend Alexander Craig. He invited us in to see and photograph the building.

An antique shop building in Dover-Foxcroft once housed a Universalist church, and Dexter still has an active Universalist congregation. We used to order Christmas puddings from the Dexter church every year until they discontinued the fundraiser. The church later sold maple syrup to raise money, but as we could procure that product locally, we did not order any.

Upper Abbot's old schoolhouse stood long abandoned in 1975.
photo by Chris Coyle

The area retains old one-room schoolhouse buildings, some named and shown on topo maps. We had several in our immediate vicinity in various stages of repair or disrepair. When I was growing up, only two buildings remained from Mayfield's former days. One was the abandoned Pooler House near the junction of Routes 16 and 151 at Mayfield Corner. The other, the old Mayfield schoolhouse, stood a little distance east of the Pooler House up the rarely used Lake Road almost directly across the road from the Flanders cemetery.

In reasonably good repair and painted white, the old Mayfield schoolhouse interested me on its site in the woods on the semi-abandoned road. Sadly, it burned or was burned in the early 1970s.

Don Walker, the local game warden, used the old school as a field office. I never knew for sure but wondered if some convicted and disgruntled poacher may have burned it down. The outhouses lasted a few years longer. I poked around the site in May, 2007 and found part of the foundation and remains of the tin roof. It would be fun to explore the grounds with a metal detector. Perhaps one could unearth an old inkwell or some other artifact used by pupils long ago. Don Walker collected old bottles, and that is why we often didn't find many bottles near old cellar holes.

A great 1890 photo of the Mayfield school in Elinor Stevens Walker's 1974 book *More About Maine* shows pupils standing on the west side of the building. Although the north side faced the road, the front was on the west side. At the time of the book's publication, two former pupils were still living. Our friend Elizabeth Jordan, retired Bingham librarian, taught school at Mayfield for a time. She told us that she stayed with the Poolers and taught school in the house one winter with only two students, one of them Charlie Pooler.

Also used as the town hall, the old schoolhouse at Kingsbury Mills was a sorry sight. The unpainted building was not locked and essentially abandoned except for election balloting one year. We ventured inside and looked around on several occasions. Wood shingles on the roof no longer kept out the elements, and rot set in, causing the building to collapse. Dad took a slide of me standing next to remaining rubble in the summer of 1973. Today, the location is largely grown-in and forgotten other than a few apple trees marking the former schoolyard.

The old schoolhouse at Kingsbury Mills also served as the town hall, a place for plantation meetings.
photo by Bob Coyle

In good repair, the old Campbell School up in East Kingsbury was used as a camp. When the owners were in residence, they hoisted an old forty-eight-star American flag up the flagpole. We often took a drive up there in the evening. I never knew when the school closed, but, because most of the remaining old homes in Kingsbury were located along the Campbell Hill Road, I suspect it was used more recently than the one at Kingsbury Mills. Another school may have stood over near Happy Corner, but I'm not sure of that.

I remember one early evening drive up to the Campbell School when my grandparent Shermans visited us. Dad drove up the hill and shut the car off for us to look at something. Our old Ford did not start very well at times, which led to my father stomping on the accelerator and cussing at it. So, on that particular night he cranked the starter, and the car refused to start. Trying to be helpful, a very young me suggested "Push on the damn-it pedal, Daddy." He was not too amused, and I was admonished later. Eventually, the car started, and we proceeded on our way.

Although it doesn't show on the area topo map, I recall remains of what we thought had been an old school at Cole Corner on the road to Abbot Village. The building had stood on the southeast corner of the intersection and disintegrated in the early 1970s. We sometimes

In the summer of 1970, crates for packing blueberries stacked up outside the old Campbell School in East Kingsbury.

photo by Bob Coyle

stopped the car and looked around. As years wore on, less and less of the structure remained, and eventually the area reverted to woods.

Another old building on the west side of Route 151 south of Brighton near the road to Mahoney Hill had a faded old red and white sign marking it as the Roosevelt School. Greta McCue, the Wellington postmaster, told us one summer that she and her husband had purchased the building to use as a family camp. They also owned a camp on Kingsbury Pond near the town line between Mayfield and Kingsbury. The McCues opened a small lunch canteen that operated out of a trailer on weekends open only for a few weeks one summer and closed for good before we got a chance to eat there. It sat right right next to Route 16 at the town line. A plank nailed between two trees marked its one-time location for years afterward.

Another former school was located on Route 15 a few miles east of the village of Monson. A sign in front of the building proclaimed it used by the Finnish Farmers Club. Many people in Monson share Finnish descent. I think many of them had worked in the slate quarries.

One day we were having a meal in the Kahvila Restaurant in Monson, and the woman working there told us she had been to a dance at the Finnish Farmers Club the night before. It had gotten so lively, she said she was concerned that the floor might collapse.

I don't remember seeing any one-room schoolhouses still in use around our neck of the woods during our days in Maine, although some may have served in the not too distant past. A two-room school in Wellington functioned until around 1970 when a new building replaced it. Caratunk, a once busy logging community north of Bingham but eventually a quiet little hamlet, closed its one-room school in 2003. At that time, the last remaining one-room school in the state was in Shirley over in Piscataquis County.

We often saw extension houses on our drives through the Maine countryside. The unique buildings looked like fun places to play hide and seek.

Two sets of extension houses abutted Route 151 north of Athens in August, 1963.
photo by Bob Coyle

Often, several sections of the house attached to each other. A shed or carriage house might attach to the last section of the house followed by one or more barns end to end. There were two extension houses across the street from each other on Route 151 between Brighton and Athens. I saw some of the oldest utility poles ever just north of the area. Grey in color and very low to the ground at perhaps only ten to twelve feet high, they lacked creosote treatment. Electric wires sat on insulators on short pieces of wood protruding from the poles rather than on crossarms. I wondered how much clearance the wires had above winter snows.

In 1980, we called a Realtor to look at a farm southwest of Abbot Village on the dirt road alongside Kingsbury Stream in 1980. We never seriously considered actually purchasing the property. It was more of a pipe dream. We admired the

Abandoned utility poles dotted the rural Maine landscape in the 1960s.
photo by Chris Coyle

huge wooden barn dating back to days of old. Portions of heavy plank flooring hinged to permit easy cleanout from housing animals. I'm not sure how many acres the property included, but I think the tract of land was fairly large with some open fields and others reverted to forest. I cannot remember much about the actual house, for the barn fascinated me more. Dave Cass, visiting us at the time, took several photos of the farm.

Cemeteries in the Mayfield—Kingsbury area provide a link to the region's past when the area had more population and families eked out a living on farms, in small mills, and at the slate operation on Cook Hill in Mayfield. Some of the old graveyards are easily accessible by auto, but others are not. There have been no recent burials in any of these cemeteries. Most are better cared for than in years past when we spent summers in Mayfield.

The Concord/Mayfield Cemetery Association
provides a listing of cemeteries in Mayfield.
Ben Adams Cemetery
Flanders Cemetery
Clark Cemetery
Hilton Cemetery
Kelley-Hall Cemetery

Kingsbury Plantation
provides a listing of cemeteries in Kingsbury.:
Foss Hill Cemetery
Titcomb Cemetery
Bede Cemetery
Kelly Cemetery
Stone Cemetery

More information about the cemeteries may be found on the Find a Grave website.

exploring what once had been

The Mayfield—Kingsbury part of Maine has slept for many decades. Civilization has not taken root there as in other parts of the state. The last permanent residents in Mayfield, the Pooler family, left in 1948. Other inhabitants of years ago had long since passed on or moved to more successful towns.

The fact that we spent summers in a ghost town was one of the things I liked about living at the cabin. "The Murmuring Past of Mayfield" is a chapter in Elinor Stevens Walker's book *In and Around Our Great Northern Wilderness* and indeed appropriately describes what once had been. I enjoyed looking for old cellar holes and imagining life a century before when people farmed the rough soil. Topo maps show some of the old houses, and I enjoyed looking at them and correlating sites with map designations.

We saw lilacs or maybe old apple trees growing in the woods, usually indicating a house nearby years before. From an early age, the folks taught me that when I saw lilacs, I should start looking close to the ground and watch for any uncovered wells—they didn't want me to fall into one. They also taught me that, should I ever become lost in the woods, I should walk downhill, find a brook, and follow it downstream. Sooner or later, streams flow into something bigger with greater likelihood of finding civilization near a river or lake.

When exploring the woods, we found old metal, tin cans, and sometimes old bottles near sites of former homes. A dump revealed artifacts that hadn't rotted or disintegrated from long gone lives. Near Route 151 just south of the Mayfield/Brighton line, my Coyle grandparents dug up a small hackmatack tree and

Chris and Bob hiked abandoned Lake Road in 1973.
photo by Chris Coyle

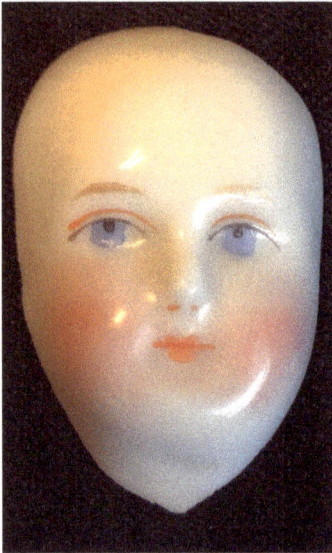

*Barbara found
a porcelain doll's head
near an old cellar hole
in Brighton.*

photo by Chris Coyle

transplanted it to their home on Harriet Avenue in Quincy. Near the same location, Mother found a porcelain doll's head, one of the more interesting finds.

Occasionally on backwoods rambles, we stumbled on old telegraph wires perhaps still attached to trees. The rusting lines had once provided a means of communication among transient lumbering operations prevalent in the area years ago.

The old Pooler house down at Mayfield Corner held a great deal of fascination for me. Fortunately, I have a couple of 35 mm slides of the Pooler house. Usually empty in my experience, the house was used as a lumber camp for men to bunk in around 1964. A couple lived in a trailer outside, and the wife cooked meals for the crew.

Norma Sawyer went down to visit with the woman but found that, like many French Canadians or some Mainers with origins in France, she spoke only French, so they could not communicate very well. The house was empty and abandoned again the next year.

I was in the Pooler house once when I was about four or five. I remember a large wood stove and that most of the plaster had fallen off the walls. I didn't like being inside and felt kind of frightened. The last of the old houses in Mayfield, the building was gone soon after.

Chris found the old Pooler house at Mayfield Corner both fascinating and frightening.

photo by Bob Coyle

One summer day, I asked Dad to drive me around Kingsbury. With the Kodak Brownie camera, I took photos of all the old-time houses in Kingsbury. I was glad I did that, as some of those old buildings were no longer maintained and didn't last much longer.

I often thought about what life must have been like in that isolated area decades before. People had to grow most of their own food and take care of themselves. Probably some of them never even ventured far from the area.

We stopped to pick berries at Mrs. Flossie Ward's fields later that summer. She was one of the last of the old-time residents of Kingsbury. I inquired who owned the various buildings, most of them along the road by her old farm. I wrote down everything she told me.

I thought Katahdin Iron Works, KIH, north of Brownville Junction, an interesting place to visit. In operation from 1845 until 1890, it had a blast furnace and charcoal kiln still standing as ghostly reminders of that past era. Though a tumbling ruin when we first visited the site in the mid 1960s, the site was cleaned up later with some stabilization work done.

We called the abandoned property on Campbell Road in East Kingsbury The Witch's House.

photo by Bob Coyle

Barbara and Chris examine butter and egg flowers at Katahdin Iron Works north of Brownville Junction.

photo by Bob Coyle

The Bangor and Katahdin Iron Works Railway operated nineteen miles of track between Brownville Junction and KIH. After KIH shut down, a few thousand feet of the spur remained at the junction. Brian Beers, a retired Canadian Pacific Railway dispatcher, told me about railroad cars stored on the track during World War II when rail traffic was extremely heavy.

Barbara, Bob, and Chris sometimes visited the stabilized blast furnace at Katahdin Iron Works, Brownville.

photos by Bob Coyle

The family also sometimes visited the stabilized charcoal kiln at Katahdin Iron Works.

photo by Bob Coyle

We also enjoyed visiting the museum of Dexter Historical Society in an old grist mill. The mill operated during the nineteenth and early twentieth centuries and today contains artifacts from the town's history. An old newspaper article on display recounts an unsolved murder in a nearby alley, a place where even today I might not want to linger after dark.

The Skowhegan History House in a nineteenth-century brick dwelling displays exhibits from that town's exciting past. The world's tallest statue of a Native American at the end of the Skowhegan municipal parking lot, formerly a small railroad yard, depicts an Abenaki Indian clutching a fish trap.

Longtime stateswoman Senator Margaret Chase Smith lived in Skowhegan. She served first as a US Representative in Congress and then as a US Senator. The first woman to serve in both houses of the United States Congress, she was also the first woman to represent Maine in either. In her younger days, she taught in a one-room schoolhouse and later worked in a textile mill. She passed away in 1995 at the age of ninety-seven. Her home, perched on the banks of the Kennebec River in Skowhegan, serves the public as the Margaret Chase Smith Library and Museum.

Most area towns of any size have historical societies worth visiting. Monson Historical Society in the former fire engine house has an old snow roller on display outside the building. Well into the twentieth century, many towns rolled snow on the main streets rather than plowing. Teams of horses pulled snow rollers. The roller compacted snow and allowed sleighs and sleds to negotiate the winter roads.

The Blacksmith Shop Museum on the outskirts of Dover-Foxcroft displays material from the bygone era. We stopped there every year or two. We took my cousins, the McCastors, there during their summer visit in 1966.

On our way to visit the blacksmith shop one day in the mid 1970s, we drove by another museum on the same road. It consisted of old machinery and similar objects. It never seemed quite finished nor open to the public. I noticed what looked quite like a two-foot gauge boxcar behind other artifacts.

Snow removal involved rolling rather than plowing in the old days on New Engand roads, including in Monson.
photo by Bob Coyle

We stopped and got chatting with the owner. Indeed, a boxcar from the Sandy River and Rangeley Lakes Railroad stood in the background. Built back in 1897 by the Portland Company, an SR&RL boxcar numbered a faded seventy-four, and measured twenty-seven feet, nine inches in length.

We told the operator of the Sandy River Railroad Park in Phillips where I had been working as a volunteer since I was about fifteen. He said the park could have the boxcar if they wanted to come and get it. Sadly, it never happened.

In the 1970s, some school buses served unorganized territories in Maine.
photo by Bob Coyle

brief history of mayfield and kingsbury

Mayfield and Kingsbury are situated east of Bingham and west of Abbot Village in a quiet part of central Maine. Located in Somerset County east of Bingham, Mayfield originally called Fordstown, was named for Enoch Ford, the first white settler. The town name was changed to Mayfield with official incorporation in 1836.

From page 358 of Varney's 1881 *Gazetteer of the State of Maine*:

> Mayfield lies on the eastern line of Somerset County, 23 miles north of Skowhegan. It is bounded on the north by Bald Mountain Township, south by Brighton, west by Bingham, and east by Kingsbury, in Piscataquis County. The town is quite hilly; Coburn Ridge, occupying nearly the whole western side of the town, being the greatest. It has two considerable ponds in the northern part, of which Austin Stream, running west to the Kennebec, is the outlet. Hayden Pond lies near the centre of the town, its outlet emptying into Kingsbury Pond in the south-east part. The last is 2½ miles long and 1 mile wide. The principal settlement is at the south-east part of the town, on the road from Skowhegan to Blanchard. The principal rock of the town is slate. The soil is quite fertile, yielding good crops of grain. Cedar and spruce are the most numerous woods. There are two lumber-mills in the town, and one mill for preparing slate, of which considerable quantities are quarried here. The town was a part of Bingham's Kennebec Purchase. It was incorporated March 7, 1836... The nearest post-office is at Brighton. The town has one public schoolhouse... The population in 1870 was 96. In 1880 it was 141.

After the quarry closed, the population of Mayfield declined to seventy-four persons as reported in the 1890 census. Mayfield surrendered its organization as a town in 1887 but reorganized into a plantation in 1892. The Maine legislature confirmed and validated the organization in 1895.

Alphonso L. Flanders, a descendant of first settler Enoch Ford, was prominent in the doings of the town. He owned Mayfield's only store, located near his residence a short distance north of Mayfield Pond. His wife, Mary E. Chamberlain Flanders, served as the longtime postmaster of Mayfield between 1886 and her death in 1924.

The Mayfield Post Office was located in the Flanders home at Mayfield Corner. Besides performing the duties of the store and post office, the Flanderses opened their large home to accommodate the chance traveler, according to Elinor Stevens Walker in her book *More About Maine*. The Pooler family later owned the house located close to the intersections of routes 16 and 151. The building disappeared by the mid 1960s.

Mayfield's population declined through the early part of the twentieth century. Mayfield's plantation status was surrendered in 1937, and since then, the Mayfield area has remained an unorganized territory.

Located due east of Mayfield, Kingsbury is part of Piscataquis County and holds plantation status.

From page 303 of Varney's 1881 *Gazetteer of the State of Maine*:

Kingsbury is situated in the south-western part of Piscataquis County, having Mayfield, in Somerset County, for its western boundary. Its other boundaries are the Piscataquis County towns of Blanchard, on the north, Abbot and Parkman on the east, and Wellington on the south. The principal ponds are Kingsbury, two miles long by one wide, Foss, about one mile each way, and (Hilton Ponds), somewhat smaller. There are two fine Cascades in town, and the streams are well-stocked with speckled trout. The town is hilly, the principal rock is slate, and the soil, where cultivated, is mostly a clay loam, good for potatoes and grass. The trees usual in the region flourish here; and the primeval forest still stands to such an extent that one road passes through it for nine miles without encountering a single opening. There is a saw mill and grist mill, built in 1835 by Judge Kingsbury; (now owned by the Hilton's) on the outlet of Kingsbury Pond. This stream forms the south branch of the Piscataquis River, while the north branch passes near the north-eastern part of the town. The stage-road from Athens to Moosehead Lake passes through Kingsbury. The village is twenty miles from Dover, and half the distance from the station of the Bangor and Piscataquis railway in Abbot.

The township was a part of the Bingham Purchase. It was lotted by Eleazer Coburn, esquire, and in 1833 was purchased by Hon. Sanford Kingsbury, of Gardiner, for the sum of four thousand dollars. William Hilton and his brother the next year made openings, and in 1836 there were so many settlers that the town was incorporated under the name of its honorable proprietor. There are now a store, hotel, mechanic-shops, and the mills already mentioned at Kingsbury Village. There is a church organization of the persuasion called Buzzellites [followers of John Buzzell, who split from the Free Baptists in 1835]. Kingsbury; has two public schoolhouses . . . The population in 1870 was 174. By the census of 1880 it was 198.

In 1786, William Bingham, a very wealthy and influential banker in Philadelphia, secured two tracts of land known as the Bingham Purchase in the District of Maine, which at that time was still part of Massachusetts. Each tract comprised a million acres. At forty, Bingham was considered the wealthiest man in the country. His circle of friends included George Washington, Alexander Hamilton, and Benjamin Franklin.

Bingham's Penobscot Purchase was located in Washington and Hancock counties with Somerset County the site of his second or Kennebec Purchase. The town of Bingham was named for William Bingham, although he never set foot within the area. The Kennebec purchase was divided into seven ranges, each with seven townships, four west of the Kennebec River and three to the east. The Bingham Purchase is still used to refer to the geographical area that includes the lands purchased. Mayfield, T2R2 BKP EKR, means Township 2 Range 2, Bingham's Kennebec Purchase, East of the Kennebec River.

In 1885, Kingsbury surrendered its organization as a town but reorganized as a plantation the following year, 1886. A plantation, a type of minor civil divisions in Maine, falls between an unorganized township and a town. The Maine legislature confirmed and validated the organization in 1895. The population of Kingsbury declined rapidly between 1910 at 108 persons to 63 in 1920.

In later years, the Kingsbury post office was located in the home owned by John Cook, which also served as a hotel. That section of Kingsbury Plantation was known as Kingsbury Mills. Effie Bean Nugent served as the last postmaster.

The eventually abandoned old Worcester home occupied the center of Kingsbury during the Coyles' years at Kingsbury Pond.

photo by Chris Coyle

In addition to that assignment, Effie helped with the work of the hostelry. The old three-and-a-half-story structure burned one blustery March day in 1931 after someone stuffed too much birch bark into the kitchen stove.

A smaller, extant building was constructed the next summer. Kingsbury Post Office was discontinued around 1957. Kingsbury's population declined over the years until 1980 at four persons, since increased to twenty-eight.

Both Mayfield and Kingsbury have seasonal camps, most of them situated on Kingsbury, Mayfield, and Otter ponds. Kingsbury's permanent residents live near Kingsbury Pond or along roads to East Kingsbury. Those living or summering in Kingsbury and Mayfield have no electricity nor telephone service, preferring to live off the grid.

On November 2, 2009, Chris presented
a program about Mayfield
at the Old Canada Road Historical Society.

poster courtesy of Old Canada Road Historical Society

blueberrying

We always spent time picking blueberries during our summers in central Maine. We quite successfully found various patches of blueberries on old roads. We could pick a few handfuls along the driveway just above where the brook ran close by. The old road up Cook Hill was also a decent spot, especially in earlier years. West Mayfield had some fine patches of berries in the old fields. We could pick there at length until we had all we wanted.

Typical attire for a lengthy blueberry-picking session included dark pants and a hat to protect each of us from the sun and orbiting black flies, sometimes jokingly referred to as Maine's state bird. If black flies or other insects were especially bad, we splashed Woodsman's Fly Dope on exposed skin and covered up as much as possible. We wore short pants and T-shirts in pleasant weather when bugs weren't an issue.

After a 1973 afternoon of blueberry picking, Barbara and Chris return to the cabin.
photo by Bob Coyle

We picked blueberries into an old set of white enamel cooking pots with red trim. I can vividly picture them. We stored the berries in our gas refrigerator to use with cereal, muffins, fruit cups, Mother's famous blueberry pie, or Dad's equally famous blueberry pancakes. The top to a great day at the cabin, Dad made blueberry pancakes for supper while I rode my bike up and down the driveway a few last times before sitting down for the evening meal.

Kingsbury had commercial blueberry fields, especially on Campbell Hill Road. Mrs. Ward retained the blueberry rights to her land when she sold her farm. Each summer, she opened her fields so people could go in and pick berries. We often took advantage of that, as the blueberries on her property were more plentiful than those we happened upon at some abandoned farm or along a back road. She collected her money when we finished.

We often felt an overwhelming temptation to snack on berries as we picked. Our tongues became rather blue after snacking, and when the time came to pay up, we tried not to open our mouths too much and reveal the unpaid consumption of berries. In retrospect, Mrs. Ward probably assumed that folks would snack while picking, and her price likely reflected that.

The Prebles lived on Cowett Hill on the side road across from the old Campbell School. They hired pickers for the high-producing fields. They opened other fields to the public for pick-and-pay harvesting. Mr. Preble ran the operation well into his nineties. I remember one day when I was around ten, we stopped at the Prebles' home and inquired about blueberries. Mrs. Preble invited us into the kitchen where she

The Prebles lived in a Cape Cod-style house on the property of their commercial blueberry fields in East Kingsbury.

photo by Jane O'Regan

worked at the sink. As we chatted about the berries, one of the farm workers came to the door. Mrs. Preble showed me her automatic door. She had a rope arrangement over to the sink where she gave it a tug and the door opened. I was quite impressed at my young age.

Most of the large fields in East Kingsbury had been used to graze sheep years before when wool had a good market in New England. Now the stark, barren landscape seemed lonely, and we wondered what it was like there a century before. We thought also what it must be like there during a winter blizzard.

The Worcesters also ran commercial fields in East Kingsbury and on the Wellington Road. All the commercial growers utilized rakes for harvesting the berries. The rakes look like dustpans with tines. In addition to picking berries, they also collected a good deal of chaff. Workers raked berries into large buckets that, when full, they dumped into a winnower machine to separate berries from chaff. We felt that the process damaged berries, and we

The blueberry crop showed at its best in summer 1966.

photo by Bob Coyle

found it best to freeze them if not using them right off. Commercial growers usually sold berries from the field after they went through the winnower. We took that option if we did not have time to pick our own. Usually, we preferred to hand-pick berries and grew quite efficient at it.

My friend Keith McGuirk from Athol rode up to Maine with us in 1971 and spent a few days at the cabin. Then we met his family at the Dutch Treat, a restaurant over in Wilton. One morning we drove down to Kingsbury Mills and saw a large black bear hanging up on the side of the shed by the Worcester operation. We were told that the bear had been raiding the Worcesters' commercial blueberry fields and had been shot the night before.

The same day we saw the bear carcass, I believe that Dad, Keith, and I hiked nearby Foss Mountain from Route 151. Dad had hiked the mountain some years before when he mapped bedrock geology of the region. He had also climbed Kelley Mountain on the west side of Route 151. Kelley Mountain sported the fire warden's lookout tower, likely no longer in use. Although Foss Mountain had no tower, we nevertheless experienced quite a nice view thanks to stunted tree growth at the mountain's summit.

Upon returning to the car, we were dismayed that the 1969

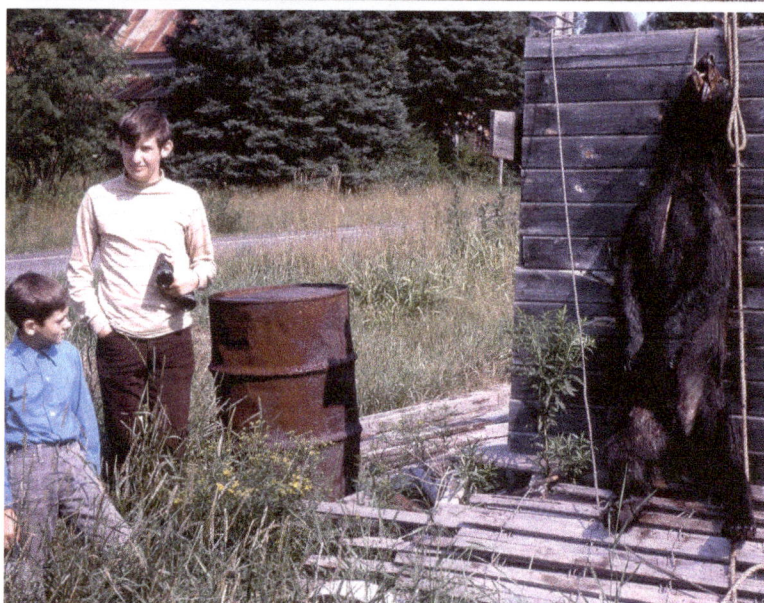

Keith McGuirk, Bob, and Chris sit among blueberry bushes at the top of Foss Mountain near Kingsbury Plantation, top. Chris and Keith see what happened to the bear that fed on commercial blueberries at Kingsbury, bottom.

photos by Bob Coyle with top photo timed

130

Plymouth Fury would not start. So ten-year old Chris sat behind the steering wheel and kept the car on the road even without power steering while Dad and Keith began pushing the disabled vehicle northward over level pavement toward the cabin a few miles away. We had not gone too far that way when a car traveling north stopped and a man got out to help us. He suggested trying to restart the car, as he thought that letting the engine sit for a time may have improved the situation.

He was right. The car started right up, and we drove merrily back to the cabin after a good workout for two of the three of us. I didn't mind the opportunity to pilot the lifeless vehicle, but I'm sure that Dad and Keith were relieved when it started up.

Fortunately during our Mayfield years, we did not get let down by car trouble. I have vague recollections that years ago when I was small, one of Dad's early cars had a problem with the gasoline tank. Wilder Rollins had him bring it across the river to Concord to a man who fixed such problems in his garage. I guess the fellow made things right, as I do not recall it ever being an issue again.

Not as good, another time we experienced some sort of problem with the 1969 Plymouth a year or two after Keith's visit. I don't remember exactly what had gone kaput with the car, but some sort of problem had to be fixed prior to our return to Athol. Although drivable, the car wouldn't necessarily endure a long trip. At any rate, we went to a dealership for repairs.

The outfit was a real Mickey Mouse place. We kept getting the runaround about fixing the car. First, the dude told us it needed a special part and that it would be very difficult to obtain the required piece because the car had air conditioning—our first car to have that option because no one in the State of Maine had air conditioning. They did let us use a loaner while they searched for the part.

As we had no telephone at the cabin, we had to drive twenty-five miles every day or two for updates at the dealership. Finally, after a week or so of such nonsense, we heard of a man over in Fairfield who repaired cars in his backyard garage. So down we went to the dealer to retrieve the Plymouth. Dad handed the dealership man the keys to the loaner. The employee immediately handed Dad a bill for storing our car for a week. Dad told him to get stuffed, and we left the lot in a cloud of tire smoke.

The Fairfield man was a real crackerjack at fixing anything. After looking the car over, he said he knew what we needed and that he would send his wife to Bangor to procure the necessary part. He said it would not take long, as his wife drove to Bangor some fifty miles away at eighty miles per hour in unpopulated areas on the parts runs.

Sure enough, we were up and running in no time, and the car never acted up again, at least not concerning that issue. Sometime over the winter months we received a bill from the dealership for doing nothing. The folks included it along with a lengthy letter describing the dealership in no uncertain terms to corporate offices. We never heard another word from anyone but noticed next summer that the dealership had lost its franchise and the building and lot were empty. No surprise there.

The car was frequently covered with dirt after driving on Maine's many unpaved roads. Dad had me wash the car, something I liked doing. I used regular pails from the kitchen. First, I rinsed the car off as well as I could with pond water. Then, I got some suds up with some soap in one bucket. After scrubbing the car's exterior, I sloshed a fair amount of pond water all over it to rinse off the soap. It looked good for a while, at least until we drove up the next dusty road.

A good time to drive on the dustiest roads was the day after an extended rainstorm. Some summers were very dry and water levels quite low in brooks and streams. Other years when it was very rainy, water cascaded down waterways much the way it probably did during the spring thaw, which of course we did not witness.

Barbara Coyle's East Kingsbury-style Blueberry Pie
**For decades, my mother baked famous blueberry pie,
best made using wild Maine blueberries.**

Ingredients:
3 cups blueberries
1/2 cup sugar
2 tablespoons flour
2 cups flour, sifted
3/4 cup vegetable oil
1/4 cup water

Procedure:

Pick over blueberries to cull out any flawed fruit and put in mixing bowl. Add sugar and 2 tablespoons flour (for thickening) to blueberries and mix well. Measure vegetable oil and water in the same measuring cup. Combine 2 cups of sifted flour with vegetable oil and water. If too dry, add more liquid. If too wet, add more flour. Mix well with spoon and then knead with clean hands and form mixture into a large ball.

With a knife, divide the ball into 2 portions, making one portion a little larger than the other. Lay a piece of wax paper on the counter and dust it with a little flour. Put the smaller portion, flat side down, on the wax paper. Lay another piece of wax paper on top of the half flour ball. Using a rolling pin, flatten it down. Peel off the top layer of wax paper. Invert the flattened flour ball into an ungreased glass pie dish. Gently peel off the other layer of wax paper.

Give the blueberry mixture a stir and pour it into the pie shell. Prepare the second flour ball in the same way as the first and place over the pie. Using a fork, crimple the edge of the crust. Then, using a knife or fork, put several holes in the crust to allow steam to escape.

Bake in a preheated 400°F oven for 10-15 minutes.
Then lower the oven temperature to 350°F and bake for another 30-35 minutes.

it happened one day

A sad and tragic accident occurred in 1959 when the folks stayed at the camp belonging to William Tibbetts down near the Kingsbury picnic ground. In the evening of August 19, two men were fishing in a small boat on Kingsbury Pond near the Do-Drop-Inn owned by John MacDonald of Guilford. One of the men apparently lost his balance as he stood in the boat to start the motor. The boat capsized, throwing both men into the water. Nearby campers heard the calls for help and raced to the scene with motorboats but rescued only one man. The other could not be found.

Dad, Don Sawyer, game wardens, sheriffs' deputies from two counties, and other residents searched frantically for the missing man.

A recovery crew located the body of the Bingham man within three hours on the following morning. A Waterville *Morning Sentinel* article from August 21, 1959 states that

Participating in the search were Game Warden Donald Walker, Rolon Collins, J. Stanton Giberson and Stanley Hill, all of Bingham, Robert Coyle of Allegheny College in Meadville, Pennsylania, and Donald Sawyer of Waterville.

Dad said that had both men worn life jackets, they'd likely have avoided the accidental drowning. Usually once or twice each summer, a seaplane landed on Kingsbury Pond and took off some time later, perhaps after the plane's occupants enjoyed lunch at the Kingsbury Picnic Area down by the dam. Seaplane activity caused loons to go berserk, noted by their great vocalization. On weekends, loud and annoying speedboats often pulling someone on water skis raced up and down the pond.

An unusual animal sighting happened in 1959, the year before I was born, when Gram and Gramp Coyle came to visit the folks. They arrived and told the folks that they had seen an elephant by the side of the road out by West Mayfield. Uncle Wilson was driving, and he had seen elephants in India during World War II and definitely knew one if he saw one.

They all quickly drove out to see it. It turned out to be a small traveling circus that had stopped to exercise some of the animals. It provided an interesting display, especially in Mayfield. Dad had been writing to his parents about all the wild animals in the area but they had not quite believed Dad's generalizations about wild animals until they saw the elephant!

One day in the mid 1960s when I was about five years old, we were shopping at Preble and Robinson in Bingham. Ruby Robinson took a telephone call from a friend up in Moscow who told her about a car coming down Route 201 with a monkey in it. The store emptied out onto the sidewalk to witness the spectacle. Soon, the convertible, an early 1960s model, came into view. I was rather disappointed to see the monkey sitting in the back seat—I had expected to see him at the wheel smoking a Cuban cigar! Anyway, it offered a rather unusual sight for rural Maine—or maybe anywhere, for that matter.

I can clearly remember my fifth birthday, August 29, 1965. It was the sole year I ever saw snow on my birthday. Since we went to Maine only in summer, it was also the only time we ever saw snow at Kingsbury Pond during a cold summer when we used the wood stove most every night.

In the morning of my birthday, Mother wanted to bake me a surprise for lunch, so Dad took me for a ride up Campbell Hill Road near blueberrying operations. The very low overnight temperature—near freezing in fact— could damage the blueberry crop. The Worcesters' crew of out-of-the area workers, possibly from Cherryfield, busily harvested berries as fast as they could go. Dad noticed that some of the young fellows in the blueberry field didn't even have shirts to wear, likely because they hadn't expected such cold. He drove back later with some old clothes to give them.

We began to notice snow flurries as we drove past Kingsbury Dam. By the time we got to the cabin, it was really snowing. It kept up for a little while. I don't remember if anything accumulated on the ground, but the view across the pond certainly looked different! We saw snow falling all the way across the pond. A whiteout nearly obliterated Skunk's Hill.

We experienced many wild thunderstorms at the cabin. The rumble of thunder in the distance usually indicated an impending storm. Dad often said, "It's coming down from Russell Mountain," north of us toward Blanchard. Dad told the story of years before when he did field work in the Russell Mountain area. When he hiked into the area where he planned to work, he hopped across a small stream. While he worked in the woods, a strong storm developed, forcing him to head back to the car. The small stream had become a raging torrent, and he experienced some difficulty in getting over it.

Thunderstorms at the cabin could be very loud, and for me, frightening. Dad seemed to enjoy them to the extent that he sometimes sat out on the porch or inside the cabin and watched the lightning. I always felt relieved when a storm had ended and the only sound was falling rain.

I remember mornings after a rainstorm when the sky had cleared. I just cannot describe the wonderful aroma of the Maine woods after a rain. The next best thing to it: small pillows of spruce or balsam fir which we got in Maine and put in our clothes drawers to keep them smelling nice.

One morning in the mid 1960s, we heard a most unusual scraping sound that seemed to originate up on Route 16. Dad and I walked up the driveway but cautiously stayed out of view from the road. The source of the odd sound soon came into view. An older car with several people in it had the left rear wheel missing for some strange reason. The car just barely moved under its own power at a top speed perhaps of five mph.

As it slowly made its way east on Highway 16, the exposed axle cut a groove into the pavement. We stayed out of view and made our way back to the cabin once the strange vehicle had gone down the road. The groove in the pavement of Route 16 remained for several years until repaving erased all signs of the unusual event.

Dad wondered if the car's occupants might be escaped convicts. After supper that evening, we drove east on Route 16 to follow the groove cut in the pavement earlier in the day by the three-wheeled car. We saw that the groove left Route 16 east of Kingsbury Mills and followed it up the old Stage Coach Road next to the Titcomb cemetery on the road to Abbot Village.

Dad cautiously drove up the dirt road. We suddenly spotted the three-wheeled car stopped a short distance in front of us. The car's occupants were making camp as we came around a curve in the road. I never saw Dad back up as fast as he did that day after he slammed it into reverse!

Other notable events transpired over the years we summered in Mayfield. My memory has faded for some of them, although I remember others clearly.

When we arrived in Bingham one year and stopped at Omar Sawyer's home on Preble Street to pick up the cabin keys, he told us there had been a break-in at the cabin during the cold months earlier in the year. Someone had entered the cabin through the window into my bedroom. The trunk where we stored some of our things was open. Nothing else seemed touched or damaged. It appeared that the person had let himself out the back door and left the area.

The folks decided that a shirt and possibly a pair of pants had gone missing. We surmised that whoever broke in needed a change of clothes. Perhaps the person had gotten wet in the woods or from ice fishing and, out of desperation, broke into the cabin in search of dry clothes to change into. At any rate, we were thankful for no damage done beyond the break-in through the window.

On a different note, I remember that Moscow celebrated its sesquicentennial in 1966. On the evening of July 22, we attended a spectacular fireworks show in a large field up near Wyman Dam. The following afternoon, we attended a parade held in Bingham to honor Moscow. Dad took slides of the parade from the end of Preble Street at the corner opposite the Bushey and Sterling store. I still have a banner from the celebration.

A green and white pennant commemorates the 1966 sesquicentennial of Moscow, Maine founded in 1816.

photo by David Cass

The Moscow sesquicential parade showcased many floats,
including, at bottom, those of the Bingham Grange.
photos by Bob Coyle

Tom Farrin's children and grandchildren spent an afternoon at Pine Cove from time to time. One day, a small group over at Tom's beach splashed around in the water. We sat on our front porch reading books we had checked out from the Bingham Union Library.

Suddenly the eldest member of the visiting Farrins called out, "Look, a black moose swimming across the pond!"

We quickly looked up and could make out the head of a moose slowly moving across the surface of the water against the background of Skunk's Hill. Dad set up the telescope, and for quite a while, we watched the animal—with antlers clearly identifying him as male as he slowly made his way to the far shore. I never thought a moose looked like it might qualify as a very good swimmer, but sure enough, that one did a good job of it.

After we stopped staying in Mayfield, Don Sawyer fortunately once captured five moose on film over in Pine Cove.

One August morning in 1971, we got into Dad's 1969 Plymouth to drive east on Route 16. We hadn't gone any distance at all when we came upon a small, light green car wrecked and propped up against a tree by the side of the road. We stopped, got out, and looked all around but we couldn't find the occupants, so we proceeded on our trip to wherever. Later we read in the *Morning Sentinel* that the car occupied by two young people on their way to hike Mount Katahdin had gone out of control, flipped over, and struck a tree and then a rock. One person suffered very minor injuries, and luckily, they were both okay. I guess the people had been removed from the scene by the time we got there, but a tow truck had yet to arrive to remove the demolished vehicle.

The very small town of Wellington had a very low gross median income. Folks there struggled to keep a roof over their heads and food on the table. We noticed one particular house gradually being disassembled and burned in their indoor wood stove as fuel over a period of several years. First a porch disappeared, then the second story went. Each summer, more parts of the house went missing. Finally one summer, only part of the first story still existed with a tarp over the top. The following year, they lived in an old small movable camping trailer next to where the house had been with only a few boards remaining of the former dwelling. The trailer had definitely seen its best days, but it evidently provided shelter and a home for the inhabitants.

Mother named a house somewhere in the area Crush-down House. Sadly, I can no longer remember the story about it. I do remember an abandoned house along the Wellington Road south of Wellington Bog. It disappeared over time, and at one point just a staircase remained standing. Maybe it's Crush-down House, but I am not certain. The folks also assigned a place the name Hummingbird House, perhaps because they often saw hummingbirds around plants surrounding the building. Unfortunately, I don't remember where that was either.

the day the dam broke

Omar Sawyer's widow Josephine called the folks one evening in late winter or early spring of 1969 when we still lived on Riverbend Street in Athol. Among other things, she told us that the Kingsbury Dam had gone out. We were very interested to see how things would look.

When we arrived at the cabin in July, the water level on Kingsbury Pond had dropped considerably lower than we had ever seen it with an additional perhaps one hundred feet of shoreline in front of us. The dock stood high and dry. We could see depressions in the ground where the kivvies normally built their nests.

After Kingsbury Dam broke in 1969, Birch Point had low water.
photo by Bob Coyle

We could also see many rocks usually hidden beneath the surface of the pond, including one large rock diagonally to the left of our shoreline toward Birch Point. One day, we got the idea to take old boards and build a boardwalk out to the rock while stepping on each board as we put it down to place the next one down ahead of it on our first day. After that, we sometimes ventured out and sat on the rock to eat a snack and watch the loons.

One interesting feature involved large rocks that almost looked like a stone wall around the new shoreline. What a mystery! Wood pilings came to light down by the picnic ground as evidence of when the lumber companies used the pond.

It began to rain during the first week of August and continued for several days. Looking out at the pond on the afternoon of August 6, we realized that rocks partially covered by water earlier in the day were out of the water—problematic since it had been raining for several days.

We hopped in the car and headed for Kingsbury dam. There we found a breach in the temporary wooden coffer dam intended to hold water back during construction of the new permanent dam.

The temporary Kingsbury Pond coffer dam broke on August 6, 1969.
top photo by Chris Coyle / bottom photo by Bob Coyle

The pond water should have exited via the usual dam gate not damaged by the original dam break. Although two cables might have raised the gate, one had broken. As a result, workers could not easily adjust the dam gate. Donald Sawyer said that chains work better than cables for the purpose. Justin Worcester, the dam keeper, said cables would be fine, but with the raised pond level from the rain, he couldn't let enough water out. Eventually, the water started going over the top of the coffer dam which proved to be too much for the structure, and it got swept away.

Beyond barriers, Chris and Barbara—tiny figures near an automobile—follow the break of the Kingsbury Pond coffer dam on August 6, 1969.
photo by Bob Coyle

We took a few photographs of a great deal of erosion around the bridge just downstream from the dam and then headed for Bingham to procure more film. We purchased the film at Moore's Drugstore and mentioned that the Kingsbury Dam had broken. At first the folks there thought we referred to when it broke in the spring, but we explained that it had broken again. Word quickly spread through town.

We returned to Kingsbury and made additional photos of the dam. Mr. Worcester walked over toward the dam and Mother said to him, "Quite a flood!" Then we drove to Abbot Village and looked at remarkably high water under the bridge on Route 15. The usually calm stream had turned into a raging torrent.

Another day, we took advantage of low water to walk counterclockwise around the perimeter of Kingsbury Pond. At the Mayfield isthmus, normally several hundred feet wide, we could easily hop over the small waterway connecting Mayfield and Kingsbury ponds.

We were invited into one of the cabins on the far shore down toward Kingsbury. Older folks, the man and woman explained that a group of retired railroad employees owned the

In 1970, Chris contemplates the view of the Farrin and Sawyer cabins on the far shore.
photo by Bob Coyle

building and that the windows came from old railroad cars. I have often wondered which railroad they had worked for. I was given a fresh peach from a tree at their cabin, and I enjoyed it very much. I could not recall ever before having a fresh peach.

Construction of the new dam finished in the summer of 1970. Slate from the old quarry in Mayfield reinforced the new dam. A new flood chute was constructed halfway across the dam with the old one still in place near the far side of the structure, but for some reason, I never saw much water go over it. An even older, wooden chute just below it had been part of some previous dam.

We experienced an interesting couple of summers with low water levels in Kingsbury Pond. We got to see and do things we would not have other-

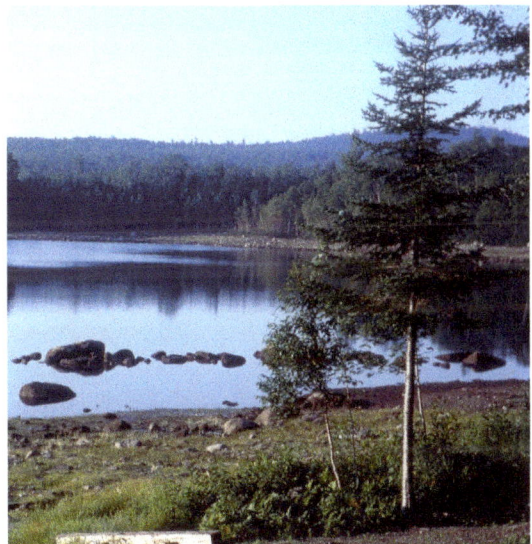

Chris watched the spruce tree shown as it grew years before from a sapling during 1969 low water.
photo by Bob Coyle

141

wise done had the dam not broken. Dad saw an uncommon Louisiana waterthrush down-stream from the dam on several occasions.

Work progressed on the permanent Kingsbury Pond dam after the temporary coffer dam broke.
photo by Bob Coyle

the log drive

Our area of Maine had long been known for its logging operations. Although no large-scale operations went on close to us during the more than two decades we stayed in Mayfield, we didn't have to travel too far to see them.

At least some small logging took place in the woods of Mayfield and Kingsbury. Through 1976, Kennebec Log Driving Company, chartered in 1835, handled large-scale movements of pulpwood from East Outlet down the Kennebec to mills down river from Bingham. Before establishment of the KLD company, individual companies themselves had to drive logs downriver. After KLD formed, it took charge of driving all logs on the river. Marks on the end of the logs allowed KLD crews to sort and deliver logs to the proper mills.

How quiet and tranquil we found it to sit on the Kennebec River banking at Riverside Restaurant in Bingham watching logs slip quietly downstream. That all changed after the fall of 1976. Never again would the call "Ice out!" resonate up and down the valley signaling the start of the drive. Crews bringing up the rear cleaned up logs that had gotten hung up on rocks or along the sides of the river. I remember seeing a chain used on the last drive for sale the next summer at the service station on the corner of Meadow Street in Bingham.

When driving north toward Skowhegan from Waterville, we often saw great numbers of logs in the river at Pishon Ferry in Hinckley. Sometimes we couldn't even see the water! Logs awaited sluicing at the dam in Skowhegan.

Revenues from logging built the region—the villages, railroads, and secondary industries. Lombard log haulers were built in Waterville from 1901 to 1917. The earlier log haulers were steam-powered and moved by means of a continuous track like that on a bulldozer. The unit steered by skis under the

In Bangor in August, 1965, Barbara and Chris waited near the statue of legendary giant lumberjack Paul Bunyan.

photo by Bob Coyle

In August 1968, pulpwood fills Kennebec River
at Pishon Ferry in Hinkley in the town of Fairfield.
Tracks for the Maine Central Skowhegan branch run along the river's edge.

photo by Bob Coyle

front of the machine. Much like cars on a train, sleds of logs coupled together from the rear of the machine. Piled with logs, the sleds pulled across snow and ice-covered frozen ground. One logging outfit estimated that three Lombard tractors did the work of sixty horses. Gasoline engines replaced steam boilers during the last years of Lombard production.

Regular river drives of long logs ended in Maine after 1925. Since then, pulpwood—logs cut into four-foot lengths—made it easier to drive wood more suited to newer mill machinery down the river.

I was fortunate to see the last long log drive on the Gatineau River near Ottawa in 1992. Pulpwood, that is logs cut to four-foot lengths, is easier to handle, especially at dams, than long logs. Handling of long logs on the drive differed considerably from maneuvering pulpwood, and crews versatile in handling one type of log did not necessarily have sufficient ability to handle the other. Skilled river driving is a lost art.

Long logs dominate a view of Kennebec River
beneath the Skowhegan railroad bridge about 1900.

postcard from the collection of Chris Coyle

The last drive of long logs in Maine that I know of is described in Louise Dickinson Rich's popular book

144

We Took to the Woods. She recounts how the Great Hurricane of 1938 dealt much damage to New England trees and infrastructure. Workers hauled fallen pine into temporary storage booms at Pond-in-the-River to await the drive down Rapid River to Umbagog Lake where other workers gathered it into government storage booms. Someone came up with the idea for great publicity with cameramen and reporters on hand to watch the brief revival of old-time long log drives in the spring of 1939.

The problem was that there weren't many men left skilled as river drivers of long logs. Legendary figures of old famous in song and story for running up and down the rivers of Maine had either long retired, died, or removed to places unknown. The one exception seemed to be a character by the name of Black John who resided at the county jail. When approached with the idea of appearing in the news footage, Black John readily agreed but wasn't due to be sprung until fall. The warden, however, let Black John be "borrowed" for a few days for the drive and then returned to finish his likely several more months in the slammer.

The arrangement came together. Away they went, Black John clad in suitable attire, including the quintessential plaid shirt. Other river drivers used to pulp assisted, but Black John was star of the show. Cameras rolled, and folks gawked.

Everything came to a screeching halt when a jam ensued as logs blocked each other in the river. One man fell into the icy water along with his hooked tool, a cant dog used by river drivers to wrestle logs or pulpwood. Black John, a river hog from 'way back, simply ran out across the logs as if he ran on pavement and opened the jam. Liberated logs raced downstream.

Louise Dickinson Rich concludes the story:

> This I will say for Black John. He didn't let the situation die like that with a bunch of logs floating off into the unknown. He threw back his head and howled, "Never mind the man! Grab his cant dog! That cost the company money!" That was the old river hogs' battle cry. It put the finishing touch on the episode. Black John had a true feeling for style. Black John was returned safely (to the county jail) and in good condition.

Such are the tales of old-time Maine.

We always saw log trucks in Maine. In the early years before the roads were improved, they tended to be smaller and didn't carry as much wood. At night, we heard log trucks climbing Cook Hill, the ruling grade on Route 16 west to Bingham. Trucks downshifted time and again to make one wonder if they would eventually run out of gears and have to back down the hill.

Nowadays, after a disastrous accident, most log trucks turn down Route 151 at Mayfield Corner. The accident occurred when a loaded log truck lost its brakes descending Bingham Hill and roared into Bingham at eighty-plus miles per hour only to fly off the north side of Route 201 and taking the porch from a house in the process.

Another time, we missed being in the path of a runaway log truck on Bingham Hill in the afternoon of July 29, 1963. A last-minute return to Bingham kept us out of harm's way. We

We arrived at the scene where a log truck overturned on July 29, 1963 on Route 16 east of Bingham.
photo by Bob Coyle

Pulpwood shuttles downriver on July 19, 1963 in the sluiceway of Ripogenus Dam on Penobscot River in Piscataquis County.
photo by Bob Coyle

realized it when we rounded one of the first steep curves in Moscow and found a truck on its side with wheels still spinning and tons of logs spilled right where we would have been. The disoriented driver wandered about aimlessly as help had not yet arrived.

Back in the early 1970s, we took a bus tour sponsored by Scott Paper Company from Greenville into logging camps above Moosehead Lake. We saw a huge machine that, in about forty seconds, could turn a standing tree into a log ready to load onto a truck. The machine grasped the tree, removed the branches, snipped off the top, and finally cut the base off in incredibly short time.

Logs cut into four-foot lengths got dumped into Moosehead Lake to become booms easily towed by the boat *Katahdin* to East Outlet of the Kennebec River, where workers sent them down the Kennebec to mills. The highlight of the Scott Paper tour was eating lunch in the lumber camp— great food! Though a rainy day, with drizzling off and on, we thoroughly enjoyed ourselves.

It always surprised me how quickly a wooded area could grow back enough to erase the scars of a logging operation. The Maine woods do indeed regenerate themselves in short order.

Hollingsworth & Whitney at Winslow once served as the destination for many log drives.
postcard from the collection of Chris Coyle

Wooden posts in the ground marked boundaries of paper companies in our area of Maine. Hollingsworth and Whitney painted all boundary markers red, and we saw them throughout the area. If I remember correctly, S. D. Warren painted markers blue, and I think Scott Paper Company painted theirs yellow. A clump of rocks usually helped hold markers up as the rocky land of Somerset and Piscataquis counties does not lend itself to digging.

The frontier days of logging in Maine lingered for decades. One late afternoon, we returned south from Indian Pond along the old railroad grade and stopped at the little supply store at Moxie Pond. The store sat just north of the dam at the northwest end of Caribou Narrows on the pond.

The store itself seemed like a relic from the olden days. Ardelle "Ida" Allen, the elderly woman who ran the store. seemed equally as old.

An outlet dam in Kokadjo at First Roach Pond marks the beginning of Roach River, used by loggers.
postcard from the collection of Chris Coyle

147

When Dad inquired if she had a particular item, I cannot remember now what, she replied that we would need to go "down river" to buy it—parlance from the days of log drives on the river. In her eighties in 1979, Mrs. Allen published her autobiography, *Ida, A Happy Life in the Maine Backwoods*—a required book for anyone's Maine bookshelf.

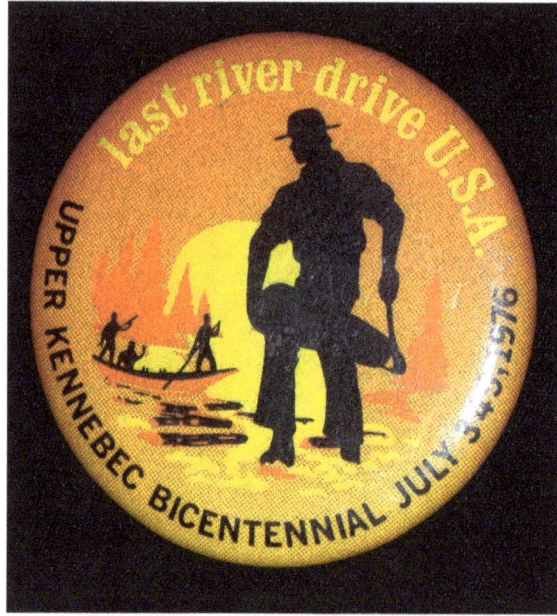

A pinback button commemorates
the final river drive on Kennebec River
and in the United States
on July 3 and 4, 1976,
during the nation's bicentennial.

photo by David Cass

the railroads

From an early age, I learned where to look for railroads each summer. The first one was the out-of-use Skowhegan branch that had run between Route 201 and the Kennebec River north of Waterville. It surprised me one summer to see it being rebuilt to service the new paper mill at Shawmut. The rails north to Skowhegan were removed, but the old railroad bridge in Skowhegan remained a footbridge until it washed away during the big floods of 1987.

The venerable old station disappeared back in the 1950s, long before our time in Maine. The yard once stood behind the information center and in front of the foot of the Skowhegan Indian statue, erected in 1969.

We clattered across the Bingham branch of the Maine Central Railroad just south of the village of Bingham. After another mile or so, the railroad crossed Route 201 again on its way to the Quimby Veneer Mill. Occasionally we saw a freight train in Bingham. I can remember a few occasions when I heard train whistles, often when we were at the Yellow Bowl.

On August 15, 1978, Maine Central GP7 575
pulls freight cars across the upper Route 201 crossing at Bingham.
photo by Chris Coyle

I sometimes saw a yellow GP7 engine pulling freight cars back and forth over the crossing for the spur into the veneer mill. Pulpwood cars sat off on sidings for loading. Although the engine house was long gone, the turntable remained in use, mainly by snowplows. One summer, many years ago, Dad shipped boxes of rocks by rail from the Bingham freight station. Our friend Wilder Rollins became interested in the railroad after he retired and used to go down to Bingham yard to watch the train when it came into town.

I ventured into the Bingham yard one afternoon in August of 1978 when I was seventeen and took photographs of the track layout. The sectionman happened to be there patrolling the track, and I told him of my interest in the railroad. He brought me into the section house and gave me several items, including a set of track plans for Bingham, some crossing signs, and a spike puller. He also let me photograph the Fairmont M19 track car in the shed.

Before they got torn up, tracks marked the view northward into Bingham yard in August, 1978.

photo by Chris Coyle

Years later, Dave Cass and I purchased the very same Fairmont car, number M1107! Section crews used such cars to maintain tracks so they did not have to be on foot for miles. Track cars could carry a few tool boxes and supplies. They could also pull one or more trailers. Although we had visions of running the car on tracks of abandoned railroads, we never did so and eventually sold the car. After that, we confined our railroading to models.

After the Quimby Veneer Mill closed in the early 1970s, there was much less railroad business in Bingham. I fortunately photographed a freight train at Bingham in the summer of 1978 when laborers took boxcars of machinery out of the old veneer mill. We went down to Riverside Restaurant for refreshments after taking my photos. The train crew also walked over for lunch. I talked with the crew for a little while, and they told me that, even though the track to Bingham was in fairly good condition, they knew it would be abandoned before long.

The freight station and log pulp cars no longer functioned after 1977 when rail service to Bingham ended.

photo by Bob Coyle

The line was indeed abandoned north of North Anson in 1979. Reverend Doug Drown later collected the Bingham Depot milepost, repainted it, and placed it in the vestibule of the new Bingham Area Health Center on the site of the depot. A plaque on the wall explains it is the milepost and provides a history of the Somerset Railway.

Although the depot at Bingham yard on Main Street has been gone for many years, the depot at Bingham Heights on Murray Street still stands in use as a residence. When they ran all the way to Rockwood, through trains used that depot on the Somerset line. An excursion group of Massachusetts Bay Railroad Enthusiasts traveled the line from Oakland to the end of track at North Anson in 1985 in the Guilford Rail System inspection train. I really wish I had gone to Maine to participate in that ride.

Robert E. Hunnewell, a lifelong resident of Bingham and Pleasant Ridge wrote the book *Bingham—Gateway to the Maine Forest*. He describes a very exciting day on the railroad south of Bingham.

Walter Hughes was about fifteen years old and was living at the Frank Curtis farm on Route 201 between Bingham and Solon. It seems one day around noon a call for help came over the Farmers Telephone Cooperative. A mix-up had been made in train orders, and a northbound freight out of Solon and a southbound freight out of Bingham were on the same track. Long-legged Walter made a streak for the distant tracks and arrived just as the northbound train came around a curve. He jumped between the rails and waved his red bandanna. The southbound train came into sight. He stood there frantically waving the bandanna. The engineers caught the signal and came to a stop only a few feet apart.

Walter certainly qualifies as the hero of that day and averted what surely would have been a head-on collision.

A little way up Bingham Hill after leaving Route 201 and beginning our bouncy ride east over Route 16, we crossed the long-abandoned roadbed of the Somerset Railway on its trek toward the shores of Moosehead Lake at Rockwood. We drove north every year along the old grade from Mayfield crossing on Route 16 to at least Lake Moxie and often farther to Harris Dam on Indian Pond in an all-day affair. We viewed various sites and usually ate a picnic lunch somewhere along the way. The route offers the best drive along an abandoned railroad in New England as one can drive some thirty miles over the old grade before reaching the foreboding waters of Indian Pond where Harris Dam of Central Maine Power has flooded out the old line.

When special company came to visit us, one landmark we often showed them was the Trestle until it was dismantled in 1976. It stood high over Gulf Stream on the line's climb in elevation up to Deadwater several miles north of Bingham Heights. With construction of the Somerset Railroad extension from Bingham north to Moosehead Lake, the crossing of Austin Stream at its widest part presented a major engineering challenge. At 700 feet long and 125 feet high, the Gulf Stream Trestle served as one of the largest such railroad structures in New England.

We often drove visitors to see the long-abandoned Gulf Streaam trestle, left.
In its heyday c. 1910, the trestle north of Bingham qualfied as one of the largest in New England.

photo, left, by Bob Coyle • postcard from the collection of Chris Coyle

Dad said that, when he first went up there, one could still drive over the formidable structure. I only remember the trestle after it was blocked off and we drove around it on a detour. The return trip from Moxie Pond usually involved driving west to The Forks and then south on Route 201. The Kennebec and Dead Rivers join to become one waterway at The Forks, making the town a stopping off point for river drivers years ago. Upon reaching Bingham, we often went to Riverside Restaurant for a pizza before heading back to the cabin.

Several other former railroad bridges along the line became fitted with planks to permit auto travel. I remember one time when we drove south from Moxie Pond to Mayfield Crossing, we found the planks across one such bridge in terrible repair. Gaping holes in the bridge marked spots where planks had rotted away. Mother got out of the car to direct Dad how to steer across the bridge and avoid the holes, which spelled trouble. I got out from the backseat, walked across the bridge, and sat down on a rock to watch the happenings. Dad got the car safely across without incident, and we proceeded on our trip.

Somerset Railway began building its line from Bingham north to the shore of Moosehead Lake in 1904 through wild country. Even the names of uninhabited townships sounded from another land—Upper Enchanted, Lower Enchanted, Misery Gore, Ten-Thousand-Acre Tract, Indian Township, East Moxie, Chase Stream, Squaretown, Soldiertown, and many others. Mosquito, a station stop on the Somerset extension, later renamed Troutdale, undoubtedly appealed more to would-be sportsmen than the thought of being eaten alive by insects while trying to enjoy the great outdoors.

Legends and stories soon grew as the railroad entered the area including tales of the dingmale, a creature heard but never seen. In his book *The Old Somerset Railroad*, Walter Macdougall tells more

> of the devil dancing on a camp roof in Enchanted Township, of phantom figures walking the tote roads, of snarled chains that foretold of death, and ghost lights that haunted the night.

Various strange occurrences befell trains operating through the area after establishment of regular service. Mr. Macdougall relates a number of such stories. Vast tracts of wilderness remained in the area when we summered in Mayfield, and I never felt the need to explore anywhere after dark.

There were still a few old railroad buildings standing and used as camps—the twin section houses at Baker Stream, Bald Mountain Station at the spur's junction with the main line, Troutdale Station, and Lake Moxie Station. One of the Baker

Around 1910, Somerset Railway renamed Mosquito Station north of Bingham, top, to Troutdale. Lake Moxie Station stood around 1920 near Caribou Narrows on the north end of Moxie Pond.

photo, top, and postcard from the collection of Chris Coyle

Stream buildings was listed for sale in 2010 with several interesting photographs along with a summary of the building's amenities such as its unique twelve-volt, direct current electrical system.

Hollingsworth and Whitney ran their own logging railroad spur in and around their Bald Mountain operation for a number of years. Omar Sawyer served as superintendent of the spur. I drove into the area with Omar's son Donald back in the summer of 1999.

Omar Sawyer, Don Sawyer's father, superintended the Bald Mountain logging spur, curving right past the site of Bald Mountain Station.

photo by Chris Coyle

We found the former railroad bed dirt all the way to Moxie Pond. It was exciting to drive through rock cuts, across fills, and over the same bridges where trains of old had run. Although paved north of Moxie Pond, the roadbed measured somewhat narrow in comparison to other secondary roads. At Indian Pond, we saw a small settlement for Central Maine Power employees who worked at Harris Dam.

At Somerset Junction, the Somerset line ran under the Moosehead subdivision of Canadian Pacific Railway. Greatly enlarged Indian Pond created by Harris Dam has submerged much of the old roadbed. One particular stop on the Somerset, Marr's Camps, remains above water but can be reached only by boat, crossing ice in the winter, or via a very long walk through the woods.

After trains stopped running north of Bingham, it took another three years to lift the rails of the upper Somerset line. To bring patrons to his isolated camp, Mike Marr, owner

An old railroad bridge south of Somerset Junction provided access for trains.
photo by Chris Coyle

of Marr's Camps made up a little contraption to run on abandoned rails. No doubt he was rather shocked one afternoon to meet a very rare freight extra.

I became keenly interested in the two-foot gauge railroads of Maine, all of them abandoned for several decades by my young teen years. Maine had a disproportionately large number of two-foot, narrow gauge railroads. In December, 1973, I purchased the January, 1974, edition of *Model Railroader* magazine. The advertisement on the back cover caught my eye for the new book *Ride the Sandy River* by L. Peter Cornwall and Jack Farrell. "Explore the past on America's largest two-footer, the Sandy River and Rangeley Lakes Railroad of Maine," said the advertisement. Well, since I was born in Maine, had always spent summers there, and had an avid interest in railroads, I decided the book and the former railroad were worth looking into. The following year, I bought the book.

I checked out Linwood W. Moody's *The Maine Two Footers* from the Bingham Union Library the following summer. My mother had read it when I was young. In fact, her name remained on the checkout pocket glued to the inside of the back cover.

We soon made a trip to see what was left of the Monson Railroad, the closest to our cabin. Monson Railroad is one of very few with all its depots, albeit just two, still standing. Once I had saved enough money, I purchased *Ride the Sandy River* the following winter.

The Monson Railroad, once considered the smallest railroad in the United States, served as a common carrier two-foot, narrow gauge railroad operating between the town of Monson and Monson Junction in the town of Abbot with many spurs serving slate quarries in the Monson area.

A two-foot gauge railroad train prepares to leave Monson Station around 1920.
photo from the collection of Chris Coyle

The railroad used old-fashioned link-and-pin couplers until the last day of operation in 1943. Yet, even though the railroad never modernized its equipment, Monson Railroad became the first railroad in Maine to have a completely rock-ballasted main line using rock as broken slate scraps from the quarries. A combination coach-baggage car provided necessary accommodations for passengers, baggage, and the US mail.

Many slate monuments, electrical switchboards, roofs, and gravestones across the country began their trip on the Monson Railroad. Locomotives 3 and 4, owned by the Maine Narrow Gauge Railroad Co. & Museum in Portland, Maine, survived at least into the third decade of the twenty-first century.

Inside the old station at Monson Junction, I picked up a handful of moldy waybills and other paperwork, all from the Bangor and Aroostook Railroad that shared the station, although I found none from Monson Railroad. Also at the junction, I found remains of the turntable used only for turning snowplows, not for locomotives as they ran forward in one direction and backwards the other way. My folks and I also located the cistern servicing water plugs for Monson's steam locomotives.

At Monson proper, the station stood unpainted but in good condition and the foundation of the two-stall engine house nearby. Gary Kohler and I found one of the Monson's unique banjo switch stands on its side with a two-inch sapling growing up through the middle. Monson Railroad used old style stub switches.

Abandoned Monson Junction Station in Abbot Village had slate shingles and Guilford yellow paint.

photo by Chris Coyle

Nicknamed the Two-by-Six a distance between the rails of two feet and the main line from Monson Station south to Monson Junction ran six miles, although the line had spurs and sidings operating over quite a deal more mileage. My folks and I explored some of the spurs. Moosehead Manufacturing Company used several former Monson Slate Company buildings in the 1970s. Moosehead made high quality furniture and operated from 1947 until about 2007.

Several very deep quarries had provided profitable slate veins in Monson in the late nineteenth through the mid-twentieth century. Some were dry by the 1970s while some had filled with water. One had become a dump. I remember throwing a rock over the edge into the abyss and waiting a considerable time until I heard it hit something down in the hole. When the slate quarries operated full time, electric two-foot gauge trains ran in the underground mines.

We drove over to Phillips where I discovered Sandy River and Rangeley Lakes Railroad, SR&RL country and the fledgling Sandy River Railroad Park. I gradually found where the railroad went through most of the towns. Before long, I volunteered at the Sandy River Railroad Park for several summers in my teens. I met Homer Beers at the Park in 1977. In 1986, Homer and I embarked on a fourteen-year, part-time project of hiking the entire abandoned 117-mile system of the SR&RL. Dave Cass joined in for several summers.

Maine had not only a disproportionate number of two-foot gauge railroads but also some other non-standard gauge lines such as the five-foot, six-inch or Portland gauge of the Grand Trunk Railway. At the other end of the track gauge spectrum ran the eighteen-inch industrial trackage of American Thread Company's spool mill in Milo.

At the Seashore Trolley Museum in Kennebec,
the family rode old-time trolleys on the former roadbed of the Atlantic Shore Line Railway.

photo by Bob Coyle

I sometimes convinced Dad to stop at the Seashore Trolley Museum in Kennebunk on our trip to the cabin. We rode the old-time trolley cars on the former roadbed of the Atlantic Shore Line Railway. The museum boasts an excellent gift shop where I purchased engrossing material to read during our stay at the cabin.

After I became an active model railroader in my teen years, I became aware of a small manufacturing firm, Dyna-Model Products Company located in Sangerville, Maine, and not all that far from the cabin. So, one afternoon in August of 1975, we drove over to Guilford and across the Piscataquis River to Sangerville. I did not have a street address, so we stopped at the Sangerville Post Office and inquired as to the firm's location. The clerk drew me a map of how to find them, and it was a good thing he did, as we never would have found the place by just driving around.

We located the small building outside the owner's house after driving over a series of back roads. Operated by Percy and Marie-Luise Kemp, the firm did not have a store or retail presence but nevertheless greeted us warmly and showed us through the small plant. They described the process of putting their kits into saleable form. They said that many of their kits, although not advertised as such, are models of specific buildings based on nearby struc-tures that they measured and, in many cases, scaled down to better fit a model railroad. One represented their grist mill located in Dover-Foxcroft.

A. W. Gilman Grist Mill at Dover-Foxcroft offered flour, grain, feed, seeds, lime, cement, hay, and straw sold wholesale and retail.

photo by Chris Coyle

Maine Central Railroad, owned by CSX in 2024, operates a few interior Maine rural branches originally constructed and operated as independent railroads. I have often thought that one of the branches would be a good prototype for a model railroad. It could include most operating highlights of the line along with a nice terminal facility at one end and a con-nection with the main line at the other end. A particular feature such as a mill or big trestle on one of the lines might serve as the highlight of the layout.

The small town of Harmony is south of Wellington, our mail hub. Harmony served as northern terminus of Maine Central's Harmony Branch until 1966. Built as the Sebasticook and Moosehead Lake Railroad and projected to reach the riches of the Moosehead Lake area, the line originated at a connection with the Maine Central in Pittsfield. It ran north through Hartland, where I was born, then along Great Moose Lake, past the Wild Goose Club, and tied up at Harmony with a compact little terminal facility.

Down East magazine once published an entertaining article about the branch entitled "When All Was Not Harmony on the Harmony Line." Some real characters worked on the line years ago, such as Conductor Bert Pettengill who appointed himself superintendent, Hartland Division, Maine Central Railroad. He proceeded to issue his own special orders much to the non-amusement of Morris MacDonald, general superintendent of Maine Central. Fuming, MacDonald finally had his business car tacked to the rear of a train destined for Pittsfield where he put things right with Mr. Pettengill.

Maine Central abandoned the nine miles of track north of Hartland when the northern portion of the line no longer turned a profit. The large tannery in Hartland kept the southern portion of the branch in the black. I remember occasionally poking into the abandoned railroad yard at Harmony in the 1970s. Not too much remained of the railroad, but I could easily see vestiges of the small terminal area with lots of cinders on the ground, as I recall.

Most of the Bangor and Aroostook Railroad, the B&A, lies within an area called The County, that is Aroostook County, the nation's largest county by land area east of the Rocky Mountains. I became familiar with what remained of B&A's nearby Greenville branch, once the Bangor and Piscataquis Railroad.

The company abandoned and removed all

Aroostook Potato — The Kind We Grow in Maine

B & A 321

In a 1930s artist's rendering, a legendary Aroostook potato dominates a flat car.

postcard from the collection of Chris Coyle

track west of Guilford in 1962. The remainder of the branch from Guilford east to Milo was gone by the end of 1964. The old freight house still stood at Guilford during the years we summered in Mayfield. I remember the B&A crossing on Route 15 near Upper Abbot in the 1960s shortly after the removal of the rails, but the ties stayed very visible.

Dave Cass, the folks, and I made a trip to Northern Maine Junction in Hermon, west of Bangor, in 1986. The B&A crossed the Maine Central at Northern Maine Junction containing a large yard, roundhouse, car storage, offices, and a long unused coal tower from the days of steam.

With direction from our friend Bob Buck, railfan extraordinaire, as to what to do, we drove into the junction that August morning and parked at the office building. I asked the receptionist for permission to walk about the yard and photograph the equipment.

Built in 1950, a Bangor & Aroostock GP7 engine waits at Northern Maine Junction in 1986.

photo by Chris Coyle

She replied that they would be pleased to host us, had us sign releases, and asked us not to go inside any buildings or climb on locomotives or cars. Then she asked if we would like to see the railroad's gift shop.

We expressed interest, of course.

As of 1986, the railroad was just exiting the passenger business in the form of buses by that time. I purchased a travel bag with the railroad insignia, a video tape of the railroad's history, and several small items. I can recall seeing several Bangor and Aroostook Railroad buses at the campus circle at the University of Massachusetts, Amherst, during my undergraduate years in the early 1980s.

We spent enjoyable hours at the Northern Maine Junction and shot several rolls of film. I recall photographing old BL2s, the only such locomotives I have ever seen; unused F units, a former World War II troop sleeper converted to a caboose; refrigerated potato cars, classic red, white, and blue State of Maine boxcars, and the old coal tower. I also photographed a Maine Central train led by the same locomotive wrecked beyond repair a year later in a three-train wreck at East Fitchburg, Massachusetts, yard.

As I grew into my teen years, I became aware that Maine had passenger rail service on one railroad. The Canadian Pacific Railway International of Maine line bisects the northern part of Maine and saves many miles of track over an all-Canada route. The Atlantic Limited, CPR's long-distance passenger train that ran between Montreal's Windsor Station and St. John, New Brunswick, served two remote stations on the Moosehead Subdivision in our area—Jackman and Greenville Junction.

One train ran in each direction daily, but station stops in Maine occurred in the middle of the night. As I never asked my folks to drive me to one of the stations to see the nocturnal train arrive, I never got to see them. I do remember seeing well-kept station buildings with train order boards into the 1980s, something by then long gone from other lines I knew.

A Bangor & Aroostock caboose converted from a World War II troop sleeper
waits at Northern Maine Junction in 1986 in front of several Maine Cenral pulpwood cars, top.
Maine's last passenger train in the 1970s stopped at the station at Greenville Junction.

photos by Chris Coyle

VIA Rail Canada, born in 1977, is the Canadian version of Amtrak. After some ups and downs, the company announced passenger service across Maine abolished forever on December 31, 1994. As I had wanted to ride this line for decades, my friend Jim Rock and I made arrangements to travel on VIA's Atlantic run in July 1993.

Although the train traversed Maine in the middle of the night, I sat up in the dome car on the return trip west until all hours. The train ran across the famous Ship Pond Viaduct also called the Onawa Trestle west of Brownville Junction. Then we sped past Onawa, a remote settlement reached only by train unless walking or with the help of an animal until 1960.

Eastbound and westbound trains swapped crews and US customs agents at Kyleton siding just east of Greenville. Then, illuminated by moonlight to reveal sights I will never forget, the train ran west along the shore of Moosehead Lake. At one point, the conductor popped his head up to the dome section where I rode alone and asked if I would like him to dim the lights so I could see better. What a great development, as I could look far ahead along the train where the headlight of the locomotive illuminated the dark countryside and lineside block signals sprang to life. I retired to my sleeping compartment at 4 a.m. for a couple hours of sleep.

The Scoot, a steam-powered mixed train, served the remote settlements of the Moosehead Subdivision until 1960. Mixed trains were freight trains with a passenger car to serve areas in which there weren't enough riders to warrant a full passenger train, but those

In the early 1980s, the station at Greenville Junction hosted one of the last train order boards.
photo by Chris Coyle

who did ride the train really depended on the service. The Scoot operated between Megantic, Quebec and Brownville Junction, Maine. The Scoot pulled Canadian Pacific's pay car, the last in use on a North American railroad. Pay cars, originating in the days of rail service to wild frontier lands, made it possible for railroads to pay cash to their employees at remote locations far from settlements and banks. Such was the case in northern Maine through the 1950s. The Scoot was the next to last steam-powered first-class train in the country. Steam locomotives needed equipment such as the octagonal enclosed water tank at Greenville Junction.

I've spent many a winter night relaxing where it is nice and warm reading about Maine's fascinating railroad and lumbering history. A particularly fascinating story involves the existence of two steam locomotives that survive far from any roadway in a remote area of the Allagash. I never did get deep into the Maine woods to see the lonely engines but read about them in old issues of *Down East* magazine and books from the Bingham library.

Track workers, top, ride a car approaching the Onawa trestle.

photo by Chris Coyle

In the early part of 1926, one of the last big time independent lumbermen, Edouard "King" Lacroix, pronounced la-CrWAH, laid out a thirteen-mile line from the west shore of Eagle Lake along Chamberlain Lake and south to Umbazooksus Lake. There, logs picked up from Eagle Lake got dumped into the Penobscot watershed and driven downriver to the huge Great Northern mill at Millinocket.

While other men might have given up building the railroad as impossible, King Lacroix succeeded. Lombard log haulers moved material and equipment under his direction across frozen ground and lakes to accomplish the task with no railroad tracks for moving them. Frozen ground and iced-over lakes made it infinitely easier to move the heavy equipment in winter rather than in warmer seasons.

Chris sits in the cab of the Maine Central 470 engine on display at Waterville in 1974.

photo by Bob Coyle

He brought two used steam locomotives converted from burning coal to burning oil. That reduced the likelihood of their cinders starting a dreaded forest fire once they were back in operation.

The line known officially as Eagle Lake and West Branch Railroad included the two converted locomotives. The railroad operated until a decline in paper prices due to the Great Depression.

In September of 1933, the two locomotives were run into the engine house at Tramway and their boilers blown down. Then they cooled off forever and remained to avoid the cost of taking them out.

Much Eagle Lake and West Branch trackwork remained in place, and forest wardens used a track car to patrol the woods. After the Maine Forest Service mistakenly burned the engine house with the locomotives inside back in 1969, volunteers have somewhat stabilized the ancient unused locomotives over the years.

As I grew older and became more knowledgeable about past and present railroads of Maine, I kept a keen eye out for them on our travels. I particularly enjoy traveling along roads that paralleled or cross railroad tracks several times. I grew skilled at spotting abandoned railroad grades and looked for remnants of bridge abutments and other artifacts.

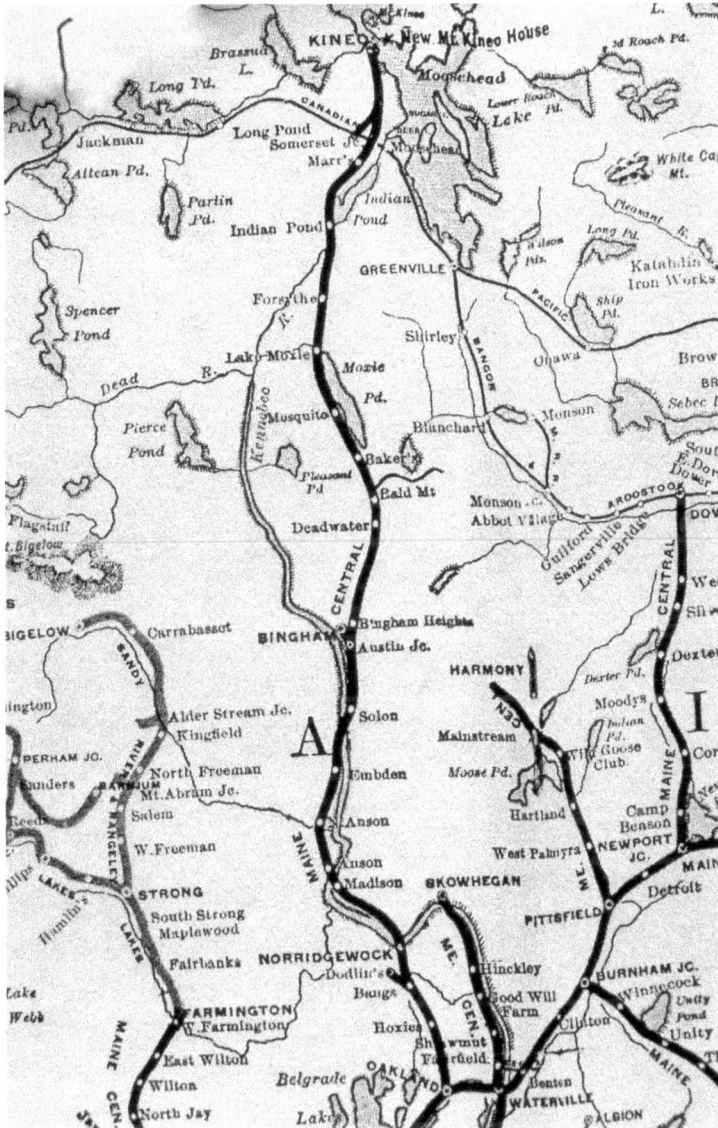

A 1915 map shows railroads in the Bingham region.

map from the collection of Chris Coyle

our maine summers conclude

We learned in 1981 that Don Sawyer planned to retire that year. The Sawyers wanted to spend summers at the cabin but told us that we could come up in the fall. As Dad still taught science in junior high school and I attended college we knew that would not work for us. Therefore, at the end of our 1981 stay, we packed up items we had kept at the cabin over the winter and said goodbye after twenty-three years to our summer home.

In twenty-three years, we had rarely missed a summer in Maine. We had not gotten to the cabin in the summer of 1962 as Dad was busy with coursework at BU, and that same August we moved to Athol from Boston.

I will never forget growing up summers at the cabin in Mayfield. Not only did I find ways to keep myself amused, but I learned how to live without a lot of material things. In the years that followed, we stopped at the cabin from time to time. One such visit remains vividly in my mind.

Barbara Coyle
photo by Chris Coyle

While doing some explorations in the area, Homer Beers and I drove down the driveway to the cabin in August of 2002. The Sawyers were just leaving for Bingham to join some friends for dinner. They invited us to sit on the porch after they left. Homer and I each opened a can of cold Moxie and sat down. As I sat looking at the familiar sights at Kingsbury Pond, everything came back to me. My body welled up with emotion, and my mind went back in time to several decades earlier.

After their passings in 2013 and 2015, I brought a portion of my parents' combined ashes back to Maine to return them to the earth via the brook that ran near our little log cabin on Kingsbury Pond. My good friend, the Reverend Douglas W. Drown, officiated at the committal service there at the brook. Doug had been minister at the First Congregational Church of Bingham from 1976 to 2008.

Homer Beers, my friend of forty years, and his

wife, Elisa, from Ontario accompanied me. Jackie Pike, who, like me, volunteers at the Sabbathday Lake, Maine, Shaker community and her friend Gerry Estabrook, joined us from the Blue Hill area.

We found a little clearing next to the brook after parking our cars near where our mailbox had stood decades before. During the service, Doug and Jackie sang "Shall We Gather at the River?" with Gerry on the Dobro resonator guitar while I gently poured my parents' earthly remains into the cool mountain stream.

Homer and Elisa scattered fresh lilac blossoms from Jackie into the water. Half a century of memories came back to me. After my birth at the little hospital in Hartland, my folks brought me to the nearby cabin in the summer of 1960 when I was only a few days old. I glanced over to the dirt driveway fifty feet away. From my mother's diaries, I had found that we spent 852 days of our lives at the cabin.

As I looked around at familiar hills and streams, I suddenly had insight into permanent and transient parts of life. Permanent are the hills, vales, streams, and ponds, but transient—indeed a glimpse in time—were our years at the cabin. I shed a tear but smiled with happiness, for I knew that my folks' lives were in the truest sense complete and they were, at long last, home.

Doug wrote to me afterward and told me that the gathering was one of the most touching and meaningful such events in all my ministry. I was very fond of Bob and Barbara and felt privileged indeed to have taken part in the service. The words you spoke were deeply moving, and I sensed keenly that you, I, and they shared, and share, that faith which is full of immortality.

I could not have agreed more.

As I write six decades after some of the events occurred, I am all too aware of how much that once remote area and, indeed, the world have changed in ensuing years. The backwoods character of Mayfield and Kingsbury is disappearing. Wind turbines stand upon mountaintops. Aerial photographs show woods roads everywhere. Cell phone service and other so-called improved methods of communication are creeping into the area. Traffic moves at quite a clip on much widened state highways where once travel went slow and leisurely with time to look around. It doesn't matter whether such changes are good or bad, for time marches on and nothing is constant but change. I am glad, however, to have experienced summers in that area of Maine when we did.

Bob Coyle
photo by Chris Coyle

How fortunate that my father's September to June teaching schedule provided the opportunity allowing us to spend part of each summer at the cabin where I shared my parents' interest and knowledge of the natural world. They imparted their knowledge to me during my growing years inimitably shaping the person I am today.

Chris displayed Mayfield memorabilia when he gave a presentation at the Old Canada Road Historical Society in 2009.

photo by Chris Coyle

our family's summer place

a reminiscence by Bob Coyle

Around 2005, my dad, Robert B. Coyle, who preferred to be called Bob, started writing stories about our many summers in the Maine woods. Some follow.

—Christopher Coyle

I found the part of Maine where our family spent summers when I took a six-week aerial geology field class in 1954. Boston University required the class of all of us undergraduate geology majors. Most of us worked our way through school, and the expensive aerial geology course, usually taken the summer between junior and senior years, meant not earning money for tuition with a summer job during that time.

Mark Emory Elementary School in North Anson provided space for classes held in one large room on the first floor with the other classroom on that level and all upstairs rooms used as dormitories for us geology majors. Dr. C. Wroe Wolfe, our instructor, had bought some not very sturdy war surplus cots that often collapsed under us as we slept. Since we worked out in the field all day, we tended to be so tired that the victim of collapse likely just slept the remainder of the night in whatever configuration he found himself. We took our meals in the basement cafeteria.

The course plan involved three all-day lectures on rainy days spread out over the six weeks. That year, we heard them all the first week, and we did most of the field work in the rainiest summer Maine had experienced in many years.

Dr. C. Wroe Wolfe's Boston University summer geology course headquartered at Mark Emory Elementary School in North Anson.

photo by Bob Coyle

Much of the time, we helped graduate students map bedrock and surface geology of several local quadrangles. For graduate students working on doctorates, quadrangle mappings would become thesis projects. The instructor also led trips to outstanding area geological sites.

Dr. Wolfe brought Bob and other BU students to study river terrace levels on North Anson farmland.

photo by Bob Coyle

The first trip involved a visit to an outcrop about halfway between Jackman and Greenville along the Canadian Pacific Railway. The rail route from west to east through Maine shortens the trip from Montreal to the Maritime Provinces by many miles. The deep cut Paleozoic rocks—old New England sedimentary rocks—had not, like most sedimentary varieties, metamorphosed. We easily recognized seashells, mainly of brachiopods, that formed limestone beds. Specimens taken close to the surface showed impressions of fossils only, while deeper in the rock, we found shells themselves intact.

The short hike to the outcrop went through thick Maine underbrush followed by a much longer walk along the railroad track. We perceived a disturbance in the bushes as we walked along. We all stopped. Out came a pair of calf moose who paid no attention to us.

We watched them feed on succulent plants along the side of the railroad and heard the sound of an approaching train. The two young animals drifted back into the underbrush. They counted as the first of many moose I would see in Maine.

Another time while climbing Tumbledown Mountain, my wife, Barbara, and I found a full-grown moose feeding high on the side of the peak in a type of lake created by the erosive activity of an Alpine glacier and called a tarn after the last Ice Age.

28 Averill Terrace
Waterville, Maine

May 12, 1958

Robert B. Coyle
Allegheny College
Meadville, Penna.

Dear Mr. Coyle:

Harold Labbee, realtor of Waterville, said you were interested in renting a camp in the Kingsbury Pond area for the summer, 1958.

I have a log cabin, built in 1951, situated on Kingsbury Pond which is for rent at $350 for the season.

It is 24 X 24 feet plus an eight foot porch across the front. There are two bed rooms, a kitchen, and a large living room, 13 X 24. It is finished off inside with knotty pine.

Cooking, lighting and refrigeration is with bottled gas. Heat is with a wood stove and there is ample supple of wood in the woodshed.

Plumbing is primitave and the little house is situated about 75 feet back of the camp in the woods. The lake water is suitable for washing purposes. We use drinking water from a spring which is at the head of the pond.

The camp is complete except for linen.

Very truly yours

Donald D. Sawyer

On May 12, 1958, Don Sawyer offered Bob rental of the Sawyers' log cabin in Mayfield. Then married to Barbara and an instructor at Allegheny College in Meadville,Pennsylvania, Bob had taken summer geology courses in and near Mayfield with Dr. Wroe Wolfe.

from the collection of Chris Coyle

We arrived at the Sawyers' cabin in Mayfield for the first time on June 20, 1958 after a drive of more than six hundred miles from our home in Pennsylvania—not that we did it in one day.

When packing to go to Maine, we knew we would be there all summer.

As summer in the north country may be very changeable, we learned fast to bring clothes for all seasons with the outdoor temperature usually cool at night and moderately warm in the day. We could seldom leave all the cabin windows open all night. I can think of only two nights over the years that we did not get up and close them before morning.

In Bingham, we went to a good old-fashioned grocery store, Preble and Robinson's housed in a large three-story wooden building. Besides purchasing our supplies there, we bought the best meat I have ever had in my life. We became friendly with the nice people who ran the store. On one of the hot days of summer, we had groused about the heat all the way to town. At the completion of our shopping, we put our goods on the old wooden check-out counter and remarked to Mrs. Robinson, how hot it was.

"My, yes," she smiled. "Isn't it wonderful?"

During cool weather that some years seemed to last the whole summer, we burned wood in the cabin's wood stove. It stood in the middle of the large living room and heated the entire building in short order. We kept a kettle of water on it, and one of the big pluses meant we could make toast on top of the stove. No toast equals stovetop toast. It's hot and moist with butter all melted into the bread. No toaster in the world makes such good-tasting fare. Doughnuts also constituted a special delight when heated on the stove.

When we had long stretches of cool weather, it seemed that I constantly brought wood in from the woodshed. When we first built a fire, we had a problem with the newspaper we used as a starter. Oftentimes, we used a *Christian Science Monitor* left over from the previous year's stay. I invariably found one or more articles I had to reread before consigning the paper to the flames. Barbara and Chris usually pressured me to finish the article quickly and get on with the job.

Sometimes in really cool weather, we had to leave the doors to the two small bedrooms open to let the heat in, and I got up once or twice in the night to add more wood. How wonderful to have the stove going, especially if the loons gave us a concert out on the lake.

Some summers, we had very few thunder and lightning storms. Other years, we might end about every day with one. They generally occurred in the middle of the afternoon and followed the slate ridges up from the southwest. The many ridges in the Kingsbury and Bingham quadrangles—Babbitt, Crockett, Coburn and Foster ridges, to name a few—are composed primarily of slate, the predominant rock of central Maine. Geologists call the area the Central Maine Slate Belt. We often heard rain pelting the lake over at Pine Point almost a half mile across the water while the sun still shone at the cabin. We found it fascinating to watch rain advance on us. Often, we could no longer see the tall trees at Pine Point.

The arrangement of underlying rocks strongly controls the topography in central Maine. Most rocks are metamorphic with lots of folded and tilted slates and quartzites, both very resistant to erosion and thus often forming hills and ridges. Often found as depressions surrounded by ridges of the harder rock, some granite, igneous intrusions do not resist erosion as well as metamorphic rocks.

One interesting result of such a rock structure involves formation of a trellis drainage pattern. Smaller streams flow into larger streams at right angles and on maps look like a trellis that someone might have in their rose garden.

One day during the summer of 1958, we explored the drainage pattern in Kingsbury Plantation when we came across an elderly man. He had stopped at one of the small streams crossed by Route 16, our main east-west road. Very friendly in a Maine sort of way, he told us he had a dipper to fulfill his mission for the day, taking a drink from each of the streams in his old town. The clear and cool water in each brook seemed pure.

His name was Adrian Robinson, and he told us that he had been born and raised in Kingsbury back when there were quite a few year-round homesteads. By the time we met him, only two or three households remained.

An elderly fellow, Manley Drake, lived alone in the old Robinson house located on the road to Campbell Hill in East Kingsbury. Mr. Robinson said that, when he was young, his parents did not have much money, that they grew most of what they ate and made most of their own clothes. He said they did not miss the worldly goods and had a very happy life on the farm.

A short way off, we saw woods fast invading a small

Adrian Robinson grew up in an East Kingsbury farmhouse later occupied by Manley Drake.

photo by Chris Coyle

cemetery on Foss Hill. Similar woods had taken over many farms and open places in town. Mr. Robinson's parents were buried in the Foss Hill Cemetery, and he wondered if he should have their remains moved to the more populous town to the south where he lived. We talked about the beautiful land in Kingsbury, how his parents had never visited the other town, and that we judged changes taking place natural as well as peaceful. Finally, the old man decided to leave them in the land they had lived on and loved.

We never met Mr. Robinson again, but often over the years we stopped at Foss Hill Cemetery and visited his family's graves.

Cook Hill has many happy memories for our family. Each year in early August with a sky good for viewing, we loaded up the car with blankets, flashlights, and food to watch one of nature's most dramatic displays. As evening came on, we drove to our favorite spot where the old and new roads met at the top of the hill. We had plenty of room to park away from "traffic," usually only three or four cars while we watched. We had plenty of room to look out at the vast sky.

From that point, we could see the ring of hills and mountains that surrounded us and below us several lakes and ponds in the valley. Many fir trees stood out on the northern horizon, and gradually, as light dimmed, they faded to black tower-like forms. They seemed to me like the Buddhist temples I had longed to see in Burma and Siam.

At last with the evening planets, we discovered the great stars—Arcturus in the west; Vega, Deneb and Altair, the summer triangle nearly overhead; red Antares to the south. One year, we saw a super brilliant red Mars, and at other times we found Venus, Jupiter, Saturn, and occasionally even Mercury.

Next, as fainter stars came out, we located familiar constellations—Lyra, Cygnus, Aquilla, Hercules, Bootes, Scorpius, and Sagittarius. We found even the faint Delphinius, Sagitta, and Corona Borealis and, to the north, the circumpolar constellations all in their proper places.

But most interesting to us were stars rising in the eastern sky—Pegasus, Andromeda, and especially Perseus, the last to appear and the focus of the display. First one to see the flash of a Perseid meteor called out, and the others tried to see it before it streaked away. As darkness of night increased, we witnessed still more and more meteors. They generally got brighter as the night wore on. Sometimes they left a glowing trail that slowly faded. Once, we even had two meteors in sight at the same time!

One excellent evening when Chris was quite small, we counted thirty-three meteors before we went back to the cabin. The display so impressed me that I got up long before daybreak. Chris and I went down to the dock to watch for more. They seemed much brighter, and we counted another thirty-three before the sky became too bright to see any more. While it was still dark and starry, the form of a night-flying great blue heron soared by over the lake. As it went by us, it gave out a loud croak!

We went back to bed with the rosy dawn after that special night.

By 1963, I had embarked on my own thesis project, mapping the bedrock geology of the Kingsbury US Geological Survey quadrangle. It required many field trips into remote woods to collect data armed with a notepad, magnifying glass, sledgehammer, and collecting bag. Knowledge of how to use a compass in conjunction with the US Geological Survey topographic map guided me on long hikes through remote territory that my research project entailed. At times, fellow graduate students, undergraduate helpers, and even Dr. Wolfe himself assisted me. Sometimes, I returned the gesture.

My undergraduate helper and I took a field trip north to Russell Mountain in Blanchard during the record wet summer of 1963. Chris and Barbara had other things to do in town and back at the cabin. A wild area composed of igneous and metamorphic rocks very much affected by glaciation, Russell stood at 2,187 feet as the highest point in the Kingsbury Quadrangle.

We had a long ride to the place where we planned to start our exploration of the mountain on the north side close to the Appalachian Trail. We began the long traverse toward the top of the mountain. We had not gone too far when a light, misty rain started. We decided to go on and hoped the precipitation would stop.

As we made our way through the woods and over the streams looking for rock outcrops, rain became heavier. After a few hours slogging through the rain, we came out to a small clearing with a log camp and outbuilding near Hussey Pond. Since the cabin's small porch provided cover, we decided to wait for the heavy rain to stop before we went higher on the mountain.

We didn't have much room there out of the rain, and after a while, it became obvious that the storm would keep on. We decided to head back to the car.

The rain got even worse. Small streams we had jumped across on the way up had become muddy, raging torrents, and we had to climb up the slope adjacent to each stream until we could find a place narrow enough to ford. Even though we went down grade, it took twice as long to get back to the car.

After reaching the car, we retraced our route toward home. When we came to the iron bridge over the Piscataquis River in Monson, we could see and hear changes that had taken place since we went over it in the morning. The stream that seemed only moderately high in the morning had grown to flood stage.

I stopped the car on the bridge. The river had cut a very handsome gorge downstream through almost vertical slates. We had previously found many potholes along the sides cut into bedrock by gravel swirled around by the current. As we watched the raging water from the bridge, we could even hear rocks grind against boulders by the river.

too late for extensive examination. Came out on trail on north side of Dead water Brook just about at beaver dam. App 2 miles back to car.
August 14 1963   Wet Wednesday   Down pour
Started at intersection 966 in Blanchard Quad. (8,8)
140 p. to Kingsbury Quad.
(600 p at brook)
station540 848 p.   oc up stream app. 10 p. of gray slate non-cal. Water very high.
Specimen K6 325   gray slate ~phyllite
1648 1st trail to west Hussey Pond   downpour went app. 600 p. to cabin on shore of Pond + waited about 2 hours for rain to stop – it did not, came back out in downpour no further outcrops
925 p. interesting pot hole in stream bed made in gray clay typical of that derived from the slate. On return trip the water was so high pothole was practically invisible.

Bob's August 14, 1963 field-notes describe
getting stuck in heavy downpour near Hussey Pond.
from the collection of Chris Coyle

175

Piscataquis River rushes through the gorge near Blanchard.
photo by Chris Coyle

What an experience! I had never before heard the formation of potholes.

We finally made it back to the dry cabin through the storm with its numerous flashes of lightning. It had, apparently, not rained at all there.

I think that summer had the most extensive lightning storm I have ever witnessed. Since the cabin lacked electricity and at the time no nearby camps had bright lights, we could easily observe electrical storms in the nighttime sky. The storm I remember never seemed to have a moment without flashes of lightning brightening the sky.

We got up from our beds and watched the tremendous storm raging all around us. Five-year-old Chris sat on a couch next to one of the windows to watch. We saw him take his flashlight and shine it out the window several times. When we asked him what he was doing, he said he was "giving it back to them!"

Fortunately, most summers in Maine are not that wet.

I don't think you can ever forget some sights. Take the time my son Chris and I decided to hike along the Appalachian Trail to the top of Bald Mountain near Moxie Pond not too many miles from the cabin. We had driven over an abandoned railroad bed to the spot where the trail crossed the former railroad transformed to a dirt road for cars and trucks.

We left the car there and climbed all the way to the crest of Bald Mountain. Long before digital cameras, we took slide images along the way and, since we were reading the J.R.R. Tolkien *Lord of the Rings* series aloud evenings at the cabin, we compared the woods we passed through with those described in these great stories.

After some time looking at the wonderful and wild view from the mountaintop, we began our descent. We considered a beautiful view of Bald Mountain Pond too good to miss, so we made the extra trek to the spectacular view where I took two remaining slide photos. Our detour proved a time-consuming mistake, and we grew very hot and tired from our long hike. We finally did make it back to the car.

On the drive home, we focused on blueberry pie and vanilla ice cream. As we reached the descent point on Cook Hill, we did not look too carefully at the dead moose illegally shot and with one leg removed and the rest of the animal left to rot. When we passed the cadaver on other days, we often saw ravens and other scavengers feeding on the carcass. That day as I glanced over my shoulder, I thought I saw a large animal at the moose.

I went a little distance down the hill before it registered on me that I had seen a big black bear feeding on the carcass. I backed up the hill and, sure enough, a large black bear held up the haunch of the moose and gnawed on the carcass. I had no film left to take a picture, but we watched for a while before the bear became aware of us. The bear dropped the moose with a loud clatter and ran off through underbrush into the woods.

We raced back to the cabin to get my wife, Barbara, and returned in short order to the moose. We could hear the bear in the woods, but it seemed reluctant to come out. About that time, a northern waterthrush, a small warbler, walked up to the moose and began to eat. I gave Barbara my field glasses, and she looked at the little bird. At that moment, the bear stood up on its hind legs in the underbrush and, glued to the field glasses, she missed the awesome spectacle. Chris and I, however, will never forget it.

One afternoon as we drove down the long driveway to the cabin, we found an immature northern goshawk up on the woodpile. It worked on a young snowshoe hare, large prey for such a young bird. It must have just caught the rabbit.

I turned off the ignition and let the car coast down to the cabin, which did not upset the hawk. It just continued awkwardly to pull apart its prey. Because of the nature of the wood-pile, the bird occasionally lost large chunks of meat through openings between the logs. When she finally finished eating the big meal, she wiped her beak back and forth on the nearest log and sailed off into the deep woods.

Very early the next morning as I went to shave at the dry sink in the kitchen with its window that looked out on the log pile, I discovered a red fox pulling out the fragments the young goshawk lost the day before. We all watched as the fox made a meal of the leftovers the bird missed. Not much goes to waste in the wild.

Owls have always been special to our family, and we have had good fortune seeing and hearing them in Maine. One day in the summer of 1973, my by then teenaged son Chris and I hiked over the abandoned stage road that connected Skowhegan with Greenville. As we ate our lunch in a small clearing, we spotted the first juvenile saw-whet owl either of us had ever seen.

The little woodland bird perched about four feet up in a spruce tree. He allowed us to get close enough to touch him, although we did not do so. I remember the rich chocolate-brown color of the bird that stood about seven inches in height and that he showed no fear of us giant strangers. It's likely he had never before seen a human.

The only other small owl we saw in Maine was the eastern screech owl. Bird publications claim they are very common. However, we have never found them easy to locate and have seen and heard only about a dozen during our years of birding. One evening when Chris was quite young, I played blocks with him on the living room floor at the cabin when I saw an uncommon shape in the swamp maple outside the window. The tree seemed to give up one lower branch each year of its life.

That year's dying branch made a favorite perch for the ruby-throated hummingbird that fed on nearby jewelweed. Flying insect eaters like the least flycatcher and alder flycatcher, eastern kingbird, and cedar waxwing often launched their sorties from that exposed perch. They grew fat and fed their young on abundant Maine insect life.

At first, I thought an owl sat on the branch but then decided it was only a bunch of dead leaves. Just as I told Barbara of my mistake, the bunch of leaves turned its head in our direction. The bird perched less than twenty feet away, and with binoculars, we could see it very clearly even in the fading light.

It was a most elf-like little bird-a screech owl. Screech owls are a little bigger than saw-whet owls and measure between seven and ten inches high. That one was a gray-phase bird. Screech owls also appear as red-phase, sort of like brunettes or blonds among people.

It's a wonder anyone ever sees screech owls, since they are so well-camouflaged and, of course, nocturnal, thus lessening the likelihood of seeing them in daytime.

The owl stayed until almost complete darkness and then took off on silent wings out over the marshy edge of the pond to search for its small prey.

We sometimes imitated screech owl calls and occasionally had a tremulous response from an owl in the vicinity.

Without doubt, we most often observed the ghostly barred owl, named for horizontal bars of dark brown on its upper chest. The word barred poorly distinguishes the bird, as several other owls show barring. When you say barred owl, people often think you are saying barn owl, and it takes a while to get it all sorted out. Barn owl qualifies as a legitimate species, but it is not the same species as barred owl.

The log walls and open windows of the cabin always let in sounds of nature. All you needed to do was become conscious of them—the lonely call of loons on the pond; snarls of bobcats, raccoons, and other mammals in the night; wind in the big white pines; rain hitting the cabin roof.

During one particular summer night, we awoke to the deep, husky calls of a barred owl—"Who cooks for you? Who cooks for you all?" We quietly put on our slippers and bathrobes and made our way onto the open front porch. The call originated from Skunk Hill, the ridge across the pond.

I returned the call.

After a response, I answered again.

A few minutes of complete silence followed.

Again the call, but then from Pine Cove—much nearer to us.

We kept up the dialogue and soon, the bird finally landed in a tree right over our heads.

Vulnerable is the word for our heads when we think of the owl's sharp talons, but we still shone our flashlights on our handsome nocturnal visitor. He had dark eyes, unusual for eastern owls. No ear tufts graced his rounded head, and we saw a striking, distinguishing pattern of so-called bars on his chest and belly.

He rotated his head in circles as he tried to find the source of the call that might have originated from a rival barred owl. The characteristic movement probably occurred because of his cone-shaped eyeballs that make it impossible to rotate his eyes as we do. Finally, as usual, he flew off, gliding on wings that seemed to measure from about four to five feet from wing tip to wing tip.

As with many other sightings, we heard him later as he made his way around the pond. And again later, farther away. We slept and heard him no more on any night that year, but every summer we renewed our acquaintance with the owl of our pond.

People do not see great horned owls, the terror of the night for many small-to-medium-sized animals, as often as they see smaller barred owls. We always consider it exciting when we do find one.

One day—July 25, 1964 at 3:25 p.m. to be exact, I went for a hike by myself down to Mayfield Corner, three quarters of a mile from the cabin. The destination still had two buildings left from the old days.

The game warden used the first building, a former small school, when he was in the area. Sometimes in fall, a deer hunter became lost. Searches got organized. The building made a good headquarters. It faced the abandoned stage road to Greenville but could be seen from the newer main route.

The other building was the abandoned Pooler farmhouse, used one summer to house a crew for a nearby logging operation. The building disappeared a year or two after that.

West of the old school, thick woods on either side of the road thinned out to former fields and orchard of the Pooler farm. I spied a huge bird sitting there in a dying Elm tree. I stopped. I realized I saw a great horned owl!

I had never before identified one of its species. I ran all the way back to the cabin, burst into the kitchen, and croaked to Barbara to come out. She promptly shut off what cooked on the gas stove, grabbed her binoculars and the toddler Chris, and rushed to the car. We drove back to Mayfield Center.

Surprisingly, the great horned owl still sat in the elm tree.

We quietly slipped out of the car and advanced to within a short distance of the magnificent bird. It turned its tufted head and looked at us, looked away for a while, and then again sought us out with his keen eyes. Then, it dropped from its perch and flew on huge silent wings into the dark forest.

Only then did I remember the camera on the front seat of the car. What a picture I could have had to show. Barbara and I have mental pictures of that memorable encounter. Chris was a little young to remember the event.

Some years later, deep calls of two great horned owls awakened me. They seemed to call from directly over the cabin. Their call is shorter and deeper than calls of the barred owl.

Both cabin doors had noisy latches, and I felt that the sound of opening them could scare the birds. I finally chose the door to the porch that faced the pond. As I opened the door, two huge owls dropped down from the roof of the cabin and flew out over the surface of the pond made golden by the dawn. Even though they flew low over the water, the sun lit up both birds from below, perhaps a reflection, as it rose over the eastern ridge.

What a sight!

They went to the huge trees at Pine Point and landed there. I roused Barbara, and she saw them through binoculars and telescope. We watched until they disappeared into the woods to sleep away the day at a secluded roost.

Probably long-eared owls inhabit the forests of Mayfield and short-eared owls hunt the bogs and meadows. Someday, we may see them, too.

In winter, snowy, great gray, hawk, and boreal owls sometimes make their way to snowy Mayfield, but so far, we have never been there at that season, so we can only speculate about their visits. I think that barn owls are so rare in New England that none visit the Mayfield area. In fact, I have seen only one barn owl anywhere in the wild, and it wasn't in Maine.

Our neighbor Tom loved the wildness of the area near our cabin and his with loons, deer, moose, and other animals. He nevertheless felt the need of some domestic animals, too. So every year he brought up two, three, or four ducks, which he called his quack-quacks. At first, he stayed at the camp only weekends, leaving the birds very lonely. They were so glad when they found we had moved in next door. Quacking all the while, they often waddled up to the cabin where we gave them some company and a handout.

Whenever we went into the pond, they joined us and tried to become human beings. Whenever we went swimming, they tried to act just like us and splash in imitation. Often, we looked out and saw them trying to join up with other species, one day with a family of wood ducks. The mother wood duck brought her ten baby ducklings into the cove in front of the cabin. At once, two of Tom's ducks joined the line and tried to do everything the ducklings did. When mother woody spied them, she drove them off with no mercy.

Next, we saw Tom's ducks with a family of mergansers, narrow-billed diving ducks. They typically find food by submerging for it. Tom's ducks were mallards, a kind of dabbling

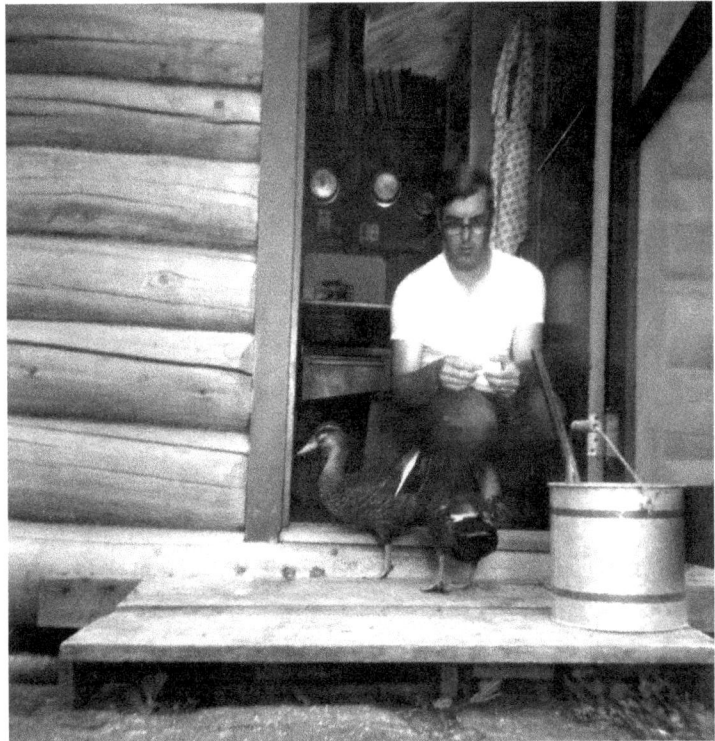

Bob feeds ducks at the cabin in 1972.
photo by Chris Coyle

duck that feeds mainly on the water surface or by turning bottoms up to feed on the shallow bottom. Tom's lonely ducks copied the mergansers and tried to dive under the surface of the pond. They followed the group for a while but did not stay with them.

Sometimes, Tom's ducks even tried to become loons. The aloof divers largely ignored them, and in short order, they came back to their favorite place in front of our camps.

Now and then, the ducks followed us when we walked up the long driveway to get our mail. As the walk became deeper into the woods, the birds grew increasingly uneasy and finally raced back in great fear to the water. Foxes, minks, goshawks, and other predators would have liked to dine on young duck, proving their fear legitimate.

Tom had planned to eat the birds for Thanksgiving that fall, but the next year when we asked about the birds, he said that some wild ducks finally accepted them and, as he had not clipped their wings, they had flown south with their adopted family.

Also when we stayed at the cabin, we sometimes took the opportunity to find moose. On occasion, we took a two-mile ride after supper to see if we might locate any moose in Bryant Bog, an old lake bed filling in with plants. It provided a great feeding place for moose, or so we thought, even though we didn't spot them there too often.

We did get to see a cow moose there several times. The first time, we were on the way to the Skowhegan Drive-In to watch a movie, and I just happened to see a dark form in the pool close to the road. We stopped and backed up. She moved a short distance away and continued to feed. Unfortunately, I did not have my camera.

But I saw her again soon after, and I did have the camera. She stood in the road a hundred or so feet ahead of us. I got out of the car and looked in the viewfinder. She appeared so small that I thought of moving nearer. She still looked small in the camera but big in the real world. She began to move off toward an old abandoned apple orchard, so I ran toward her and got my first good picture of a moose. Barbara called me to stop and return to the car.

What an exciting experience that was!

After our son Chris was born, we brought him to the cabin, and he loved it there most of the time. But one thing he especially did not like to do was to go down to Bryant Bog to look for moose. Even so, often after we ate supper, did the dishes, and cleaned up, we drove to the bog, parked in a spot we anticipated might reward us with a sighting, and waited. Chris soon got bored and asked to go back to the cabin.

One day we heard him say under his breath, "I will go quietly down to Bryant Bog and shoot all the moose!"

1964

The following birds were seen within the Kingsbury Quadrangle primarily around the Sawyer Cabin on the west end of the north shore of Kingsbury Pond in Mayfield, Maine. Time of observation was July and August 1964. The observer was Robert Coyle.

Date	Species	Where seen
7/1	Common loon	On Kingsbury Pond.
8/2	Great blue heron	Flying from Cook Hill toward ponds, p.m.
7/12	American bittern	On marshy ground e. of cabin on K. Pond
7/23	Black duck	Flying over Kingsbury Pond.
7/14	Wood duck	Female and 9 young in front of cabin.
8/16	Goshawk	Immature individual eating on log pile, in back of cabin. (well seen)
*8/6	Broad-winged hawk	In tree on way to King Hill with snake in talons.
7/19	Osprey	Over Kingsbury Pond from cabin.
8/23	Sparrow hawk	Nw of Wellington near waterfall, a family of 4 or 5 birds.
7/4	Ruffed grouse	Mother and young near game warden's station, Mayfield.
7/25(3:25pm)	Great horned owl	In dead tree app. 300 ft. from rt. 16 at Mayfield Center.
8/19	Common nighthawk	Pr. over Kingsbury Pond at dusk.
7/12	Chimney swift	Over K. Pond in front of cabin.
7/3	Ruby-throated hummingbird	Nest 20' up on branch in drive at camp.
7/12	Belted kingfisher	Over K. Pond from cabin.
7/4	Yellow-shafted flicker	At 2nd bend in drive to cabin.
7/1	Yellow-bellied sapsucker	Around cabin.
7/2	Hairy woodpecker	On log pile in back of cabin.
7/23	Downy woodpecker	In tree near Bryant Bog - a pr.
7/27	Eastern kingbird	Kingsbury Pd. picnic ground.
*8/4	Yellow-bellied flycatcher	At first bend in drive to cabin.
7/1	Least flycatcher	Edge of K. Pd. around cabin.
7/2	Tree swallow	Over K. Pd. in front of cabin.
7/14	Bank swallow	About a dozen nests in new gravel pit at Mayfield Center.
7/1	Barn swallow	Nest on front porch of cabin (4 young) first time - house torn down in May.Cen
7/9	Blue jay	On road toward Kingsbury.
7/1	Common raven	At Pine Point across from cabin, K. Pd.
8/27	Common crow	Pr. on cabin roof op. picnic grounds in Kingsbury.
7/9	Black-capped chickadee	On rt. 16 near cabin.
7/21	Boreal chickadee	Hill top west of Foss Pond.
7/1	White-breasted nuthatch	Tree beside cabin.
7/9	Red-breasted nuthatch	Rt. 16 near mailbox at end of drive.
8/14	Winter wren	Pair seen on granite hill in sec. 2 of Quad. while on traverse.
7/14	Catbird	In brush in front of cabin, K. Pond.
7/1	Robin	Nest at first bend of drive.

Page 1 of Bob's list of birds of the Kingsbury Quadrangle

Date	Species	Where seen
8/13	Wood thrush	Old road at Mayfield Center.
*8/4	Gray-cheeked thrush	On long trip to Mayfield Center.
7/2	Veery	Back of cabin.
*8/29	Ruby-crowned kinglet	On rd. to old gravel pit Mayfield.
7/1	Cedar waxwing	Nest 40' high in front of cabin.
7/2	Red-eyed vireo	In trees in back of cabin.
7/16	Black-and-white warbler	Old rd. Mayfield Center.
8/11	Nashville warbler	2nd curve on driveway, cabin.
7/9	Magnolia warbler	Near mailbox, cabin.
7/16	Black-throated blue warbler	Woods toward Kingsbury.
7/23	Myrtle warbler	Driveway 1st bend.
7/9	Blackburnian warbler	Family near mailbox, cabin.
7/9	Chestnut-sided warbler	Next camp down toward Kingsbury.
7/3	Ovenbird	Woods near cabin.
7/16	Yellowthroat	Mayfield Center near old barn.
7/19	Canada warbler	Female hit west window of cabin. Ok.
7/16	American redstart	Driveway at cabin.
7/1	Red-winged blackbird	Kingsbury Pd., Birch Point. Nest.
*8/28	Rusty blackbird	Small flock on Brighton rd. near Bryant Bog.
7/3	Common grackle	Flying over pond in front of cabin.
8/25	Brown-headed cowbird	Near small camp Kingsbury end of pond.
7/9	Rose-breasted grosbeak	Clearing near mailbox.
8/6	Indigo bunting	In brush below Game Wdn. cabin, Mayfield
7/9	Evening grosbeak	Pr. in driveway near mailbox, cabin.
7/3	Purple finch	Mayfield Center.
7/2	American goldfinch	On shore in front of cabin.
7/9	Slate-colored junco	On rd. toward Kingsbury.
8/6	Chipping sparrow	Pr. at Mayfield Center.
7/9	White-throated sparrow	Nest 2nd bend in driveway.
*7/22	Swamp sparrow	Bryant bog.
7/1	Song sparrow	Front of cabin.

A water thrush (probably Louisiana) was seen 8/2 near Mayfield Center but could not be positive of which species.

The following birds were heard but not observed this summer:
* 8/29(3 a.m.) Barred owl (once only) 8 hoots at least 3 times from pine tree right in back of cabin.

many times Pileated woodpecker   Heard in woods many times especially in early July--did not list dates as thought I would see during summer.

8/11   Wood pewee   Heard many times before date listed and many times after.

several times Scarlet tanager   Across street from mail box; heard in first half of July.

*Birds seen and/or heard in Quadrangle for first time this year.

Birds listed below have been seen in Quadrangle other years but were missing this year: red-breasted merganser, red-tailed hawk, red-shouldered hawk, killdeer, American woodcock, spotted sandpiper, great crested flycatcher, Eastern phoebe, alder flycatcher, cliff swallow, brown creeper, brown thrasher, hermit thrush, golden-crowned kinglet, Philadelphia vireo, warbling vireo, black-throated green warbler, northern water thrush, mourning warbler, bobolink, Eastern meadowlark, white-winged crossbill.

Page 2 of Bob's list of birds of the Kingsbury Quadrangle

The Years We Spent in Mayfield
by Barbara J. Coyle

These are the days we arrived and left the cabin each year. When we mention the cabin, it means only one place, the Sawyers' little log cabin in Mayfield, Maine, on Kingsbury Pond. Occasionally, we traveled from the cabin to another location, such as Bar Harbor or Quebec City, and stayed overnight, but our primary residence for the time was still Mayfield

year	arrived	left	days
1958	Friday, June 20, 1958	Tuesday, September 02, 1958	74
1959	June 8, 1959/Tibbetts June 20, 1959	Tuesday, September 01, 1959	86
1960	Tuesday, June 14, 1960	Sunday, September 11, 1960	89
1961	Monday, July 24, 1961	Wednesday, September 06, 1961	44
1963	Monday, July 01, 1963	Monday, August 26, 1963	56
1964	Wednesday, July 01, 1964	Tuesday, September 01, 1964	62
1965	Thursday, July 01, 1965	Tuesday, August 31, 1965	61
1966	Friday, June 24, 1966	Monday, August 22, 1966	59
1967	Monday, July 31, 1967	Thursday, August 31, 1967	31
1968	Wednesday, July 31, 1968	Thursday, August 29, 1968	29
1969	Friday, July 18, 1969	Tuesday, August 26, 1969	39
1970	Monday, July 20, 1970	Wednesday, September 02, 1970	44
1971	Thursday, August 05, 1971	Wednesday, September 01, 1971	27
1972	Friday, July 14, 1972	Thursday, August 17, 1972	34
1973	Thursday, July 12, 1973	Monday, August 20, 1973	39
1974	Thursday, July 25, 1974	Tuesday, August 27, 1974	33
1975	Friday, July 25, 1975	Wednesday, August 27, 1975	33
1976	Wednesday, August 11, 1976	Thursday, August 26, 1976	15
1977	Wednesday, August 03, 1977	Thursday, August 18, 1977	15
1978	Tuesday, August 08, 1978	Wednesday, August 23, 1978	15
1979	Thursday, August 02, 1979	Wednesday, August 22, 1979	20
1980	Monday, August 04, 1980	Sunday, August 24, 1980	20
1981	Thursday, August 13, 1981	Wednesday, August 26, 1981	13

Total number of days in Mayfield   852

*1959: arrived Bingham June 8, arrived Tibbetts June 20, left Sept. 1

Barbara's record of days spent in Maine

acknowledgments

First and foremost, I sincerely thank the late Donald and Norma Sawyer for sharing their wilderness retreat with us as we rented it for nearly a quarter of a century.

I corresponded with Don in later years, and he answered many questions about the area's history. I also thank Don for taking Homer Beers and me up to the old Hollingsworth and Whitney operation on Bald Mountain back in 1999. Don's son Dan Sawyer cleared up several matters as I wrote We Lived in the Woods, and I appreciate it. Don's nephew Don Nodine was also very helpful in answering more of my queries.

I am very grateful to the Reverend Douglas W. Drown for clearing up many questions I had about the part of Maine near the cabin on Kingsbury Pond. I am thankful as well for numerous discussions with Douglas Drown on ways to improve We Lived in the Woods.

Thanks also to the many kind people of central Maine who always made us feel welcome in the Pine Tree State.

Several friends from Bingham helped me over the years in my quest to learn about the history of the area. Thanks to the late Marilyn Sterling-Gondek of Bingham's Old Canada Road Historical Society for answering many questions and confirming other information.

The late Elizabeth Rollins Cummings sent me many articles from the Waterville Morning Sentinel about railroads. I appreciate her thoughtfulness. I have kept most of the things she sent me.

When I was in my teen years, the late Elizabeth Goodrich Jordan, former Mayfield teacher and later librarian of Bingham Union Library, answered a lot of questions about Mayfield's history.

I also extend appreciation to Dr. Everett Parker, Kelvin Kindahl, and Brian Damien of Maine Philatelic Society for clearing up several unanswered questions. Thank you to my publisher Marcia Gagliardi and my copy editor Debra Ellis for their many hours of editing. They have kept me on the straight and narrow.

A special thanks to the late Charlie Pooler, proudly self-described as the best poacher around who in 2011 at age ninety-five provided me a tour of old roads and sites of former homes in his old town of Mayfield. Charlie and his family were the last permanent residents of Mayfield. They left their old home in 1948 and moved to Bingham.

I extend sincere appreciation to David K. Cass for expert digitizing of images, discussion, and review of the manuscript.

And a big thank you to Susie Gaglia for inspiring me to see We Lived in the Woods through to completion.

maine bookshelf

The reader will find Maine topics of interest covered in further depth here.

Allen, Ardelle, called Ida. *Ida: A Happy Life in the Maine Backwoods*. Thorndike, ME. The Thorndike Press, 1979.

Benson, James E. *Postcard History Series: Along Old Canada Road*. Portsmouth, NH. Arcadia Publishing, 2008.

Blanchard, Fessenden S. *Ghost Towns of New England: Their Ups and Downs*. New York. Dodd, Mead & Company, 1960.

Calvert, Mary R. *The Kennebec Wilderness Awakens*. Lewiston, ME. Twin City Printery, 1986.

Coffin, Robert P. Tristram. *Kennebec: Cradle of Americans*. Camden, ME. Down East Books, 1965.

Coyle, Chris. "The Post Offices and Mail Delivery to Mayfield and Kingsbury, Maine." *The Maine Philatelist*. 42 no. 3. (July 2023): pp. 3-7.

Dow, Sterling T. *Maine Postal History and Postmarks*. Lawrence, MA. Quarterman Press, 1976.

Duplessis, Shirley. *Hidden in the Woods: The Story of Kokad-jo*. Greenville, ME. Moosehead Communications, 2001.

Fendler, Donn (as told to Joseph B. Egan). *Lost on a Mountain in Maine*. Rockport, ME. Picton Press, 1993.

Gagnon, Lana. *Chesuncook Memories*. Oscar Gagnon, 1974.

Gould, John. "The Train Ride that Mattered." *Christian Science Monitor*. April 11, 1974.

Gould, John. "The Wildest Ride in the History of Goatdom." *Christian Science Monitor*. November 7, 1986.

Grant, Gay M. *Images of America: Along the Kennebec*. Dover, NH. Arcadia Publishing, 1995.

Hall, Jon. F. *Images of America: The Upper Kennebec Valley*. Dover, NH. Arcadia Publishing, 1997.

Hall, Jon. F. *Images of America: The Upper Kennebec Valley*, vol. 2. Portsmouth, NH. Arcadia Publishing, 1999.

Hamilton, Nathan D. and Cynthia A. Thayer. *Images of America: The Moosehead Lake Region*. Dover, NH. Arcadia Publishing, 1995.

Hempstead, Alfred Geer. *The Penobscot Boom and the Development of the West Branch of the Penobscot River for Log Driving: 1825-1931*. Alfred Geer Hempstead, 1975.

Hilton, C. Max. *Woodsmen, Horses, and Dynamite: Rough Pulpwood Operating in Northwestern, Maine, 1935-1940*. Orono, ME. University of Maine Press, 2004.

The History Committee of the Bingham Sesquicentennial. *Bingham Sesquicentennial History: 1812-1962*. Skowhegan, ME. Skowhegan Press, 1962.

Hunnewell, Robert E. and Bea Bridges. *Bingham: Gateway to the Maine Forest*. 2006.

Jones, Robert C. *Two Feet to the Quarries*. Burlington, VT. Evergreen Press, 1998.

Kidney, Dorothy Boone. *Away from It All*. New York. A.S. Barnes and Company, 1969.

Kohler, Gary. *A Pictorial History of the Monson Railroad*. Washingtonville, OH. Pine Lake Publishing, 2011.

Macdougall, Arthur R. Jr. *The Old Lake Road*. Arthur R. Macdougall. 1977.

Macdougall, Walter M. (compiled and introduced by). *Remembering Dud Dean: Arthur Macdougall's Famous Tales of Everybody's Favorite Maine Guide*. Camden, ME. Countrysport Press, 2001.

Macdougall, Walter M. *The Old Somerset Railroad: A Lifeline for Northern Mainers*. Camden, ME. Down East Books, 2000.

Moody, Linwood W. *The Maine Two-Footers: The Story of the Two-Foot Gauge Railroads of Maine*. Berkeley, CA. Howell-North Press, 1959.

Moscow History Committee. *Makers of Moscow*. Skowhegan, ME. Skowhegan Press, 2015.

Parker, Dr. Everett L. *Railroads of the North Woods*. Greenville, ME. Moosehead Communications, 2002.

Pike, Robert E. *Spiked Boots: Sketches of the North Country*. Woodstock, VT. The Countryman Press, 1999.

Pike, Robert E. *Tall Trees, Tough Men*. New York. W. W. Norton & Company, 1999.

Reed, Jean Brown; French, Althea Haggstrom; and Emanuelson Davis, Elizabeth. *History of Monson, Maine: 1822-1972*. 1972.

Reynolds, Clifford S. *Of Love and the Kennebec*. Manchester, ME. Falmouth Publishing House, 1952.

Rice, Douglas M. *Log and Lumber Railroads of New England*. 3rd ed. Portland, ME. The 470 Railroad Club, 1982.

Rich, Louise Dickinson. *We Took to the Woods*. New York. J.B. Lippincott Co., 1942.

Sawtell, William R. *Katahdin Iron Works Boom to Bust*. Milo, ME. Milo Printing Co., 1982.

Sawtell, William R. *Onawa Revisited*. William R. Sawtell, 1989.

Sleeper, Frank H. *Images of America: Margaret Chase Smith's Skowhegan.* Dover, NH. Arcadia Publishing, 1996.

Soderberg, Norman R. "Ice-Cutting Time in Abbot Village." *Down East* 21 no. 6. (March 1975): 36-39.

Sterling-Gondek, Marilyn. *The Forks of the Kennebec.* Marilyn Sterling-Gondek, 2017.

Stuart, Al. *Pierce Hill.* South Portland, ME. Pilot Press, 1981.

Various authors. *All Aboard for Yesterday: A Nostalgic History of Railroading in Maine* (reprints of articles from *Down East Magazine*). Camden, ME. Down East Books, 1979.

Walker, Elinor Stevens. *In and Around Our Great Northern Wilderness.* 3rd ed. Lisbon Falls, ME. Eastland Press, 1977.

Walker, Elinor Stevens. *More About Maine.* Rumford, ME. Rumford Publishing Company, 1974.

Whitney, Roger A. *The Monson Railroad: Maine's Two-Foot Narrow Gauge Railroad to the Slate Quarries.* Westbrook, ME. Robertson Books, 1989.

Whitten, Margaret V. *A Bit of History of the Moosehead Lake Area.* Greenville, ME. Moosehead Graphics, 1992.

Wilson, Dorothy Clarke. *The Big-Little World of Doc Pritham.* New York. McGraw-Hill Book Company, 1971.

Workers of the Federal Writers' Project of the Works Progress Administration for the State of Maine. American Guide Series: *Maine—A Guide 'Down East.'* Boston. Houghton Mifflin Company, 1937.

Zimet, Abby. "Four's a Crowd at Town Meeting." *Maine Sunday Telegram,* May 6, 2000.

about the author

*Chris Coyle takes his place with the locomotive
he ran as a volunteer for visitors at
Sandy River Railroad Park in Phillips, Maine.*

photo by Susie Gaglia

After his birth in a small, country hospital in Hartland, Maine, in 1960, Chris Coyle grew up summers in a log cabin in central Somerset County, Maine, where he developed a great appreciation for the world around him and the people of the Pine Tree State.

Retired from some forty years at the University of Massachusetts, Amherst, as a researcher, he managed veterinary and animal sciences laboratories and later inventoried chemicals for environmental health and safety. He holds an associate's degree in animal science from the UMass Stockbridge School of Agriculture, a bachelor's degree in animal science from UMass, and a master's degree in library and information sciences from the University of Rhode Island.

He served on the railroad advisory board of Palmer Public Library and authored parts of the book *One Town and Seven Railroads*. Always interested in New England history, especially of railroads, he has also authored articles for magazines and other publications.

colophon

Text and captions for *We Lived in the Woods* are set inBookmania, developed in 2011 by Mark Simonson Studios. Bookmania combines the sturdy elegance of the original Bookman Oldstyle, developed in 1901, with the swashy exuberance of the Bookmans of the 1960s. With more than 680 swash characters—more than any previous Bookman, possibilities are endless. The broad range of weights makes it great for display use, but it also works well for text. Unlike some Bookman revivals, it retains the original classic sloped roman for the italic. Bookmania includes all the features of a modern digital font family.

Titles for *We Lived in the Woods* are set in Cooper Standard, originated from from Oswald Cooper's career as a lettering artist in Chicago and the Midwest in the 1920s. Cooper was advertised as being "for far-sighted printers with near-sighted customers." While very bold, Cooper is based on traditional old-style serif lettering rather than the hard-edged fonts popular in the nineteenth century, giving it a soft, muddy appearance with relatively low contrast between thick and thin strokes.

www.ingramcontent.com/pod-product-compliance
Lightning Source LLC
Chambersburg PA
CBHW041017280326
41926CB00094B/4661